THE SCALE OF PERFECTION

THE ORCHARD BOOKS

Our Lady of the Genesee

THE SCALE OF PERFECTION

by

WALTER HILTON

Translated into Modern English,
with an Introduction and Notes,

by

DOM GERARD SITWELL, O.S.B.

THE NEWMAN PRESS
WESTMINSTER, MARYLAND

PERMISSV SVPERIORVM O.S.B.

NIHIL OBSTAT: PATRICIVS MORRIS, S.T.D., L.S.S.

CENSOR DEPVTATVS

IMPRIMATVR: E. MORROGH BERNARD

VICARIVS GENERALIS

WESTMONASTERII: DIE VII APRILIS MCMLIII

MADE AND PRINTED IN GREAT BRITAIN BY
THE BROADWATER PRESS LTD, WELWYN GARDEN CITY, HERTFORDSHIRE

First published 1953

INTRODUCTION

§1 : PRESENT EDITION

THE fourteenth-century English treatise, *The Scale of Perfection*, is extant in about fifty manuscripts. It was printed as early as 1494 by Wynkyn de Worde, and this edition was reprinted four times before 1533. In 1659 it was printed in a somewhat altered form,[1] and this text was twice reprinted in the seventeenth century (1672 and 1679), while in the nineteenth century it was reproduced by Dom Ephrem Guy in 1869 and by Fr Dalgairns in 1870. In 1923 Dom Noetinger and Dom Bouvet brought out a French translation of Wynkyn de Worde's edition, and in the same year Miss Evelyn Underhill produced her English edition. While making no claim that this was strictly critical, she did consult a selection of manuscripts and based her text on Harleian MS. 6579. The English is partially modernized. In 1927 another partially modernized edition appeared in the Orchard Series made from Wynkyn de Worde's version. All of these versions are now out of print with the exception of Miss Underhill's which has recently been reissued (1950). It is evident that a full critical edition is much to be desired, but in view of the number of manuscripts its production will not be an easy or speedy matter, and as, if it does appear, it will of course be in the original language and spelling, it will hardly be of a nature to appeal to the general reader. But in the meanwhile, as *The Scale* contains much valuable spiri-

[1] This edition has generally been attributed to Serenus Cressy, but his name does not appear on it, and Dom Noetinger showed that the changes introduced into the text are not altogether satisfactory from a theological point of view, and suggested that Cressy may not have been responsible for it. (See *Downside Review*, June 1923.)

tual teaching which can still make an appeal in its own right, it seemed worth while to produce a new popular version, and in completely modern English. All the modern versions hitherto have been in an adaptation of the original language which is properly speaking neither Middle English nor modern English, and though it soon becomes intelligible in the main, the general reader does, I fancy, in spite of a certain attraction in the archaic forms, find it balking. And though with a little practice and the use of a glossary it is not difficult to understand the words in the semi-modernized editions, the real meaning of many passages is not so easily obtained. Admittedly a translation such as I have made involves a selection in difficult passages of one interpretation rather than another, but in the more doubtful cases I have given my reasons for adopting the interpretation that I have chosen and the original text is given in the notes. It is always difficult when turning Middle English into modern to know how far to let the colour of the original show through and I am conscious that I may have done so in varying degrees, but my primary purpose throughout has been to make the text intelligible, and I believe this version is a faithful rendering of what Hilton meant.

Apart from the question of the language there is a certain difficulty in following the argument, for although Hilton has a plan, it is not immediately obvious,[1] and the reader who is left to proceed from chapter to chapter may fail to see how the work hangs together. I have accordingly supplied a general plan of both Books, which it is hoped will enable the reader to understand the articulation of the whole work.

The version is based on the Underhill text checked by the Wynkyn de Worde (Orchard) edition. There is in fact practically complete agreement between them except in the

[1] The useful analysis at the beginning of the French edition is not reproduced in the first Orchard Series edition.

division of the chapters and the chapter headings, which differ considerably in the two versions. On both these points there is great variety in the manuscripts and on the face of it one version does not seem to have more authority than the other. I have followed the Wynkyn de Worde text in the chapter divisions as these seemed more in accordance with the actual divisions of the subject matter. For the headings I have used those which best explained the content of the chapters, taking them indifferently from either version and without comment. Although there are evidently, as is to be expected, variant readings in the manuscript texts, it is, I think, certain that none of these is so great, or differs to such an extent from the already printed texts, as to make these substantially unreliable, and it did not, therefore, seem necessary to wait for a critical text before proceeding to a translation. In the few cases where there seemed obvious textual difficulty I am indebted to Miss R. Birts for very kindly giving me information on the manuscript readings.

Notes inevitably seem either too full or not full enough, but I have tried to explain the theological implications of Hilton's remarks where these seemed necessary for understanding the text, to elucidate the terms he uses, and the meaning of particular texts where this was obscure. In addition I have tried to provide a minimum of running commentary on the actual teaching.

No serious study of the sources has been attempted, though here and there I have been able to connect his teaching up with that of other medieval writers. The French editors drew attention to parallels in the writings of the Fathers which I have sometimes quoted, but it is difficult to say how far these were really sources in many cases. The fundamental ideas of Hilton's spirituality belong to what had already in his day become traditional, and indeed they grow inevitably from the whole Christian conception of man's life and its relation to God. It is obvious from the general plan of the work, and from the first twenty chapters of the second Book in particular, that he was trained in the theology of the Schools, and by the late fourteenth century he had a considerable body of theological speculation upon which to draw. To attempt to disentangle the particular trends of theological thought which lie behind his work would, however, be a difficult business in the light of our present knowledge of the by-ways of medieval theology and no attempt has been made to do it here.

St Anselm seems to have been a real source, as the French editors noted, and Hilton's teaching on the sort of contrition required for confession was certainly outside the main stream, but, though subsequently condemned, had its medieval authorities. The parallels with *The Cloud of Unknowing* are many and most of them have been noted, though I believe that he did not accept the main thesis of that work. There is nothing to show that he owed anything to Rolle, but on the contrary it would seem extremely likely that he was critical of his teaching in some respects.

His work is thoroughly medieval, and yet in spirit it is in many ways suggestive of much that came after it. "Always gently, sweetly, and peacefully" was a maxim of St Francis de Sales, and it would serve to sum up Hilton's attitude to the spiritual life.

§2 : LIFE AND WORKS

Nothing is known of the life of Walter Hilton except what can be gleaned from the manuscripts. It is generally accepted that he was an Augustinian canon of Thurgarton in Nottinghamshire and that he died in 1395 or 1396. Many manuscripts state that he died on the vigil of the Annunciation, 1395, that is on 24 March 1396 by our reckoning. John Greenhalgh, however, a monk of Sheen, in a colophon dated 1499 in Trinity College, Cambridge, MS. 354 gives the vigil of the Assumption 1395 as the date of his death, but it looks as though Assumption here was an error for Annunciation. He is nearly always referred to as a canon of Thurgarton, and some manuscripts add that he died there. He is generally given the title of Magister, which at this time was reserved for doctors of theology. One manuscript, Marseilles 729, calls him Parisius, implying that he had studied at the university of Paris. A certain amount more can be gathered from his unpublished Latin works which have been examined by Miss H. L. Gardner. Two Latin treatises, *De Imagine Peccati* and *Epistola Aurea*, seem unquestionably to be his both from manuscript tradition and internal evidence, and they reveal two important facts about his life. The first is that he was at one point of his career himself a hermit. The extracts from the *De Imagine Peccati* and the *Epistola Aurea* quoted by Miss Gardner[1] seem to indicate that he was leading the eremitical life himself when he wrote these works. And this receives some corroboration from the fact that MS. Digby 115 of the *De Imagine Peccati* refers to him in the title as hermit, and one manuscript of *The Scale* (Harley 2397) does the same. The *Epistola Aurea* is addressed to one Adam Horsley who was proposing to become a Carthusian at Beauvale, and this gives us a valuable indication of date. Horsley was made Controller of the Great Roll in 1375, so the *Epistola Aurea* must have been written after that date, if he was on the point of becoming a Carthusian when he received it. It also seems clear from Miss Gardner's quotations that Hilton was not himself a religious when he wrote the work. If these facts be so, then it would seem that in early life Hilton must have been a hermit, possibly of the Richard Rolle free-lance type, and that he must have been one long enough to acquire a personal

[1] *Essays and Studies of the English Association*, 1936, pp. 108–12.

authority sufficient to warrant his writing a book of spiritual advice for a friend. Further, he can only have become a Canon Regular in the last twenty years of his life. In view of the maturity of the spiritual teaching of *The Scale* it is fair to assume that he wrote it towards the end of his life at Thurgarton. From the considerable manuscript evidence for Hilton as Magister and the undoubted fact that *The Scale* was written by someone with a considerable knowledge of theology, it would seem that Hilton must have become a hermit after taking his doctorate. Such a course must have been uncommon, though there were apparently hermit priests at this date.[1] The alternative, that he began the course leading to a doctorate in theology in middle life, seems most unlikely. The date of his ordination may yet be discovered, but in the meantime we can only conjecture at what his career may have been before he entered Thurgarton.

Apart from *The Scale*, there is convincing manuscript attribution to him for the *Epistle on Mixed Life*, a book written for a devout layman, and for the treatise *Of Angels' Song*,[2] and there is little doubt of his authorship of four other small treatises which are known as *Eight Chapters on Perfection*, *Qui habitat*, *Bonum est*, and *Benedictus*.[3] An English translation of the *Stimulus Amoris* seems also to have good manuscript attribution to him and has been published by Miss Kirschberger.[4] In Harley MS. 2406 there exists an anonymous commentary on an epistle of Hilton's addressed to a nun, but nothing is known of this work. There is also an unnamed tract in Brit. Mus. MS. Add. 33971 to a friend troubled in his conscience

[1] See the names and descriptions of hermits given in Appendix C to Miss R. M. Clay's *Hermits and Anchorites of England*.

[2] Both are printed in Horstman's *Richard Rolle of Hampole* (London, 1895), vol. 1, pp. 264 and 175.

[3] These have been printed together with the *Epistle of Mixed Life* in the Orchard Series, *Minor Works of Walter Hilton*, 1929.

[4] *The Goad of Love* by Walter Hilton (London, 1952).

in the matter of confession. *The Scale* was translated into Latin, possibly as early as 1400,[1] and several manuscripts of this translation exist. In addition to his English works he also wrote the two Latin treatises to which reference has been made above.

§3: THE SPIRITUALITY OF "THE SCALE"

An attempt has been made to explain in the notes all the passages which are really significant for an understanding of Hilton's spirituality, and it is hoped that these explanations with the aid of the general plan of the two Books will enable the reader to get a clear idea of Hilton's view of contemplation and how it is to be obtained. There are, however, some general aspects of his teaching which it may be useful to mention here.

For Hilton, as for all Catholic mystics, contemplation means some kind of direct knowledge of the Godhead, and it is an essentially supernatural experience. The distinctive and valuable contribution that he makes to the idea is the conception of it as an awareness of the life of sanctifying grace within the soul (see Bk. II, chap. 40, and nn. 4 and 5). Such a view follows, I think, necessarily from what any of the Catholic mystics on the one hand say about the union between God and the soul in contemplation, and from what theology on the other teaches about the union between God and the soul effected by sanctifying grace, but I do not think that any writer on the subject has drawn attention to it so clearly as Hilton has done. To use his own terminology, sanctifying grace *reforms*[2] the soul in the image of God, but

[1] See an article on "The Text of the *Scale of Perfection*" by Miss Gardner, *Medium Aevum*, February 1936, p. 22.

[2] In the sense, of course, of re-forms or re-fashions, but I have retained Hilton's word throughout as a technical term.

while the ordinary Christian is aware of this only through faith, and is what Hilton calls *reformed in faith* alone, the contemplative has achieved some sort of direct awareness of it and is *reformed in faith and feeling*. The idea is important because it brings out clearly the fact that contemplation is not a sort of "mystery" to which only the initiated can attain, but is simply the manifestation of a more than ordinary degree of holiness to which everyone should, at least remotely, aspire. This conception of contemplation as an awareness of the life of grace within the soul will further enable us to see the emphasis he lays on its achievement in its proper perspective. Writing, it is true, for a recluse, he is quite explicit that contemplation should be her aim. "I have told you something of the nature of true contemplation in order that you may hold it before you as an end for which to strive" (Bk. I, chap. 14, p. 20). But he is equally explicit (Bk. I, chap. 10) that it is not for its own sake as an experience that it is to be sought. What the soul is to desire is not an experience but God—or Jesus, as he puts it. "I would rather have a true and pure desire of Jesus in my heart, though with very little spiritual enlightenment, than practise all the bodily mortifications of all men living, enjoy visions," etc. (Bk. I, chap. 47, p. 75). Essentially the end of the soul's activity for him as for any other spiritual writer is simply the highest degree of knowing and loving God of which it is capable, and in the last analysis the means by which this is to be achieved are always the same. There must be (1) prayer, and (2) some sort of ascetic training; prayer and mortification, in Father Baker's words.

A very slight acquaintance with *The Scale* will reveal the fact that Hilton has something to say about both these subjects. To deal with the second of them first, Hilton's insistence on the necessity for mortification hardly needs pointing out. He devotes nearly half of the first Book to it (from

chap. 55). It is to be noted though, that it is internal mortification with which he is concerned, the overcoming of vice,
what he admirably describes as destroying the roots of sin.
In the matter of external mortification he is very moderate,
and goes so far as to say that hunger and great bodily suffering will hinder the soul from contemplation (Bk. I, chap.
75). In that he may be said to look forward to the age that
was to come after him. It was characteristic of Counter-
Reformation spirituality to concentrate on the intense cultivation of private prayer, and it is no doubt true that extreme
bodily mortification will interfere with this. In general,
though, the extreme asceticism practised at some periods
of the Church's history found no place in the fourteenth-
century English school of spirituality.

The part which Hilton makes prayer to play in the work
of transforming the soul may not be so immediately obvious,
but it is in fact, I think, fundamental. It will be seen from the
plan of the first Book that the first means of achieving this
reform in feeling, which is contemplation, is simply "seeking Jesus", that is desiring Him (sect. IV, 1) and it is pointed out in note 3 to chapter 46 that this necessarily means
prayer. There can be no doubt, I think, that in the terminology of today what Hilton is advocating when he exhorts the
soul to desire God is a direct approach to Him in affective
prayer, that is a prayer in which affections, or acts of the
will, predominate. It is at this point that the medieval character of Hilton's work becomes most marked. A modern
reader who is at all acquainted with current spiritual literature will expect to be instructed in methods of making a
meditation, that is he will expect to be told how to use the
methodical and systematic consideration of points of doctrine or of our Lord's life in order to excite the will to make
acts—of love, sorrow, etc.—in which prayer properly consists. Hilton says nothing of all this because it was a practice

which grew out of the formal Spiritual Exercises which were only developed in the century after his death. These consisted of a course of meditation and prayer calculated to give a new orientation to life, to bring about a "conversion" to a life fully directed to the service of God. Such Exercises were the outcome of the movement which reformed the religious houses of Europe from within during the fifteenth and sixteenth centuries, and they are first to be found among the Canons Regular of St Augustine at Windesheim and the Benedictines of the reformed Congregation of St Justina at Padua in the fifteenth century. The first full-dress example of a course of Spiritual Exercises was the *Ejercitatoria* of Garcia de Cisneros who reformed the monastery of Montserrat about the year 1500. They differ much no doubt from the more famous Exercises of St Ignatius by which they were later eclipsed, but they are of the same *genre* and it is one which was unknown a hundred years earlier. This new spiritual technique, the so-called *devotio ,noderna*, was a powerful instrument of reform, and was in fact the instrument by which it was effected within the religious houses.[1] The whole art of prayer was elaborately worked out and analysed, much stress laid on meditation, and a set period put aside for it each day. All this was unknown to Hilton. The traditional programme of the religious houses allowed only for the recitation of the Divine Office and spiritual reading, though obviously private vocal, and also mental, prayer was practised, as Hilton's second and third degrees witness. Nevertheless, I think it is substantially true to say that the

[1] In this connection it is interesting to note that when the community was restored to Westminster Abbey in Mary's reign, Cardinal Pole was anxious to obtain some Italian Benedictines to give them Spiritual Exercises, and the community undertook to introduce the "ways of the Italian Congregation"—which would include regular meditation. See *Ampleforth and its Origins* (Burns Oates, 1952), chap. 4 p. 64.

sort of prayer which he not so much taught as took for granted was that which came later to be called affective. We can
see what I take to have been very much his approach to the
spiritual life in general, and to prayer in particular, expounded and, so to speak, rationalized by the English Benedictine writer, Father Augustine Baker, in the seventeenth
century. Father Baker reacted strongly against the spirituality of his day and maintained that, at least for those who had
what he called a "propension" to be contemplatives, meditation should at an early stage be given up in favour of affective
prayer. This would at first consist of what he calls "forced
acts", perhaps taken ready-made from the psalms or some
book, but in time these might be expected to give place to
a greater or lesser extent to spontaneous acts, which he calls
aspirations, "the constant exercise of which," he says, "is
proper and perfect contemplation." In accordance with the
spirit of the age in which he lived, and in spite of the fact
that he reacted against it in the main, Baker analyses the processes of prayer and systematizes them much more than
Hilton did, but there can be no doubt of the kinship between
the two. Baker himself cites the fourteenth-century English
treatise, *The Cloud of Unknowing*, as one of his chief sources,
and we know that he was acquainted with Hilton for he
quotes him explicitly, lifting indeed the whole of the parable of the pilgrim—with acknowledgements—from chapter 21 of the Second Book of *The Scale*. Apart from this he
himself made a "modernization" of *The Scale* into seventeenth-
century English which is preserved in a manuscript at Downside. His views, however, met with much opposition in the
newly founded English Benedictine Congregation, many of
whose members, including Baker himself, had been trained
in the Congregation of St Justina.

At this distance of time we should be able to regard the
controversy dispassionately, and although it is not my pur-

pose to go into it at length here, a few observations about it may be relevant in view of the fact that Baker was undoubtedly carrying on the Hilton tradition. In the first place there is no doubt that the new methods of prayer and meditation were suited to the needs of the new age, the age of the Renaissance and the Reformation, and secondly there was, and is, room for the old methods. There are some who more easily approach prayer through a method that is predominantly affective—and in truth it is a question of emphasis. The intellect may well be used on the matter of affective prayer when the will is sluggish and this is in effect meditation; on the other hand an over-rigid adherence to set schemes of considerations may be enforced to the detriment of real prayer. The great spiritual directors have, of course, always been aware of this, but they have not always been available.

However, Hilton still lived in the Middle Ages and he cannot fairly be criticized for not having anticipated the achievements of a later age. But the fact that he does essentially belong to the Middle Ages means that some aspects of his work are bound to appear unsympathetic to the modern reader who is not acquainted with medieval ways of thought. The trick of using the allegorical interpretation of Scripture texts to illustrate points of morality or doctrine, for example, is apt to appear both irritating and unconvincing to those who are unaccustomed to it. More serious, perhaps, is the uncompromising attitude he takes up about heretics and infidels, about which something is said in the notes to the relevant passages. But on the other side of the balance and far outweighing these defects is the essentially sound foundation of prayer and mortification on which he bases his teaching and of which I have already spoken, and added to that a certain native sanity and good sense which constantly manifest themselves. It is not that he says anything new. In a sense there is not anything new to be said about the pursuit of virtue and the cultivation of prayer, for the raw material of either process is human nature, which does not change. There may be superficial differences of technique, but the ultimate reality of these activities remains the same. Already the desert fathers had a certain homely yet profound wisdom in these matters, and Hilton had his share in the inheritance of it. His teaching on humility in Book I (chap. 16) for example might seem unreal or even fantastic at first sight—though it is not—but his application of it in chapter 19 is full of wisdom. If you cannot feel this sort of humility, he says, "humble yourself in your will by reason, believing that you ought to be humble in the way that I have described". And if you cannot do even this—"though nature rebel and refuse its assent to your will—do not be anxious, but accept your rebellious nature as a trial". Rightly understood there is great wisdom in accepting the situation, and Hilton stresses the advice again and again. Perhaps the most striking example is in Book II (chap. 24, p. 206) where he is speaking of the worldly and even sinful thoughts which will press in on the soul newly turned to God and from which it cannot escape: "Nevertheless, if you find it so, do not be too depressed, and do not struggle too much, as though you would put these things out of your mind by force, for you cannot do that. Wait till grace comes, be patient, and do not let your efforts be too violent; if you can, quietly turn your will and your thought to Jesus as though you attached no importance to these feelings." That advice will be found repeated in one form or another in chapters 22, 23, 27, and 41 of the second Book, and of a piece with it is what he has to say about not fighting directly against temptations in Book I (chap. 38).

If any testimony to the genuineness of Hilton's teaching were wanted it could be found in the reiterated emphasis which he puts on humility and charity. Again there is nothing new in this—God forbid that there should be—but those two virtues are surely the hall-mark of the Christian life at its fullest. Hilton is not the sort of writer whose personality stands out vividly in what he writes, but we do in the end, I think, get a very clear impression of a kindly, understanding man, one in whom it would be easy to confide, well informed too—indeed, in spite of his disclaimers, an expert in what St Gregory called the art of arts, that of guiding souls. It has already been suggested that he shows understanding of the difficulties of others—an understanding which nowhere shows itself so disarmingly perhaps as in his chapter on distractions in prayer (Bk. I, chap. 33)—and it is this combination of high spiritual ideals with a great sympathy for human weakness that makes him, in my opinion, such an attractive writer on the spiritual life.

Much of the matter in the notes and nearly all the Appendix has appeared in articles in *The Downside Review* and I am indebted to the editor for permission to make use of it.

GERARD SITWELL.

St Benet's Hall,
Oxford.
30th April 1952.

PLAN OF BOOK I

PLAN OF BOOK II

PLAN OF BOOK II

BOOK I

THE FIRST CHAPTER

That the inner life of a religious must correspond with the outer

DEAR Sister in Jesus Christ, I beg you to remain contented and steadfast in the vocation to which our Lord has called you. By the grace of Jesus Christ strive with all the powers of your soul to live up to the state of life which you have undertaken. You have forsaken the world, turning to our Lord, and are as it were dead in the sight of men. Accordingly let your heart be dead to all earthly attractions and anxieties, wholly turned to our Lord Jesus Christ. For you must know that an exterior turning to God is mere fantasy, unless the heart turns too. And so she is in a wretched state who fails to keep an inward watch over herself, and lives a life which is only outwardly devoted to religion; who is a religious only in dress and speech and external behaviour; who scrutinizes other men's actions, and judges their failings, thinking herself to be something, when in reality she is nothing. Such a one deceives herself. Do not you act thus, but turn both internally and externally to God, and conform yourself inwardly to His likeness by humility and charity and the other virtues, and so you will be truly converted to Him. I do not say that you can straightway be as easily and perfectly converted to Him in your soul as your body may be enclosed in a house, but you ought to realize that the reason of your being physically enclosed is that you may more easily come to be so spiritually; that as you are outwardly cut off from the conversation of men, so your heart should be cut off from worldly attractions and anxiety about all earthly things. And my purpose in this little work is to tell you how, in my opinion, you may best achieve this.

3

THE SECOND CHAPTER

Of the active life and its works

You must understand that, as St Gregory[1] says, there are in the Church two ways of life which lead to salvation. One is called the active life, the other the contemplative. Every man who is saved is so by one or other of these. The active life consists in love and charity manifested exteriorly by good works. It means the keeping of God's commandments and the performance of the seven corporal and spiritual works of mercy for one's fellow-Christians. This is the life proper to men of the world who are rich and have plenty of worldly goods; and it belongs also to those who hold office and authority over other men, and have the administration of property or wealth, whether they are learned or ignorant, laymen or ecclesiastics. Such are bound to fulfil these duties to the best of their abilities, as reason and discretion shall dictate. If they are possessed of great fortune, it will be their duty to do much good; if their fortune is small, less is expected of them. If they possess nothing, they must at least have good will. These are the works of an active life, whether it is exercised in temporal or spiritual authority. Exercises of bodily mortification, such as fasting, vigils, and other severe forms of penance, also pertain to the active life. The flesh must be chastised, with discretion, to atone for past sins, and to restrain sinful inclinations, and to make the body obedient and compliant to the soul. These works, active though they are, dispose a man in the early stages to come to the contemplative life, provided that they are used discreetly.

[1] *Hom. in Ezech.*, Bk. II, Hom. II. (P.L., LXXVI, col. 952).

THE THIRD CHAPTER

Of the contemplative life and its works

THE contemplative life consists in perfect love and charity, manifesting itself by the spiritual virtues,[1] and by a true knowledge and sight of God and spiritual matters.[2] This is the life which belongs to those who for the love of God have left worldly riches, honours, and external activity, and devoted themselves body and soul to the service of God in the interior life. Now since your state demands that you be a contemplative—for that is the object of your enclosure, that you may more freely and completely devote yourself to spiritual matters—it behoves you to strive continually, body and soul, to attain to as much of that life as lies within your capacity—using what means seem best to you.

However, before I tell you of the means, I shall tell you first a little more about the life itself in order that you may have some idea of what it is, and put it before you as the object of all your efforts.

[1] *Spiritual virtues*. Hilton uses this expression several times. The spiritual virtues are opposed to the spiritual vices, which are those which have not got for their object any sensible pleasure. They are particularly pride and hatred, and the spiritual virtues opposed to them are humility and charity.

[2] Hilton frequently uses the expression "ghostly things" as a sort of pendant to the idea of God, and it is often difficult to know exactly what he means by it. One cannot escape the conviction that he habitually added the phrase without adverting clearly to its meaning in a particular context, and I have accordingly allowed myself some latitude in giving it what seemed an appropriate translation in each case, though it is frequently not possible to leave its meaning otherwise than vague.

THE FOURTH CHAPTER

The first degree of contemplation

THE contemplative life has three degrees. The first consists in the knowledge of God and spiritual matters which can be attained by reason. We get this through the teaching of other men and our own study of the Scriptures. This sort of knowledge is not accompanied by any devotion or interior consolation brought about by a special gift of the Holy Spirit, but it is proper to learned men who have long studied Holy Scripture. In varying degrees it is the result of application and the natural intelligence which God gives in different measure to all those who have the use of reason. Such knowledge is a good thing, and may be called a sort of contemplation inasmuch as it is a certain realization of truth and a knowledge of spiritual things. But it is only a figure and shadow of true contemplation, for it carries with it no inward experience of God and no interior sweetness. Only he can feel these consolations who has great charity, for charity is the true fountain of God to which no stranger can come. But this sort of knowledge that I have been speaking of is common to good and bad, for it does not demand charity. And for that reason it is not true contemplation, for often heretics, hypocrites, and carnal-minded men have more of it than good Christians, and yet these men have no charity. Of this sort of knowledge St Paul says: *Si habuero omnem scientiam et noverim mysteria omnia, caritatem autem non habuero, nihil sum* (1 Cor. xiii. 2).[1] If I had full knowledge of all

---

[1] "*Si habuero omnem scientiam*, etc." Hilton always gives his quotations from the Bible in Latin and then translates them, sometimes so freely as to provide an interpretation, or almost an adaptation, rather than a translation. In some cases he adapts and shortens the Latin, as here. I have thought it best to give the Latin text as he gives it, and then to give as close a rendering as possible in modern idiom of his translation. He of course

things, and knew all secrets, and had not charity, I am nothing. Nevertheless, if those who have this sort of learning keep themselves in humility and charity, and avoid worldliness and sins of the flesh to the best of their ability, they are pursuing something which is good and which will dispose them for true contemplation, if they will devoutly ask that grace from the Holy Spirit.

There are those who have this knowledge and make use of it, either as a source of pride in themselves, or as a means of seeking worldly position, honours, and riches, instead of using it humbly for the praise of God and charitably for the benefit of their fellow-Christians. When such is the case, they fall into errors and heresies, or other public sins, by which they become a scandal to themselves and the whole Church. Of this sort of learning St Paul said: *Scientia inflat, caritas autem aedificat* (1 Cor. viii. 1). Knowledge alone lifts up the heart into pride, but join it to charity, and it turns to edification. By itself this knowledge is like water, tasteless and cold. But if those who have it would offer it humbly to our Lord and ask His grace, He would with His blessing turn the water into wine, as He did for His mother at the feast. He would turn their savourless knowledge into wisdom, and cold naked reason into spiritual insight and burning love by the gift of the Holy Ghost.

---

wrote before the Vulgate text had been stabilized by the revisions under Sixtus V and Clement VIII, and it will be found that his text often differs verbally from ours. In some cases it suggests that he is quoting from memory, but no study of his Vulgate text has been attempted for this edition.

THE FIFTH CHAPTER

The second degree of contemplation

THE second degree of contemplation consists principally in the act of love, and the intellect receives no special light on spiritual matters. It is given generally to simple, unlearned people who devote themselves wholly to God, and these are the sort of ways in which it makes itself felt. When a man is thinking about God, the Holy Ghost inspires him with a feeling of fervent love and great devotion at the thought of the passion or some scene in our Lord's life, or with a feeling of great trust in the goodness and mercy of God and His willingness to forgive our sins; or else with great thankfulness for His gifts to us, and a filial fear of the hidden judgements of God and His justice. Then, again, sometimes when a man is praying, he feels his heart completely detached from earthly things; with all its power it strains after our Lord with fervent desire and great joy. And yet there is no special illumination of the intellect in all this, no secrets of Scripture are revealed, but for the time being a man wants nothing more than just to pray and feel as he does, such great joy and comfort does it bring him. He cannot explain it, but he is quite sure of what he feels. From this feeling spring sweet tears, burning desires, silent sorrow, all of which purify the soul from sin and make it melt with the love of Jesus Christ, pliant and obedient to God's will. So much so, that a man has no care what becomes of him, if only God's will is fulfilled. All this, and more, will he feel, and it is all the outcome of great grace. Whoever has this experience is in charity, and this charity may not be lost or diminished except by mortal sin, even though the fervour pass[1] away.

[1] *Even though the fervour pass.* In Bk. II, chaps. 33, 34, 35, Hilton will develop the idea of contemplation as an awareness of an intense

And that is a comforting thought. This may be called the second degree of contemplation.[2]

THE SIXTH CHAPTER

Of the lower stage of the second degree of contemplation[1]

BUT this second degree has two stages. The lower stage may be experienced as strongly by men leading an active life, when the grace of God visits them, as by those who give themselves entirely to contemplation and have received the

---

degree of the life of grace in the soul. The awareness comes and goes, but this intense degree is itself dim or secret contemplation, whether it is felt or not. See Bk. II, chap. 41, n. 1.

[2] For the relation of the various stages of contemplation and of prayer as set out by Hilton see n. 1 to next chapter.

[1] It is of interest to connect up these stages of contemplation with his teaching on the subject in the second Book. He has there discarded these rigid divisions, but he likens the contemplative life to the passage from the false day of the love of this world to the true day of the vision of God (Bk. II, chap. 24). In order to pass from the one day to the other it is necessary to go through the night. This passage through the night is contemplation, and it will not be a uniform process. The soul will only gradually become immersed in it. In the beginning its experiences will be sometimes painful, sometimes pleasant. Painful, because, while it desires God, its old familiarity with sin will draw it away from Him (Bk. II, chap. 24, p. 205). It is still outside in the false day but it is entering into the darkness. "This darkness is not peaceful, because you are not accustomed to it and because of the lack of knowledge and the impurity in you" (p. 206). Nevertheless it is in this period that the soul will experience at intervals the feelings of devotion that Hilton refers to in this chapter as the lower stage of the second degree of contemplation. With persevering effort, however, it will come in time to rest peacefully in the night, no longer looking back to the light of the false day of this world (pp. 206–7). This is when it has come to the higher stage of the second degree of contemplation described in chap. 7—a certain habitual rest in God. When it is

gift of it. However, this feeling of fervour does not always come when a man would have it, and often it does not last long. It comes and goes at the good pleasure of Him who gives it. And so let him who receives it humble himself, and give thanks to God, and keep it secret, unless he reveals it to his confessor, or to some other wise man, and let him retain it as long as he can without violent effort. And when it is withdrawn, let him not be too anxious but remain humbly in faith and hope, patiently waiting till it comes again. It is a little foretaste of the sweetness of divine love, of which David said in the Psalter: *Gustate et videte quoniam suavis est Dominus* (Ps. xxxiii. 9).[2] Taste and see the sweetness of our Lord.

THE SEVENTH CHAPTER

Of the higher stage of the second degree of contemplation

But the higher stage of this second degree of contemplation may only be achieved by those who live in great tranquillity of body and soul, and who by the grace of Jesus Christ and long bodily and spiritual exercises have attained peace of heart and a good conscience, so that their greatest happiness is to remain tranquil and continually praying, keeping their minds on our Lord. And they like to think of the Holy Name of Jesus, for they find it comforting. The remembrance of it feeds their love. And not only the Holy Name, but other prayers, such as the Our Father and Hail Mary, hymns, and

---

established in this state, there will penetrate to it from time to time glints and gleams of the light of God's true day, and this is the third degree of contemplation described in chap. 8.

[2] Psalm references throughout are to the Vulgate.

psalms, and all the other forms which Holy Church employs, become as it were a spiritual joy and melody, which console them and strengthen them against sin, and even relieve physical distress. Of this degree St Paul says: *Nolite inebriari vino sed implemini Spiritu sancto, loquentes vobismetipsis in hymnis et psalmis, et canticis spiritualibus, cantantes et psallentes in cordibus vestris Domino* (Eph. v. 18, 19). Be not drunk with wine, but be filled by the Holy Ghost, singing to yourself in hymns and psalms and spiritual songs, singing and psalming in your hearts to our Lord. Whoever has this grace, let him be humble and take care that he is always desiring to come to greater knowledge and enjoyment of God in the third degree of contemplation.

THE EIGHTH CHAPTER

Of the third degree of contemplation

THE third degree of contemplation—which is the highest that can be reached in this life—consists of both knowledge and love; in knowing God and the perfect love of Him. And that comes about when a man, first of all reformed in the image of Jesus by the practice of virtue, then visited by grace, is detached from all earthly and carnal love, from useless thoughts and imaginations, and is carried out of his bodily senses. By the grace of the Holy Ghost his intellect is illumined to see Truth itself, which is God, and spiritual matters, and his will is inflamed with a soft, sweet, burning love. So powerfully does this come about that by an ecstasy of love the soul for the time being becomes one with God and is conformed to the image of the Trinity. The beginning of this contemplation may be felt in this life, but the fullness of it is kept for the bliss of heaven. Of this union with our Lord St Paul says: *Qui adhaeret Deo unus spiritus est cum illo*

(1 Cor. vi. 17). Whoever in ecstasy of love is joined to God, then God and his soul are not two but one. And in truth in this union a marriage is made between God and the soul, which shall never be broken.[1]

THE NINTH CHAPTER

Of the difference between the third degree of contemplation and the second, and praise of the third degree

THE second degree of contemplation might be called love aflame with devotion, and it is inferior; the third is love aflame with contemplation, and it is on a higher plane. The former brings more satisfaction to the senses, the latter to the spirit, for it is more interior and spiritual, altogether worthier and more admirable. In so far as it goes it is a true foretaste and pledge of the joys of heaven. Those things are seen, not clearly but hazily, which in the bliss of heaven will be fully revealed. As St Paul says: *Videmus nunc per speculum in aenigmate; tunc autem videbimus facie ad faciem* (1 Cor. xiii. 12). We see God now by a mirror, as it were in darkness, but in heaven we shall see Him openly face to face. This is the illumination of the intellect accompanied by the joy of love, as David says in the Psalter: *Et nox mea illuminatio mea in deliciis meis* (Ps. cxxxviii. 11). My night is a light to me in my pleasures. The other degree of contemplation is milk for children, this is meat for perfect men who have judgement to distinguish good from evil, as St Paul says: *Perfectorum est solidus cibus qui habent sensus exercitatos ad discretionem boni et mali* (Heb. v. 14).

No man may have this gift actively within him unless he is first reformed in the image of Jesus by the practice of virtue.

[1] See chap. 45, n. 1.

And no man living in a mortal body can have it continually in its supreme degree, but only when he is visited by special grace. And as I judge from the writings of holy men, this is only for a very short time, for we soon return to the sobriety of nature. This contemplation is the fruit of charity, and it is thus, if I am not mistaken, that St Paul says of himself: *Sive excedimus, Deo, sive sobrii sumus, vobis; caritas Christi urget nos* (2 Cor. v. 13, 14). Whether we raise ourselves above our bodily senses to God in contemplation, or whether for you we remain in the sobriety of our natural senses, it is the charity of Christ that urges us. Elsewhere he describes openly the manner of this contemplation and conforming to God: *Nos autem revelata facie gloriam Domini speculantes, transformamur in eamdem imaginem, a claritate in claritatem tamquam a Domini Spiritu*[1] (2 Cor. iii. 18). He says, in effect, of himself

---

[1] "*Nos autem revelata facie,* etc." Hilton has been particularly free in interpreting St Paul here. Possibly I have been too free in interpreting him, but it is not easy to be sure of what he means. His text in E. Underhill's version is: *We, first reformed by virtues, the face of our soul uncovered by opening of the ghostly eye, behold as in a mirror heavenly joy, full shapen and oned to the image of our Lord, from clarity of faith into clarity of understanding or else from clarity of desire to clarity of blessed love.* I have taken "full shapen and oned to the image of our Lord" to refer back to "we".

Hilton certainly seems to have adopted a very bold interpretation of the last part of the phrase: *transformamur in eamdem imaginem, a claritate in claritatem tamquam a Domini Spiritu.* Mgr Knox translates, "and so we become transfigured into the same likeness, borrowing glory from that glory, as the spirit of the Lord enables us." That is, as we become more and more united to God through grace, our souls acquire glory, which is a reflection of the glory of God Himself. Hilton seems to go much further than this, and to say that we pass from a view of God in faith, "clarity of faith", into "clarity of understanding", which can only be a knowledge of God which is at least in some degree direct and in contrast to that of faith. It is the opinion of theologians that the veil of faith is never entirely removed in this life, and the phrase I have used about passing from the knowledge of faith to that of the intellect could not be taken as implying the direct knowledge of God in the Beatific Vision. On the

and those who have attained perfection: we, reformed by the acquisition of virtues, the eyes of our souls opened, see as in a mirror the heavenly joy. We are transformed into His image and pass from the knowledge of faith to that of the intellect, from desire to fruition. And all this is wrought in a man's soul by the spirit of love says St Paul. This degree of contemplation God gives where He will, to learned and to ignorant, to men and to women, to prelates and to solitaries. But it is a special gift and not a common one. And though a man in active life may have it by a particular favour, the plenitude of it is reserved for the contemplative and the solitary.

THE TENTH CHAPTER

That sensible experiences may be good or evil[1]

FROM what I have said you may understand that neither apparitions of spirits in corporeal form nor imaginary visions, whether they come to us in sleep or when we are awake, constitute, properly speaking, contemplation. And that is

other hand it is the claim of the mystics, and is indeed the whole point of the mystic experience, that the veil of faith is at least partially withdrawn, and the soul does acquire some measure of direct knowledge of God. We must take it that this is what Hilton means, and there is in fact no difficulty about admitting progressive knowledge of the Godhead. His further phrase about passing from desire to love seems to imply, as I have taken it, passing from desire of what is not possessed to enjoyment of what is. This too can only be taken in the partial sense indicated above.

[1] The suspicion which Hilton shows in chaps. 10 to 12 of any sort of physical phenomena which appear to be manifestations of mystical experience is in accordance with all the best tradition. It is Richard Rolle's enthusiasm for some of these experiences (see the next note) that makes him always slightly suspect. Such phenomena may no doubt accompany genuine contemplation, but they may also be the manifestation of very curious and unhealthy psychological states or even of diabolical illusions.

true of impressions in the other senses, whether of sound, or taste, or smell, or heat felt in the breast[2] or in any other part of the body, or, in a word, of anything that may be perceived by the bodily senses. However delightful these things may be, they are not true contemplation. Even when these things have a good origin, they are less valuable than the practice of virtue and the knowledge and love of God, for in these latter there is no deceit. But experiences of this sort may be good, the work of a good angel, or they may be illusions brought about by a wicked angel, who transforms himself into an angel of light. And since they may be good or evil, it is clear that they are not the most valuable. For the devil, when God gives him leave, can bring about the same sensible experiences that a good angel can effect. A good angel can appear in the midst of light, and so can the devil, and it is the same with what appeals to our other senses. The man who has experienced both knows how to distinguish the good from the evil, but he who has experienced neither, or only one, may easily be deceived. They are alike as far as the outward senses are concerned, but there is much difference in the inward effects. And for this reason they should neither be greatly desired nor carelessly received, but the soul must have discretion to know the good from the bad, and to avoid deception. As St John says: *Nolite credere omni spiritui, sed probate si ex Deo sint* (1 John iv. 1). St John tells us that we should not believe every spirit, but should first test it to see whether it be of God or not. And so I shall tell you

---

To the men of Hilton's age, of course, if they were not genuine they were necessarily diabolical.

[2] It looks very much as though Hilton is referring here to Richard Rolle. The sensible experience of heat, song, and sweetness was for him an important part of the mystical experience. See especially chap. 14 of the *Incendium Amoris*. Hilton devotes the whole of chap. 26 in the first Book of *The Scale* to the fire of love. See note on this chapter.

of one way, as it seems to me, in which you can distinguish the good from the evil in experiences of this kind.

THE ELEVENTH CHAPTER

How to distinguish the good from the evil in sensible experiences

BE on your guard if you perceive either with your bodily eye or with your imagination any light or brightness not apparent to other men, or if you hear any pleasant sound, or experience any sweet savour in your mouth without a natural cause, or feel heat in your breast, or any other sensible pleasure in any part of your body. In the same way, if an angel appears to you in bodily form to comfort and instruct you, or if you are conscious of anything which does not come from yourself or any bodily creature, be on your guard and examine your interior dispositions. If the pleasure that you feel causes you to give up the thought and contemplation of Jesus Christ, to forgo your spiritual exercises and prayer, if it hinders you from examining yourself and your faults, from seeking virtues and the spiritual knowledge and enjoyment of God, then there is good reason for thinking it is from the enemy. And that is true, too, if you are led to set too much store by these experiences and to enjoy them for their own sake, thinking that this sensible experience is a part of the joy of heaven and the happiness of the angels, so that you do not want to pray, but all your thoughts dwell on these experiences and all your efforts are to preserve the enjoyment of them. In this case, however great the attraction, do not assent to them, for it is a deception of the enemy. He is angered when he sees a man give himself entirely to spiritual occupations, for he hates nothing more than so see a soul in this sinful body enjoying the knowledge and love of God, which he in his spiritual state lost through his own fault. And so if he may not harm such a soul by open sins, he would like nothing better than through sensible sweetness to lead it into spiritual pride and false security, making it think that it was experiencing heavenly joy and was already half in paradise, when in fact it was near the gates of hell. And the result would be that the man through his pride and presumption would fall into errors and illusions, and might even suffer in the body as well as in the spirit.

On the other hand it may be that these experiences will not hinder your spiritual life, but make you pray more devoutly and fervently, and feed your mind with holy thoughts. And even if you are somewhat taken aback by them at first, nevertheless you soon find your heart quickened to a greater desire of virtue, your love of God and your neighbour increased, and your opinion of yourself lowered. In that case you may know that they come from God and are produced through the agency of a good angel.[1] That is God's goodness; He sends these things either to increase the trust and desire of Himself in simple, devout souls, and so to make them seek Him more perfectly, or in the case of perfect souls, to give an earnest and, as it were, a foreshadowing of the bodily glorification which they will have in heaven. Yet I know not if there be any such man living on earth. Mary Magdalen had this privilege it seems to me, when she was alone in the cave for thirty years, and every day was carried up by angels, and fed both body and soul by their presence.[2]

[1] Hilton refers frequently in the second Book of *The Scale* to this idea of the ministry of angels in producing mystical phenomena. See Appendix. In warning against attaching much importance to experiences of this kind he is in accordance with all the best tradition, and he applies what might be described as the standard test, namely, "by their fruits you shall know them".

[2] The reference is to the legend that St Mary Magdalen came to

St John speaks in his epistle of this manner of testing the effect of spirits on us: *Omnis spiritus qui solvit Jesum, hic non est ex Deo* (1 John iv. 3). Every spirit which divides Jesus is not from God. These words may be understood in many ways, but I am justified in taking them thus.

THE TWELFTH CHAPTER

What unites Jesus to a man's soul and what separates Him from it

THAT which unites Jesus to a man's soul is good will and a great desire to possess Him and to see Him spiritually in His glory. The greater this desire, the closer the union of Jesus with the soul; the lesser the desire, the looser the union. So any experience which lessens the desire and draws the soul down from the constant thought of Jesus Christ and from its natural aspiration to Him separates Jesus from the soul and so is not of God, but it is the work of the enemy. But if on the other hand a sensible experience or a revelation increases this desire, knits the knot of love and devotion to Jesus faster, opens the eye of the soul to spiritual vision more clearly, and makes the soul more humble in itself, then it is of God. From this you may understand that you are not to allow your heart to rest and take its pleasure wholly in any sensible delights of this sort, even though they are in fact the product of good spirits. But you must consider them of little or no importance in comparison with the spiritual

Provence and spent the last thirty years of her life there in a cave on the Sainte Baume near Marseilles. Modern scholarship, Catholic as well as non-Catholic, rejects the whole story. See *Butler's Lives of the Saints*, Thurston and Attwater edition (London, 1932), vol. VII, p. 315.

desire and constant thought of Jesus Christ, and you must
not let your heart become too much attached to them.

THE THIRTEENTH CHAPTER

The work of a contemplative

BUT your constant endeavour shall be through much prayer
to attain to the experimental knowledge of God in your soul.
By this I mean that you may come to know the wisdom of
God, the infinite power of our Lord Jesus Christ, His great
goodness in Himself and to His creatures. For in this is contemplation, and not in the manifestations I have mentioned
above. Thus St Paul says: *In caritate radicati et fundati, ut pos-
sitis comprehendere cum omnibus sanctis, quae sit longitudo, et lati-
tudo, sublimitas et profundum* (Eph. iii. 17, 18). Be rooted and
grounded in charity, not that you may perceive sounds or a
sweet savour or any other sensation, but that you may know
and experience with all the saints, what is the extent of the
infinite being of God, the breadth of His wonderful charity
and goodness, the height of His almighty majesty, and the
bottomless depths of His wisdom. It is in the knowledge and
experience of these things that the work of a contemplative
consists, for in these the full extent of spiritual matters is
comprised. This is that one thing which St Paul coveted,
saying: *Unum vero, quae retro sunt obliviscens, in anteriora me
extendam sequor si quo modo comprehendam supernum bravium*
(Phil. iii. 13, 14). That is as much as to say: one thing I
desire, namely to forget all things behind me and reach out
with my heart to grasp and to enjoy the sovereign reward of
eternal happiness. Behind us are all material things, in front
all spiritual ones, and therefore St Paul would forget all
material things, including his own body, so that he might
see the things which are spiritual.

THE FOURTEENTH CHAPTER

How virtue begins in the reason and the will and is made
perfect in love

I HAVE told you something of the nature of true contemplation in order that you may hold it before you as an end for which to strive, and that all your life you may desire by the grace of our Lord Jesus Christ to attain to at least one degree of it. It is this which makes the soul conform to God, and it may not be achieved until the soul has been remodelled by the practice of virtues loved for their own sake.

Many a man practises virtues, such as humility, patience, charity to his neighbour, and others, but he is moved only by his reason and will, and finds no spiritual pleasure in them. Often indeed the performance of them is heavy and bitter, and yet his reason leads him to exercise them for the fear of God. Such a man possesses virtues in reason and will, but he has no love for them. But when, by the grace of our Lord and by spiritual exercises and the practice of asceticism, what was purely an act of reason becomes an act of spiritual enlightenment, and what was done through pure determination becomes a labour of love, then he has an affection for virtue.[1] He has gnawed through the bitter shell and come to the kernel. Virtues which were at first bitter for him have become delightful, so that he takes as much pleasure in humility, patience, purity, temperance, and charity as in any earthly pleasure. Indeed until virtues thus become attractive to him, he may have the second degree of contemplation, but he will not attain the third. Now, since virtues dispose us for contemplation, it behoves us to use proper means for arriving at them.

[1] It is the particular effect of the Gifts of the Holy Spirit to produce a certain facility in practising the virtues. Hilton will develop this point in the second Book, chap. 36.

THE FIFTEENTH CHAPTER

Of three means to attain contemplation

THERE are three means that contemplatives generally make use of, reading the Scriptures and books of spiritual instruction, meditation, and assiduous and devout prayer. You cannot very well make use of reading the Scriptures, [1] and therefore it behoves you to occupy yourself more in prayer and meditation. By meditation[2] you will see how much you

[1] This sentence is omitted in the text of the first Orchard edition which follows Wynkyn de Worde's 1494 printed text. I am indebted to Miss R. Birts for the information that the manuscript evidence on the whole supports Hilton's authorship of the sentence, but the exact implications of it are not clear. The most probable explanation is that the person for whom Hilton was writing did not read Latin—which is what we should expect from the fact that *The Scale* is written in English—and that there were no English versions of the Bible available. At least at the beginning of the second half of the fourteenth century this was true, as far as we know, of versions of the complete Bible. No doubt, as Gasquet pointed out (*The Old English Bible and other Essays*, 1897, p. 109), the explanation is that from the Conquest until this time those who could read at all read Old French or Latin—though one should not forget the existence of the *Ancren Riwle* in thirteenth-century English. It was only in the second half of the fourteenth century that at all a widespread demand for an English version would be felt, and then it was unfortunately met by versions largely inspired by the Lollard movement. Such versions would evidently not be acceptable to Hilton. See note on chap. 58.

[2] From what Hilton says here about meditation it might be thought that he meant by it very much what we mean today, but when he comes to treat of it explicitly in chaps. 34 and 35, there can be no question, I think, but that he uses the word to mean contemplation of one sort or another. It would have been more satisfactory in some ways to substitute the word contemplation for meditation throughout these chapters, but this could not have been done without begging the question of the meaning of the term raised in chaps. 34 and 35, and on the whole it seemed better to retain Hilton's word, but the difference between his and the modern use of it must be remembered.

The idea of meditation, in the sense of some sort of contemplative

need virtues, and by prayer obtain them. By meditation you will recognize your misery, your sins of pride, covetousness, gluttony, and luxury, evil motions of envy, anger, hatred, melancholy, bitterness, sloth, and unreasonable depression. You will see your heart full of foolish shame, and anxiety for your body and what the world thinks of you. All these movements will boil up in your heart like turbid water from a fouled spring. And they will cloud the eyes of your soul so that you will have no sight or enjoyment of the love of Jesus Christ. For be sure of this, that until your heart is cleansed from such sins through a firm grasp of the truth, and consideration[3] of Christ's humanity, you cannot come to any true spiritual knowledge of God. He Himself bears witness to this in the Gospel: *Beati mundo corde quoniam ipsi Deum videbunt* (Matt. v. 8). Blessed are the clean of heart, for they shall see God. In meditation also you will see the virtues which you ought to have: humility, gentleness, patience, righteousness, fortitude, temperance, purity, peace, and moderation, faith, hope, and charity. It is in meditation that you will see these virtues, their goodness, their beauty, and their value. And by prayer you will come to desire, and at last to obtain them, without which you cannot become a contemplative. For Job says: *In abundantia ingredieris sepul-*

---

prayer, leading to the recognition of our faults and the virtues of which we stand in need is, of course, essential to Hilton's spirituality. It is the seeking Jesus that he will advocate in chaps. 46 to 54, and in particular we may compare what he says here with chap. 52 where he speaks of discovering the image of sin within the soul (p. 83). Cf. chap. 46, n. 3.

[3] Hilton's word here, which I have translated *consideration*, is *beholding*. On the face of it this might mean contemplation, but then he uses meditation with this meaning (see previous note), and if we are to suppose that he used the word *beholding* rather than *meditation* deliberately, it would seem that he can only have meant by it meditation in the sense we give to the word today. I have used the word consideration in order to avoid confusion with meditation used in his sense earlier in the chapter.

crum (Job v. 26); that is, with abundance of good bodily works and spiritual virtues you shall enter your grave, that is the rest of contemplation.

THE SIXTEENTH CHAPTER

The attitude of the humble man

Now, if you would use these spiritual exercises wisely and safely, it behoves you to lay a sound foundation. There are three things that you need as a foundation of all your endeavours, and they are humility, firm faith, and a right intention. First of all you should have humility in this manner.[1] By an act of your will and, if you can, because you really feel it, you should consider yourself unworthy to dwell among men and to serve God in the company of His other servants, you should think of yourself as useless to your fellow-Christians, lacking both the skill and the strength to perform good works for the benefit of your neighbour in the active life as other people do. And therefore, a miserable being and an outcast from your fellow-men, you are enclosed in a cell alone, so that you should not hurt anybody by your bad example, since you cannot help them by your good works. And beyond this you ought to consider that since you cannot even serve our Lord in outward works, you should think yourself all the more unworthy and unable

[1] Hilton's remarks about humility may appear far-fetched, but in fact it is impossible to over-stress its importance, and he will devote two chapters (62 and 77) to it later in this Book. If his doctrine seems harsh and inhuman it is counteracted by the example he himself gives of the virtue in this chapter and by the very wise attitude he adopts in chap. 19. Humility can in fact only come with a certain growth of spiritual insight and in its most profound form from the enlightenment of the Holy Spirit. See chap. 18, n. 1.

23

to serve Him inwardly. For our Lord is a spirit, as the prophet says: *Spiritus ante faciem nostram Christus Dominus* (Lam.
iv. 20). Christ our Lord is a spirit before our face. And
the service we properly owe to Him is spiritual, as He Himself says: *Veri adoratores adorabunt patrem in spiritu et veritate*
(John iv. 23). True servants will worship Him in spirit and
in truth. Then you who are so uncouth, so sensual, so blind
in spiritual matters, and especially about your own soul—
which is the thing you ought to know first, if you would
come to any knowledge of God—how should you feel yourself worthy of the contemplative life, which consists precisely in knowing God and experiencing His presence?
I say all this to you not that you should give up your purpose
and be discontent with your enclosure, but that you should,
if possible, really feel this humility in your heart, for it is no
more than the truth. And even though you feel unsettled,[2]
you should constantly desire and strive, as far as you can, to
live up to your state, believing firmly that by the mercy of
God it is so that you can best live your life. And though you
may not reach perfection in this life, you should desire
to make a beginning, and trust surely to have perfection
through God's mercy in heaven. For indeed that is how it
is with me; I feel myself so wretched, so frail and carnal, so
far from the true realization of what I am talking about, that
I can do nothing else but cry mercy, and sigh after this perfection, and hope that our Lord will bring me to it in
heaven. Do the same, and do better, if God gives you grace.
This sense of your unworthiness will put out of your heart
all rash consideration of other men's lives and judging of
their actions, and it will lead you to concentrate only on
yourself, as though there was no one in the world but God

---

[2] Taking the reading of Miss Underhill's manuscripts 2 and 3, which
runs: "And though thou feel thus, yet . . ."; I take *thus* to refer back to the
phrase about being discontented (mis-paid) with her state.

and you. And you should judge yourself viler and more wretched than any living creature, so that you can hardly put up with yourself, so great is your sin and corruption. All this you ought to feel, if you would be truly humble. For I tell you the truth when I say that, if you will have true humility, you shall think a venial sin in yourself a more serious matter than the mortal sins of other men. Because whatever defiles your soul and hinders it from this experimental knowledge of God ought to be most grievous and painful to you. But a venial sin of your own hinders you more from the enjoyment and perfect love of Jesus Christ than any other man's sin may do, be it never so great. So you must strive against yourself and the sins which impede you from the sight of God more assiduously than you do against the faults of other men. For if your own heart is free from sin, other men's sins will not hurt you. And so if you will find rest both here and in heaven, say every day as one of the holy fathers[3] advised, "What am I?"—and pass no judgement on your fellow-men.

THE SEVENTEENTH CHAPTER

The right to reprove the faults of others

But now perhaps you say, how may this be? For it is an act of charity to reprove men for their faults, and to pass judgement upon them that they may amend is an act of mercy. It seems to me that the answer to this is, that it does not belong to you or to any other contemplative to neglect yourself and to criticize and reprove other men for their faults, unless the need were so great that a man's eternal salvation

---

[3] The reply of the Abbot Pastor to the Abbot Joseph in the *De Vitis Patrum*, Lib. V, Libel. 9, n. 5 (P.L. LXXIII, col. 910).

should depend upon the reproof. But men who are leading
an active life and who have authority over others, as prelates and those that have the cure of souls, are bound in
charity by their office to inquire into and condemn other
men's faults. Not that they are to do this for the mere pleasure they take in correcting them, but only because necessity demands it: and they must do it in the fear of God and
His Holy Name for love of the salvation of souls. Others,
who are leading the active life but have no authority over
their fellow-men, are bound in charity to reprove their
faults only when the sin is mortal and cannot otherwise be
corrected, and also when they think that reproof will lead
to amendment. Else they had better refrain. The truth of
this appears from the conduct of St John, who was a contemplative, and of St Peter, who led the active life. When
our Lord at the Last Supper, at Peter's private instigation,
told St John how Judas would betray Him, St John did not
tell St Peter, as he asked, but turned and laid his head on
Christ's breast and was carried away by love into contemplation of God's secrets. And so great was his reward that
he forgot both Judas and St Peter. Thereby he taught other
contemplatives that they should act in the same manner.

THE EIGHTEENTH CHAPTER

*Why those who are humble should honour other men and
consider themselves beneath them*

So you may learn that you should neither condemn other
men, nor entertain evil suspicions against them. But you
should love and honour particularly those that lead an active
life in the world, and who suffer many difficulties and temptations, which you in your enclosure do not feel. They have

to work hard for their own and others' living, and many of
them would rather, if they could, serve God in tranquillity
as you do, and nevertheless in their worldly activity they
avoid many sins, which you, if you were in their state, would
fall into, and they do many good actions which you could
not do. There is no doubt that this is the case with many,
and who they are you know not. And for this reason you
should honour all men and from the bottom of your heart
consider them your betters, and you should put yourself
under their feet as being in your own sight the vilest and
lowest of creatures. For you have nothing to lose however
much you abase yourself, even though in God's sight you
have in fact more grace than another. But it is dangerous for
you to exalt yourself deliberately in thought above any man,
though he were the most wretched sinner alive. For our
Lord says, *Qui se humiliat exaltabitur, et qui se exaltat humili-
abitur* (Luke xiv. 11). Whoever exalts himself shall be
humbled, and whoever humbles himself shall be exalted. It
behoves you to have this sort of humility at first, and
through it and the grace of God you will come to the perfection of it, and of all other virtues.[1] For whoever has one
virtue has all.[2] As much as you have of humility, so much

[1] In the second Book of *The Scale* (chap. 37) Hilton will distinguish
between humility that is attained only by reason—the sort of humility he
has described in chap. 16 above—and humility that comes from the enlightenment of the Holy Spirit. The latter is of an altogether deeper kind,
and it is this which he holds out now as the perfection of humility.

[2] *Whoever has one virtue has all.* On the face of it this statement does
not appear to be true. The kindly man is not always temperate, the honest
man not always diligent, and so on. But if these cases are considered it will
be found that it is a matter of natural virtue or temperament, a mere
matter of disposition. There is no doubt, I think, that Hilton has in mind
something deeper, and there is a sense in which it is true to say that he
who has charity has all virtues. Charity is the virtue by which all the acts
of a man's life are ordered to his last end, which is God, and it is true to
say that no one has any virtues—in the supernatural sense, virtues meri-

have you of charity, patience, and the other virtues, although they do not appear outwardly. Strive then to get humility and to keep it, for it is the first and last of all virtues. It is the first for it is the foundation of them all; as St Augustine[3] says, if you think to build a high house of the virtues, first lay a firm foundation of humility. It is also the last, for it is what secures and makes safe all the others; as St Gregory[4] says: He who cultivates virtues without humility, is like one who carries powder in the wind. Whatever your good deeds may be, fasts, vigils, or any others, they are nothing without humility.

THE NINETEENTH CHAPTER

How to remedy a lack of love for humility, and that it is necessary to avoid excessive anxiety on this point

NEVERTHELESS, if you are unable to feel this sort of humility in your heart as you would like, do what you can, humble yourself in your will by reason, believing that you ought to be humble in the way I have described, even though you do

---

torious of eternal life—without charity. He who has charity by that very fact directs all the actions of his life to God and in this sense has all virtues *in voto*, even though his practice of some of them may fall short of the ideal. It is to be noted further that he cannot fail in them to the extent of committing mortal sin, or else he loses charity, and so it is true, absolutely, that he who has charity has all the other virtues in a real, even though an imperfect, sense. Cf. chaps. 40, n. 4, and 66, n. 2.

[3] St Augustine, *Serm.* LXIX, chap. 1, n. 2 (P.L., XXXVIII, col. 441).

[4] St Gregory, *Hom. in Evang.*, Hom. VII (P.L., LXXVI, col. 1103). See also *Expos. in Psalm. Paenit.* Ps. XXXVII, n. 3. (P.L., LXXIX, col. 569.) This work is probably to be attributed to a certain Eribert, bishop of Reggio in the eleventh century, but by Hilton's day it is commonly attributed in the manuscripts to St Gregory, and it appears among his works in Migne. See Mercati, *Revue Bénédictine*, t. XXXI, pp. 250–7.

not feel it. And hold yourself all the more unworthy in that you feel yourself better than you are. And though nature rebel and refuse its assent to your will, do not be anxious, but accept your rebellious nature as a trial, and despise and reprove it, as though you would be happy to be trampled and spurned under every man's foot as an outcast. And so by the grace of Jesus Christ through constant consideration of the lowliness of His humanity you will much reduce the movements of pride. Humility attained at first by mere will-power will become attractive to you. Without this virtue, at least in will, whoever seeks to serve God in the contemplative life will stumble like a blind man and never reach his goal. The higher a man lacking humility seems to climb by bodily penance and other virtues, the lower he falls. As St Gregory[1] says, the man who cannot truly despise himself never yet found the humble wisdom of our Lord Jesus.

THE TWENTIETH CHAPTER

How for lack of humility hypocrites and heretics prefer themselves to all others

HYPOCRITES and heretics[1] lack this humility in their will, and still more in feeling. Their hearts, dry and cold, feel none of its sweetness, and they are all the further from it in that they think they have it. They gnaw at the dry shell of the nut, but they cannot come to its sweet kernel. They make a parade of humility outwardly in dress, and speech, and a modest manner, and they appear to have many corporal and spiritual virtues. But nevertheless in their will and their feeling, where humility should chiefly be found, it is

[1] St Gregory, *Moral. in Job*, Bk. XXXIV, n. 43 (P.L., LXXVI, col. 742).
[1] For Hilton's views on heretics see note on chap. 58 (Bk. I).

only simulated. For they condemn and despise and hold as of no account those who will not imitate them or conform to their teaching. In their opinion such men are either merely foolish or else blinded by sensual living. So they exalt themselves in their own opinion above all others, thinking that theirs is the only way of life, and that they have received peculiar gifts of light and unction from God. And they take pleasure in honouring and praising themselves as though there were none like them. They praise God with their lips, but in their hearts they steal the honour and the thanks due to God and give it to themselves. And so they neither have nor feel humility. A poor sinner who falls daily and is sorry that he does so, though he may not feel humble, is humble in his will. But a heretic or a hypocrite has it neither way. These are in the same state as the pharisee who came, as our Lord says in the Gospel, into the temple with the publican to pray. And when he came there, he said no prayers and did not ask God for anything, for he thought he had no need, but he began to thank God thus: "Lord, I thank thee that thou givest me grace above others; that I am not as other men are, robbers, sensualists, and the like." And he looked about him and saw the publican, whom he knew for a wretch, beating his breast and crying for mercy. Then he thanked God that he was not such a one as he was. For, "Lord," he said, "I fast twice in the week, and I pay my tithes regularly." And when he had finished, our Lord said, he went home without grace as he came, and gained nothing. But now you say perhaps, "Where did this pharisee sin, since he thanked God, and what he said was true?" And to this I answer that the pharisee sinned inasmuch as he condemned and reproved the publican, who was justified in the sight of God. And sinned also because he only thanked God verbally, while he took pride in the gifts of God, stealing the honour due to God and giving it to himself. Heretics

30

and hypocrites are in the same state as this pharisee. They do not pray gladly, and when they do pray, they do not humble themselves, acknowledging their misery, but they only make a pretence of thanking and praising God, and all the honour they give Him is with their lips. In truth their pleasure is useless and false and not in God at all, although they themselves think overwise. They cannot praise God, for as the wise man says: *Non est speciosa laus in ore peccatoris* (Ecclus. xv. 9). The praise of God in the mouth of a sinner is neither fair nor seemly. And so poor sinners like you and me ought to avoid the state of this pharisee, and a feigned praise of God, and follow the publican in humility, asking mercy and forgiveness of our sins and the grace of spiritual virtues. And when we have done this we can indeed give Him thanks and praise with a pure heart, and attribute all to Him without pretence. For our Lord asks by His prophet: *Super quem requiescit Spiritus meus nisi super humilem et contritum spiritu et trementem sermones meos?* (Isa. lxvi. 2). Upon whom shall my spirit rest? and He answers Himself and says, upon none but the humble, the poor, the contrite in heart, and those that fear my words. So if you will have the Spirit of God rule in your heart, first get humility and the fear of God.

THE TWENTY-FIRST CHAPTER

What ought to be believed with firm faith[1]

THE second thing that you must have is a firm belief in all articles of faith and in the sacraments of Holy Church, be-

[1] In this chapter Hilton is not arguing about the truths of religion, but is giving practical advice about meeting temptations against faith and hope to a soul whose whole way of life implies that it is in fact deeply imbued with those virtues.

lieving in them firmly with your whole will. And if by the
suggestion of the enemy you feel your heart stirred to doubt
any of them, stand firm and do not be over-anxious about
such feelings, but without disputing and analysing them renounce your own judgement. Identify your faith with that
of the Church without paying any attention to the movements of your heart which seem contrary to it. For those
feelings that arise in you are not what you believe, but the
faith of the Church is what you believe, though you neither
see it nor feel it. Accept these disturbances patiently, then,
as a trial sent from God to purify your heart and confirm
your faith. You should love and respect also all the laws and
ordinances made by prelates and those that rule the Church
concerning the faith, the sacraments, or the conduct of
Christians. Assent to them humbly and sincerely. Even
though you do not know their cause and some seem unreasonable to you, do not condemn or criticize them. Respect them all, though they concern you very little. Do not
receive under colour of greater holiness, as some foolish
people do, any opinion, whether it comes from your own
imagination or the teaching of other men, if it is contrary
in any way to the law or teaching of the Church. And beyond
this you should confidently believe that you are chosen by
the mercy of God to be saved as one of His elect. Never
depart from this hope whatever you see or hear, or whatever
temptations come upon you. And even though you think
yourself a sinner only worthy of hell, because you do no
good and do not serve God as you ought, hold fast to this
faith and hope, ask mercy, and all shall be well. Yes, and if
all the devils of hell appeared to you in bodily form and told
you that you should be damned, if all men on earth and all
the angels in heaven, if such a thing were possible, told you
the same, you should not believe them, or allow yourself to
be shaken from this hope of salvation. I tell you this, because

some are so weak and so foolish, that having dedicated themselves wholly to the service of God, they are troubled and
made anxious, if the devil from within, or his prophets,
which men call soothsayers, from without raise doubts
about their salvation or whether their way of life is pleasing
to God. And this ignorance of theirs causes great depression
and almost a despair of salvation. And so there is no question
but that a firm trust of salvation befits everyone who by the
grace of God is determined to forsake sin, and who according to the light of his conscience will not remain in a state
of mortal sin, but has recourse humbly to confession and the
sacraments of the Church. And all the more is this so in the
case of those who give themselves wholly to God and do
their best to avoid venial sin. And on the other hand it is as
perilous for one who remains in a state of mortal sin to be
assured of salvation, and relying on that assurance not to
forsake his sin and submit himself humbly to God and
Holy Church.

THE TWENTY-SECOND CHAPTER

*How a right intention is necessary for those who would please
God*

THE third thing which you must have at the beginning of
your spiritual life is a right intention, that is to say a determination and a desire only to please God; for that is charity,
without which all your efforts will be of no avail. Your purpose should be always to seek to please Him, and never
deliberately to cease from good works, either corporal or
spiritual. And you must not make a time-limit—thus long
you will serve God and then you will deliberately give yourself to useless thoughts and idleness, thinking that this re-

33

laxation is necessary for human nature.[1] You must not lose the guard over your heart and give up good works in order to obtain momentary external relief by indulging your senses and occupying yourself with worldly interests. You may do this under the pretext of recreating yourself so as to be able to return afterwards more keenly to your spiritual exercises, but I am convinced that it is an illusion. I do not say that you can in fact always carry out your intention; often the needs of the body—food, sleep, necessary conversation, all the frailty of human nature—will intervene in spite of all your efforts. But you should have the intention of being always occupied bodily or spiritually and never idle, always raising your heart by desire to God and the joys of heaven, whether you are eating or drinking or occupied in any other bodily action. As far as possible do not depart from this rule, for with this purpose before you you will always apply yourself to your work. And if by frailty or by negligence you fall into any useless occupation or speech, your conscience will prick you. You will be led to find all trivial interests irksome and to turn again at once to the thought of Jesus Christ, occupying yourself with some good work. With regard to your body, you should be discreet in eating, drinking, sleeping, and all sorts of bodily penance, and also about long vocal prayers or great sensible devotion which seeks to express itself in tears or violent efforts of the

[1] Hilton here seems to preach a severe doctrine which would forbid any recreation. The difficulty, of course, is to decide what thoughts are "useless" and what occupations "idle". Anything which really dissipates the mind is certainly bad for the spiritual life and must be avoided by anyone who seeks to lead it seriously. On the other hand the tension must be relaxed at intervals. What provides a reasonable and beneficial relaxation and what causes harmful distraction will vary with each individual case, and it is for the soul, aided by its director, to make a prudent judgement of its own needs. Hilton, it must be remembered, was writing for a strictly enclosed anchoress.

imagination. Unless a man is moved by a special grace it is
good to observe discretion in these matters, for moderation
is best. But when it is a question of destroying sin by custody
of your heart, of a lasting desire of virtue and the joys of
heaven, of acquiring inner knowledge and love of Jesus
Christ, observe no moderation, for the more these are
sought the better. You must hate sin and all carnal loves and
fears without ceasing, and love and desire virtues and purity
of heart without measure if possible. I do not say that this is
necessary for salvation, but it is profitable. And if you have
this intention, you will advance more in virtue in a year
than you will in seven years without it.

THE TWENTY-THIRD CHAPTER

A recapitulation of what has been said

Now I have told you what is the first end you should hold
before yourself; and strive for it as much as you can. I have
also told you what you need to have as a foundation, namely
humility, firm faith, and an intention directed wholly to
God. And on this foundation you shall build your spiritual
edifice by prayer and meditation[1] and the spiritual virtues.
And I offer you this further advice: whether you pray or
meditate,[2] or whatever else you do, good by grace or
marred by your own frailty; whatever you feel, see or hear,
smell or taste, either in your senses or in your imagination,
whatever you know by your reason; bring it all to the bar
of the Church, throw it into the mortar of humility and
grind it with the pestle of the fear of God, cast the powder

---

[1] See chap. 15, n. 2.
[2] His word here is *think*, which I take to mean "meditate" in the
modern sense.

35

into the fire of desire and offer it all to God. And in truth
that offering will be pleasing in the sight of our Lord and the
smoke of it will find favour before Him. To sum up—test
all that you feel interiorly by the truth of Holy Church;
break yourself by humility, and offer to our Lord what
should be the only desire of your heart, the desire to possess
Him and nothing else. If you do this, then you will never be
overcome by the enemy. St Paul teaches us this when he
says: *Sive manducatis, sive bibitis, sive quid aliud facitis, omnia
in nomine Domini facite* (1 Cor. x. 31). Whether you eat or
drink, or whatever you do, do all in the name of our Lord
Jesus Christ; forsake yourself and offer it up to Him. The
means that you should make most use of, as I have said before, are prayer and meditation. First I shall show you something of prayer and then of meditation.

THE TWENTY-FOURTH CHAPTER

*Of prayer: its use in obtaining purity of heart
and virtues*

PRAYER helps you to come quickly to purity of heart by the
destruction of sin and the acquisition of virtues. Not that
its purpose is to show our Lord what you desire, for he
knows your needs already, but it is to make you a fitting
vessel to receive the grace He will freely give you. And this
grace may not be felt till you have been purified by the fire
of desire in devout prayer. For though prayer is not the
cause of grace in the soul, yet it is a means by which the free
gift of grace comes.

THE TWENTY-FIFTH CHAPTER

How to pray and on what the mind should be fixed
in prayer

BUT now perhaps you want to know how to pray and on what you should fix your mind in prayer; and also what is the most suitable prayer for you to use. To the first of these questions I reply that, when you wake up and are ready to pray, it may be that you will feel heavy and weighed down by the body, full of useless thoughts and imaginations, or worried by worldly affairs. You need then to enliven your heart by prayer and to stir it to devotion. And when you pray withdraw your heart from all earthly things. All your effort should be to leave these behind so that your mind, free from all distractions, may rise up continually to Jesus Christ. Your eyes will never be able to see Him as He is in His divinity, nor will your imagination ever be able to form an adequate image of Him.[1] But through devout and persevering consideration[2] of the humility of His precious humanity you may come to feel the goodness and grace of His divinity. If your prayer is of this sort, if your soul rises easily above all worldly thoughts and affections, and by the power of the spirit comes to dwell with pleasure in God's presence and to rest there, so that you have little remembrance of the things of earth, or this remembrance troubles you little, then you can pray well. For prayer is nothing but the rising of the heart to God leaving all earthly thoughts behind. And so it is compared to fire which of its nature springs up into the air. In the same way prayer, when it is enkindled by God's spiritual fire, is always rising up to Him from whom it came.

[1] That is, of the divinity.
[2] Hilton's word is *beholding*. For my rendering of it see chap. 15, n. 3.

37

THE TWENTY-SIXTH CHAPTER

Of the fire of love[1]

NOT all those who speak of the fire of love understand properly what it is. I myself cannot tell you what it is, but I can tell you this, that it is not corporeal, nor felt in the body. A soul may feel it in prayer or devotion, and the soul is in the body, but it does not feel it through its bodily senses. For though the presence of this fire in the soul may produce bodily heat, as if the body strove in harmony with the travail of the spirit, nevertheless the fire of love is not in the body, but only in the spiritual desire of the soul. Nobody who has this sort of devotion is in doubt about this, but simple people think that, because it is called fire, it should be hot like material fire, and that is why I have said this.

THE TWENTY-SEVENTH CHAPTER

How vocal prayers, inspired by God or composed by the Church, are best for those who begin to turn to God and give themselves to devotion

IN answer to the second question (see chap. 25), my opinion as to what prayer is best for you is this. You must know that there are three degrees of prayer. There is first

[1] This chapter is an interpolation in the subject matter of the book. It is difficult to believe that Hilton is not tilting at Richard Rolle, who, as has been mentioned (chap. 10, n. 2), attached great importance to this phenomenon. Hilton's idea seems to be that the "fire of love" is an effect of grace in the soul and is only metaphorically called fire. This experience in the soul may, however, re-act on the body and cause a feeling of heat. This no doubt is the truth, and a more accurate way of stating what occurs than to say that the bodily heat is itself of divine origin. That a feeling of bodily heat accompanies certain mystical experiences is well known.

vocal prayer, either given us directly by God Himself, as the
Paternoster, or by the Church, as matins, vespers, and the
other canonical hours, or else composed by holy men and
addressed to our Lord, our Lady, or the saints. Now with
regard to this vocal prayer, you who are a religious and are
bound to the divine office, should say it as devoutly as you
can.[1] In your matins you say in particular the Our Father,
and also psalms and hymns, to stir you to devotion, all of
them inspired by the Holy Spirit. And for this reason it is
not fitting to say the divine office hurriedly and carelessly,
as though the obligation which you have were an unwanted
burden, but recollect yourself to say it more devoutly than
any other prayer, believing that since it is the prayer of the
Church, there is no vocal prayer so profitable. And so put
off all heaviness and by God's grace do that to which you are
bound with a good will and as a free act, lest it be a hindrance
instead of a help to your spiritual life. And apart from this
you may say, if you like, the Our Father or any other such
prayer. And I should consider that best for you in which you
find most devotion and spiritual refreshment. Generally
speaking this kind of prayer is most suitable in the early
stages of conversion.[2] For to begin with, unless by a special
grace, a man's thoughts are worldly and carnal, and he

[1] It appears that the person for whom Hilton was writing was a mem-
ber of some religious community and from chap. 61 (Bk. I) and many
other passages it is evident that she was an anchoress. It seems to have
been not unusual for spiritual treatises to be written for particular members of religious houses. Richard Rolle's *Ego Dormio* and *The Commandment*
are cases in point. Equally, members of religious houses could and did
obtain permission to live as anchoresses. Margaret Kirby, the nun of
Hampole for whom Rolle wrote *The Form of Living*, received such permission. Cf. Clay, *The Hermits and Anchorites of England*, chap. 8.

[2] The Latin word *conversio* was habitually used to describe the complete
orientation of life to God which marks the beginning of the religious life.
It could imply merely the change from a good to a better form of life.

cannot think of spiritual things, because his soul is not yet cleansed from sin. And so it is that prayers such as the Our Father, Hail Mary, and the psalter are best. For he who cannot run lightly in the way of contemplative prayer, because the feet of his knowledge and love are lamed by sin, needs a firm staff to lean on. This staff is the vocal prayer ordained by God and the Church for man's assistance. By this prayer the soul of an earthly minded man, that is always falling into worldly thoughts and carnal affections, is raised up and as it were supported on a staff. Such a man is fed by the sweet words of prayer as a child with milk, and is guided by it so that he does not fall into errors or vain imaginations. For deception is impossible to anyone who will humbly persevere in this sort of prayer.

THE TWENTY-EIGHTH CHAPTER

The danger of leaving the ordinary prayer of the Church for meditation too soon in the religious life

So you see that those are misguided who, when they have felt some devotion at the beginning of their conversion and are not yet established in it, leave vocal prayer or other external exercises too soon and give themselves wholly to meditation.[1] For often in the quiet of their meditation, relying on their own efforts and their feelings, they imagine they

[1] It is evident that in this chapter Hilton is using meditation for some sort of contemplative experience (see chap. 15, n. 2). His use of the word has the curious effect of making his advice appear the very opposite of that which is usually given today. He warns the soul against taking up meditation too soon. We warn against *giving up* meditation too soon— and mean exactly the same thing that Hilton meant, namely that it is dangerous to imagine that we are the recipients of some sort of infused prayer before in fact we are.

have spiritual experiences for which they have not in fact received the grace. And by this indiscretion they overtax their minds and break down their bodily powers, and so they fall into fantasies and strange imaginations, or into open errors, and they hinder the grace that God is giving them by these vain efforts. The cause of all this is a secret pride and presumption. They have felt a little grace and they think it is so exceptional that they fall into vain glory and so lose it. If they knew how little it was that they feel in comparison to what God gives or may give, they would be ashamed to speak of it, unless it was for some very good reason. Of this kind of vocal prayer David speaks in the psalter thus: *Voce mea ad Dominum clamavi; voce mea ad Dominum deprecatus sum* (Ps. cxli. 1). To stir other men to pray with heart and voice David said: With my voice I cried to God and in speech besought our Lord.

THE TWENTY-NINTH CHAPTER

The second degree of prayer, which is vocal but follows the stirring of devotion without a set formula

THE second degree of prayer[1] is vocal, but without any set formula. This is when a man by the grace of God feels devotion, and out of his devotion speaks to Him as though he

[1] Hilton's second degree of prayer, that in words but without any set formula, appears to be precisely a description of what we mean by affective prayer, speaking to our Lord as though He were present and using such words as come to the mind; a prayer of acts in fact. But it is to be noted that he thinks of this prayer as being very definitely infused (chap. 30). The prayer of acts may indeed be so; the acts are then no longer "forced", but flow spontaneously, and are what Fr Baker called aspirations. Hilton seems to envisage a form in which the inspiration is very marked, so much so that it reacts on the body and involves some sort of rapture or ecstasy. This is clearly a fully contemplative form of prayer,

were bodily in His presence, using such words as come to his mind and seem to be in accord with his feelings; recalling his sins and wretchedness, the malice and tricks of the fiend, or the goodness and mercy of God. And out of the desire of his heart he calls out to our Lord for help, as a man might do surrounded by enemies, or in sickness, showing his wounds to God as to one who can heal them—saying as David said: *Eripe me de inimicis meis, Deus meus* (Ps. lviii. 1). Ah Lord, deliver me from my enemies; or else: *Sana animam meam quia peccavi tibi* (Ps. xl. 5). Heal my soul for I have sinned against thee, or some such prayer that comes to his mind. He is so conscious of the goodness and grace and mercy of God that he feels his heart stirred to love Him and thank Him with such words and psalms as will express his feelings. As David said: *Confitemini Domino, quoniam bonus, quoniam in saeculum misericordia ejus* (Ps. cxxxv. 1). Love and praise our Lord for He is good and merciful.

THE THIRTIETH CHAPTER

How this second degree of prayer is very pleasing to God: its effects in the body and the soul

THIS kind of prayer is very pleasing to God for it comes straight from the heart, and for that reason it is never made in vain. It belongs to what I have called the second degree of contemplation. When this gift of God actually makes itself felt, it is necessary to withdraw from the company of

---

and in chap. 31 he points out that in its more extreme forms it will not be of long duration. If the second degree of prayer is contemplative the third will be so no less, and it is in keeping with the general teaching on the subject that this highest form, the third degree, is characterized by great peace, and the violent bodily reactions no longer occur (chap. 32).

men and to be alone, so that it may not be hindered. Whoever has it let him keep it while he can, for it will not long remain in its intensity. For when the influence of grace becomes strong, it is surprising how exhausting it is to the spirit, even though it causes pleasure. And it is very exhausting to the body too, if it is felt often. When this influence of grace comes on strongly, it throws the body into convulsions suggestive of madness or drunkenness. Passionate love of this sort completely takes away the love of earthly things; the soul is as it were wounded with the sword of love, and the body collapses under the strain. This "touching" is of such power that the greatest sinner on earth, if he came under its influence, would be a changed man for long enough. The pleasures of the flesh and of the world, which before he delighted in, would lose all their savour.

THE THIRTY-FIRST CHAPTER

How the fire of love destroys all desires of the flesh as material fire destroys material objects

THE prophet Jeremias says of this experience : *Et factus est in corde meo quasi ignis exaestuans, claususque in ossibus meis, et defeci, ferri non sustinens* (Jer. xx. 9). That is to say, the love and realization of God became not fire merely but a glowing fire. For as material fire burns and destroys all material things with which it comes into contact, so spiritual fire, which is the love of God, burns and destroys all carnal love and pleasure in the soul, and this is the fire that is hidden in my bones, as the prophet puts it. That is to say, this love completely fills the powers of the soul—memory, understanding, will—with grace and spiritual sweetness as marrow fills a bone. And all this action is within—not in the senses. Nevertheless the power of this love is so great that it affects the body to the extent of making it tremble. The effect is so far removed from any natural experience and so unfamiliar that the soul is dazed and the body cannot bear it. And so our Lord tempers this experience and withdraws the fervour and brings the heart into a calmer and sweeter state. Whoever can pray thus advances very quickly in the spiritual life. He will acquire more virtues in a short time than an equally zealous man without this gift will acquire through the long practice of penance. And if anybody has this gift, at least regularly, he has no need to indulge in great bodily penance.

THE THIRTY-SECOND CHAPTER

The third degree of prayer, which is only in the heart and without words

THE third degree of prayer is in the heart and without words. It is characterized by great peace and rest in soul and body. The man who would pray in this manner must have great purity of heart, for it is only possible to those who, either by long spiritual and bodily exercise, or else by those sudden movements of love that I spoke of before (chap. 30), have come to great inward peace. It brings a taste for spiritual things, so that they are constantly praying in their heart, loving and praising God without being hindered by temptations and distractions, as I said before when speaking of the second degree of contemplation. Of this sort of prayer St Paul says: *Nam si orem lingua, spiritus meus orat, mens autem mea sine fructu est. Quid ergo? orabo et spiritu, orabo et mente; psallam spiritu, psallam et mente* (1 Cor. xiv. 14, 15). If I pray with my tongue only, by my own efforts, the prayer is meritorious but my soul is not nourished, for it does not taste the

44

fruit of spiritual sweetness by understanding. What then shall I do? says St Paul; and he answers: I will pray by travail and desire of the spirit. And my prayer will be more interior and effortless, tasting spiritually the sweetness of the love and sight of God. And it is this apprehension of the love of God that will feed my soul. As I see it, this was how St Paul himself prayed. God speaks figuratively of this sort of prayer in Holy Scripture thus: *Ignis in altari meo semper ardebit, et cotidie sacerdos surgens subjicit ligna, ut ignis non extinguatur* (Lev. vi. 12). That is to say: the fire of love shall ever be lit in the soul of a devout and pure man or woman; the soul is the altar of God and the priest shall every morning lay on sticks and feed the fire. That is, a man shall by psalms, pure thoughts, and fervent desire feed the fire of love in his heart that it go not out at any time. This peace our Lord gives to some of His servants as a reward for their labour and a foreshadowing of the love which they shall have in the happiness of heaven.

THE THIRTY-THIRD CHAPTER

What those should do who are troubled with distractions at prayer

But now you may say that I take too high a line in this matter of prayer, for it is one thing for me to speak about it, but it is quite another to carry it out. You say that you cannot pray so devoutly or undistractedly as I have said you should. For when you would raise your heart up to God in prayer, many idle thoughts come into your mind, of what you have done, or what you are going to do, and what other men are doing, and the like. These hinder and bother you so much that you feel no pleasure or peace or devotion in your prayer. And often the more trouble you take to keep your heart recollected, the more it becomes dissipated—sometimes from the beginning to the end of your prayer—so that you think your whole effort is lost.

As to taking too high a line in this matter of prayer, I admit that I cannot myself practise the sort of prayer I have been describing. But I have described it for this reason, that we should know what praying well really means. And since we cannot in fact achieve it, we should humbly recognize how feeble we are and cry to God for mercy. Our Lord Himself told us as much when He said: *Diliges Dominum Deum tuum ex toto corde tuo, ex tota anima tua, et ex omnibus viribus tuis* (Luke x. 27). You shall love God with your whole heart, and your whole soul, and your whole strength. No man carries that out perfectly while he is here on earth, and nevertheless that is the way our Lord bade us love. And the reason is, as St Bernard[1] says, that we should recognize our weakness and then humbly cry for mercy, and we shall have it.

Nevertheless I shall give you my opinion in this matter. When you begin your prayer, direct your intention quite briefly to God as purely as you can, and then begin and do your best. And though your original intention seems entirely frustrated, do not be too much upset, nor too angry with yourself, nor impatient against God, because He does not give you that sensible devotion and spiritual sweetness that you think He gives to others. But see in all this your own weakness, and bear it easily, holding humbly to your prayer, feeble as it is, and trusting securely that our Lord in His mercy will make it good and profitable, more than you know or feel. For you ought to know that your effort is taken in payment of your debt, and it is as meritorious as any other good deed done in charity, even though you were distracted when you were doing it. Therefore play your part,

[1] St Bernard, *in Cant*. Serm. L, n. 2 (P.L., CLXXXIII, col. 1021).

and let our Lord do what He will, and do not try to instruct Him. And even though you seem to yourself to be careless and negligent and much to blame for this inability to pray, nevertheless for this, as for all venial sins which you cannot escape in this wretched life, lift up your heart to God, acknowledging your wretchedness, and beg for mercy with confidence. And do not struggle with yourself, dwelling on your weakness, as though by your own effort you could avoid feeling it. Leave your prayer and go to some other good work, spiritual or corporal, and resolve to do better another time. But though you fall in just the same way another time, yes, and a hundred or a thousand times, do as I have said, and all shall be well. And a soul that never does find rest of heart in prayer, but all her life is striving with distractions and troubled by them, if she keep herself in humility and charity, shall have great reward in heaven for her efforts.

THE THIRTY-FOURTH CHAPTER

Of meditation for sinners after they have turned wholly to God

Now I will tell you something of meditation.[1] You must understand that in this matter no certain rule can be laid down for everyone to keep. It is in the free gift of God and

---

[1] It is clear from this and the following chapter that Hilton means something quite other by the word meditation than we mean today. In modern usage it connotes in such a context as this the methodical use of the discursive reason on some point of faith or of our Lord's life, which is undertaken with the purpose of exciting the will to acts of love, sorrow, etc. Hilton says of it, "You must understand that in this matter no certain rule can be laid down for everyone to keep. It is in the free gift of God and is given according to the different dispositions and the states of chosen souls. And as souls acquire more virtues and advance to higher states He

is given according to the different dispositions and the states
of chosen souls. And as souls acquire more virtues and advance to higher states He increases the knowledge and love
of Him that they have in meditation. For it would seem
that a man who does not grow in the knowledge of God and
spiritual matters does not grow in love either. And that can
be seen clearly in the apostles; when they were filled with
burning love by the Holy Ghost on the day of Pentecost,
they did not become foolish, but on the contrary were filled
with as great wisdom as a man might have on earth, both to
know God and to speak of Him. Scripture says of them:

---

increases the knowledge and love of Him that they have in meditation"
(chap. 34, p. 48). "Our Lord gives . . . a meditation on His humanity—
His birth or passion—or the compassion of our Lady, St Mary. When this
meditation is the work of the Holy Spirit it is truly valuable and comforting" (chap. 35, p. 50). And he goes on to describe what occurs when the
soul is stirred to such a meditation. "Your mind is suddenly detached from
all worldly and material things, and you seem to see Jesus in your soul as
He appeared on earth; you see Him taken by the Jews and bound as a
thief, beaten and despised, scourged and condemned to death" (chap. 35,
p. 50). And later in the same chapter: "When, then, the memory of
Christ's passion or any event in His life arises in your mind through such
a spiritual vision, with a corresponding devout affection, you ought to
understand that it is not of your own bringing about, nor is it feigned by
a wicked spirit, but it is brought about by the grace of the Holy Ghost;
for it is an opening of the eyes of the spirit on to Christ's humanity"
(chap. 35, p. 50–1). Such texts make it perfectly clear that he is referring
to some sort of contemplation, and the phrase "an opening of the eyes of
the spirit on to Christ's humanity" may be compared with what he says
in the second Book, "This opening of the eyes of the spirit to the knowledge of the Godhead I call reform in faith and feeling" (Bk. II, chap. 33,
p. 246). There he is talking about the higher kinds of contemplation, here
he is evidently referring to imaginative visions of the humanity of Christ
which might be expected to precede the higher ones of the divinity, as
indeed he says they do. "For a man will not have spiritual delight in contemplation of Christ's divinity, unless he first dwells in imagination and
with compassion on His humanity" (chap. 35, p. 51). Cf. chap. 15, n. 2.

Repleti sunt omnes Spiritu sancto et coeperunt loqui magnalia Dei
(Acts ii. 4 and 11 [2]). They were filled with the Holy Ghost
and began to announce the great marvels of God. And all
that knowledge came to them in an ecstasy of love through
the operation of the Holy Ghost.

There are various meditations which our Lord puts into
a man's heart. I shall tell you of some so that, if you experience them, you may the better profit by them. At the
beginning of his conversion a man who has been much
stained with worldliness and sins of the flesh generally dwells
most on his sins. He feels great compunction and sorrow;
he weeps abundantly, humbly and earnestly asking mercy
and pardon of God. And if he is strongly touched with compunction, because God wishes to cleanse him quickly, his
sins will seem to be always in his sight, and to be so foul and
horrible that he hardly knows what to do with himself. And
however exactly he confesses, his conscience will prick
him, so that he thinks he has not made a good confession. He
can feel no rest, and the strain would become intolerable, if
God in His mercy did not sometimes comfort him with feelings of great devotion—it may be to the passion, or whatever seems best to Him. God works in some men's hearts in
this way—to a greater or less degree, according as He wills.
And this is the great mercy of God, that He will not only
forgive the sin but will remit also the pain of purgatory for
a little pain of conscience here. Also, if God wishes to prepare a man to receive a special gift of His love, He must first
cleanse him by making him feel the fire of compunction for
the great sins he has committed. David speaks of this work
in many places of the Psalter and especially in the psalm
Miserere mei Deus (Ps. l).

---

[2] Hilton has conflated two texts here.

THE THIRTY-FIFTH CHAPTER

That the meditation of the humanity and the passion of Christ is a gift of God, and how a man may know when he has received it

AFTER this trial, and sometimes during it, our Lord gives to the converted sinner, or equally to the man who has always kept his innocence, a meditation on His humanity—His birth or passion—or the compassion of our Lady, St Mary. When this meditation is the work of the Holy Spirit, it is truly valuable and comforting, and this is the sign by which you may recognize it. Your mind is suddenly detached from all worldly and material things, and you seem to see Jesus in your soul as He appeared on earth; you see Him taken by the Jews and bound as a thief, beaten and despised, scourged and condemned to death; with what humility He carried the cross on His shoulders, and with what cruelty He was nailed to it. You see, too, the crown of thorns upon His head and the sharp spear that pierced Him to the heart, and at this sight you feel your heart moved to such great compassion and pity for your Lord Jesus, that you mourn and weep and cry out with all the power of your body and soul, marvelling at the goodness and love, the patience and humility of your Lord, that He would for so sinful a wretch as you are suffer such great pain. And nevertheless you feel so much the great goodness and mercy of our Lord that your heart overflows with love and gladness, and you shed many sweet tears. And you have great confidence in the forgiveness of your sins and the salvation of your soul by virtue of His precious passion. When, then, the memory of Christ's passion or any event in His life arises in your mind through such a spiritual vision, with a corresponding devout affection, you ought to understand that it is not of your own bringing about, nor is it feigned by a wicked spirit, but it is brought about by the grace of the Holy Ghost; for it is an opening of the eyes of the spirit on to Christ's humanity. It may be called the carnal love of Christ as St Bernard[1] called it, in as much as it has for its object the human nature of Christ. It is truly good and a great help in destroying sin and acquiring virtue, and so later in coming to the contemplation of the Godhead. For a man will not have spiritual delight in contemplation of Christ's divinity, unless he dwells first in imagination with anguish and with compassion on His humanity. St Paul did this, for he said first: *Nihil judicavi me scire inter vos, nisi Jesum Christum, et hunc crucifixum* (1 Cor. ii. 2). I showed you nothing of all that I knew, but Jesus Christ and Him crucified. As if he had said: My knowledge and my trust is only in the passion of Christ. And therefore he said also: *Mihi autem absit gloriari, nisi in cruce Domini nostri Jesu Christi* (Gal. vi. 14). Let all manner of joy and delight be far from me but in the cross and the passion of our Lord Jesus Christ. And nevertheless afterwards he said: *Praedicamus vobis Christum Dei virtutem, et Dei sapientiam* (1 Cor. i. 23, 24).[2] As who says: First I preached the humanity and passion of Christ, now I preach the divinity; that is Christ, the power and endless wisdom of God.

THE THIRTY-SIXTH CHAPTER

That the meditation of the passion of Christ is often withdrawn for various reasons from those who have received it

A MAN does not always have this sort of meditation at will, but only when our Lord chooses to give it. Some men and women have it at intervals all their lives, when He visits them. For some have such tender affections that when they

---

[1] St Bernard, *in Cant.* Serm. xx, n. 6 (P.L., t. CLXXXIII, col. 870).
[2] A conflated text again.

hear the passion spoken of, or when the thought of it comes
to their minds, their hearts melt with devotion and are comforted against all manner of diabolical temptations; and that
is a great gift of God. To others He gives it at first freely,
and afterwards withdraws it for various reasons. It may be
because a man takes pride in it, or commits some other sin
which makes him unable to receive the grace. And sometimes our Lord withdraws it and all other feelings of devotion from a man to allow him to be assailed by temptations
of the devil. And in this way He brings him to a more spiritual knowledge of Himself. For He Himself said to His disciples: *Expedit vobis ut ego vadam; si autem non abiero, Para-
cletus non veniet ad vos* (John xvi. 7). It is profitable that I
go from you in my bodily form, for if I go not the Holy
Ghost may not come to you. For as long as He was with
them they loved Him much, but it was His humanity they
loved. And therefore it was profitable to them that He
should withdraw His bodily form from their sight, in order
that the Holy Ghost might come to them and teach them to
love Him and know Him more spiritually, as He did on the
day of Pentecost. In just the same way it is for the good of
some that our Lord should withdraw a little His bodily
image from the eyes of the soul, that the heart may desire
and seek His divinity more assiduously.

THE THIRTY-SEVENTH CHAPTER

Of various temptations of the devil[1]

NEVERTHELESS a man must first suffer many temptations.
And these temptations, through the malice of the enemy,
will afflict him in various ways when consolation has been

[1] These violent temptations, whether to bodily or spiritual sins, to
sensuality or to blasphemy and despair, may afflict any who give them-

withdrawn. For example, when the devil perceives that devotion has been taken away, so that the soul is left as it were naked for a time, he sends some men such fierce temptations to sensuality and gluttony that they think they never felt any so grievous before in all their lives—not even when they gave themselves most to sin. So much so that it seems impossible to endure them and that they must fall, unless they have help. And so they are much afflicted, both by the lack of consolation and devotion which they previously had, and by the fear of falling from God by such manifest sins. And the devil works all this in them by the sufferance of God to make them forgo their good intentions and turn to sin as they were wont to do. But if a man will wait patiently and put up with a little suffering, and refuse at all costs to turn to sin again, the hand of the Lord is near him and will soon give help. For God keeps him safely and the man knows not how. As the prophet David said in the person of our Lord: *Cum ipso sum in tribulatione, eripiam eum et glorificabo eum* (Ps. xc. 15). I am with him in his tribulation, and in temptation I shall deliver him and shall establish him gloriously in my bliss. Some men are maliciously tempted by spiritual sins, as by doubts about the faith, or about the Sacrament of our Lord's Body; also by despair, or blasphemies against our Lord and the saints, or by loathing of life, or bitterness and unreasonable depression, or by too much anxiety about themselves and their bodies when they devote themselves wholly to God's service. Some again— and those namely who lead a solitary life—are tempted by great fears and horrible apparitions, either in bodily form or in their imagination, sometimes in their sleep, sometimes when they are awake. And they are so troubled by these

selves seriously to the pursuit of holiness. In chap. 38 Hilton draws on the age-long wisdom of the Church in his advice on how to meet them.

things that they can hardly have any rest. And in many other ways, more than I can or may say, the devil tempts them.

THE THIRTY-EIGHTH CHAPTER

Various remedies against temptations of the devil

ONE remedy for such as are afflicted in this way is to put all their trust in our Lord Jesus Christ, and often to recall His passion and the pains He suffered for us. Then they should believe that all the sorrow and affliction that they feel in such temptations—which to the inexperienced seem to mean that God has forsaken them—are in fact neither a reproof nor a forsaking, but are a trial sent for their improvement; either in expiation of the sins they have committed, or to increase their reward, or to prepare them for further grace. The one thing necessary is that they should suffer patiently and not turn again deliberately to sin. Another remedy is that they should not fear, or consider as sin, or take to heart, any evil inclination to despair, or blasphemy against the Sacrament, or any other disquieting experience, for to undergo these temptations no more defiles the soul than the barking of a dog or the bite of a flea. They torment the soul but do it no harm, if they are despised and set at nought. It is not wise to fight directly against them and to seek to be rid of them by force, for the more one fights against such thoughts, the more they return. And so, as far as possible, distract your mind from them and occupy it with something else. And if they yet persist, do not lose patience or become depressed, but bear them with a firm trust in God, as you would a bodily pain or an affliction sent by God for the cleansing of your sins. Bear them for love of Him and for as long as He wills, as He was scourged and bore the cross for the love of you. And furthermore it is a good thing in the beginning, before they have taken root, to open your heart to some wise man, and renouncing your own judgement to follow his advice. And do not easily reveal them to an inexperienced or worldly man who never felt such temptations, for such a one could easily bring a simple soul to despair through his lack of knowledge. For the consolation of those who are tempted in this way, so that they seem forsaken of God, our Lord said by His prophet: *In modico dereliqui te, et in momento indignationis meae percussi te, et in miserationibus meis multis congregabo te* (Isa. liv. 7). For a little time I forsook you, that is to say, I allowed you to be tormented a little, and in a moment of indignation I struck you; that is to say all the penance and the pain that you undergo here is but a moment of my indignation compared to the pain of hell or purgatory; and yet in my manifold mercies I shall enfold you, and when you think you are forsaken, I shall in my great mercy gather you again to me. For when you think you are lost, our Lord will help you, as Job says: *Cum te consumptum putaveris, orieris ut lucifer et habebis fiduciam* (Job xi. 17). That is to say, when you are brought so low by the affliction of temptation that you think you have no help and no consolation but are as it were forsaken, yet stand firmly in hope and pray to God, and in truth you shall suddenly spring up as the day star in gladness of heart and have true confidence in God according to the word of Job.

THE THIRTY-NINTH CHAPTER

How God allows His elect to be tried and tempted, and how He afterwards consoles them and confirms them in grace

To console such men that they may not despair in temptation the Wise Man says of our Lord: *In tentatione ambulat cum eo. In primis eligit eum. Timorem, et metum, et approbationem inducet super illum; et cruciabit illum in tribulatione doctrinae suae, donec tentet illum in cogitationibus suis, et credat animae illius. Et iter directum adducet ad illum, et firmabit illum, et laetificabit illum; et denudabit abscondita sua illi, et thesaurizabit super illum scientiam et intellectum justitiae* (Ecclus. iv. 18–21). That is as much as to say: The Wise Man, because he would that no man should despair in temptation, says for his comfort: our Lord does not forsake a man in temptation, but is with him from the beginning to the end. For he says that first He chooses him—that is when He draws him to Himself by the consolation of devotion—and afterwards He brings upon him sorrow and fear and trials—that is when He withdraws devotion and allows him to be tempted. Also, he says that He pursues him with tribulation, until He has tested all his thoughts, and until he will trust in Him completely. After this our Lord makes the way straight before him, and attaches him to Himself, and gladdens him and shows him His secrets, and enriches him with the knowledge of righteousness.

By these words of Holy Scripture you may see that any temptations, however disquieting they may be, are profitable to a man who by the grace of God has a real determination to leave sin. But he must patiently abide God's will, and neither sorrow, nor pain, nor the fear of temptation, must make him turn again to the sin he has forsaken; on the contrary he must ever persevere in the fight and in prayer with a firm hope. Our Lord in His endless goodness, having

56

pity and mercy on His creatures, when He sees the appropriate time, lays to with His hand and strikes down the devil with all his power. He lightens the affliction, and puts away anxieties and sorrow and darkness out of the heart. He brings the light of grace into the soul and opens the inward eye to see the value of all this suffering. He gives men a new spiritual power to withstand easily all the efforts of the devil and to avoid all mortal sins; He confirms them in virtue and the good life, and, if they are humble, He will preserve them in it to the end, and then take them entirely to Himself. This, then, is my advice to you: if you are afflicted with any such temptations, do not be too anxious, but do as I have said, and better if you can, and I hope by the grace of Jesus Christ you will never be overcome by your enemy.

THE FORTIETH CHAPTER

That a man should not give himself up to idleness or neglect the grace given him by God[1]

WHEN you have escaped from these temptations, or if our Lord has preserved you from being much troubled by them —as in His mercy He preserves many—it is well that you should not allow your peace to degenerate into idleness; for

---

[1] The general advice which Hilton gives in these chapters (40–1) is wise and traditional and is to be found already in Cassian (*Collat.* XIV, chap. 5; P.L., t. XLIX, col. 959). It is clearly a matter of prudence to recognize what is the best method of serving God, not in itself, but for us. And having chosen our way of life we have still to recognize the limits of our capabilities. The indiscriminate imitation of the actions or devotions recorded in the lives of the saints, for example, would be disastrous.

However, it is to be noted that when Hilton speaks in chap. 40 of entering into the consideration of one's own soul, he does not merely mean "recognizing one's gift from God", the limits of one's capabilities in the spiritual life. See the following note.

many rest too soon. But you may begin a new exercise and a new labour, and that is to enter by meditation into the consideration of your own soul[2] in order that you may learn its nature and thereby come to the knowledge of God. St Augustine[3] says: By knowing myself I shall come to the knowledge of God. I do not say that it is necessary for you or any man to strive for this, unless he feels moved to it by grace. For our Lord gives various gifts as He sees fit, not all to one man, or one to all men; save charity, which is common to all.[4] And therefore if anyone has received a gift of

[2] When Hilton speaks of getting to know the nature of our own soul in order that thereby we may come to know the nature of God, it seems to me that there are two distinct processes to which he may be referring. One is the sort of consideration of the state of our soul in relation to God of which he gives an example in chap. 43, the other is the much deeper knowledge of ourselves and of what he calls the roots of sin in us, which comes as the result of the seeking God described in chaps. 46–54. No doubt both processes are necessary, but that he has in mind also the second is, I think, clear from his use of the word meditation at this point, which it is to be remembered means for him some kind of contemplation or at least affective prayer (see chap. 29, n. 1, and chap. 34, n. 1). So, too, he speaks here of the exercise as itself a gift from God, not to be undertaken till the grace for it has been received.

[3] Perhaps the reference is to the *Liber de spiritu et anima*, chap. 52: *Et ita per cognitionem nostram ad cognitionem Dei pervenire* (P.L., t. XL, col. 818). The work is by an unknown author but has often been attributed to St Augustine. It is, in fact, a compilation largely made up of extracts from St Augustine. See Wilmart, *Revue d'ascétique et de mystique*, VIII, p. 251.

[4] Hilton means, of course, that charity is common to all men in grace. When God gives grace He infuses the supernatural virtues of faith, hope, and charity into the soul, and of these virtues it is charity which directs the soul to God as its ultimate good. It is therefore at the root of all virtues and no virtue is meritorious supernaturally unless it is "informed" by charity, that is directed to God as its last end. It must then be the fundamental gift of God to man without which all other gifts would be meaningless in the supernatural order, and in this sense it is common to all men in grace. Cf. chaps. 18, n. 2, and 66, n. 2 (Bk. I).

God—as devotion in prayer or to the passion of Christ, or any other however small—let him not leave it too soon for another, unless he is certainly conscious that a better is being offered him. But let him keep the one that he has and cultivate it perseveringly, ever desiring a better when God wills to give it. Nevertheless, if after a time his gift is taken away and he sees a better one and feels drawn to it, then it would seem that God is calling him to the better, and it is time for him to pursue it and to cultivate it as quickly as he can.

THE FORTY-FIRST CHAPTER

That each should know the measure of his gift from God that he may desire a better one and receive it when God will give it to him

THE holy fathers[1] who went before us taught that we should know the measure of the gift God has given us, and act accordingly; not pretending to more than we have in fact. We may always desire the best, but we may not always achieve it, because we have not received the grace for it. A hound that only runs after the hare because he sees other hounds run, rests and turns home again when he is tired. But if he runs because he sees the hare, he will not stop, although he is tired, until he has caught it. It is the same in the spiritual life. Whoever has a grace, however small, and deliberately gives up acting on it, and strives after one that

[1] Cassian, *Collat.*, Coll. XIV, chap. 5 (P.L., XLIX, col. 959). By the gift is meant the general degree of perfection to which a man may feel himself equal. There is great wisdom in Hilton's advice for there is need of discretion and humility in this matter.

The example of the hound running because he sees other hounds running is found in the *Vitae Patrum*, Lib. V, cap. 7, n. 35 (P.L., LXXIII, col. 901).

has not yet been given to him, because he sees or hears that other men have it, may indeed run awhile, until he is tired, but then he will turn home again, and he will be lucky if he does not get home lame as a result of his fancies. If on the contrary he acts according to the grace that he has, and seeks greater by humble and persevering prayer, then when he feels moved to follow the grace he desired, he may safely do so, on condition that he preserves his humility. And therefore, as far as in you lies, desire without measure or discretion to obtain from God all that pertains to His love or the joy of heaven. For who desires most from God will receive most. Act as you are able, and beg God in His mercy to make up for your deficiencies. This seems to be what St Paul meant when he said: *Unusquisque habet donum suum ex Deo, alius autem sic, alius vero sic* (1 Cor. vii. 7). *Item unicuique nostrum data est gratia secundum mensuram donationis Christi* (Eph. iv. 7). *Divisiones gratiarum sunt, alii datur sermo sapientiae; alii sermo scientiae* (1 Cor. xii. 4 and 8). *Item ut sciamus quae a Deo donata sunt nobis* (1 Cor. ii. 12).

St Paul says that each man has his gift of God, one this and another that. For to each man who will be saved is given a grace after the measure of Christ's gift, and therefore it is good that we should know the gifts which God has given us that we may make use of them. For by these we shall be saved—some by external acts and works of mercy, some by great bodily penance, some by spending their lives in sorrow and weeping for their sins, some by preaching and giving instruction, some by various gifts of devotion.

THE FORTY-SECOND CHAPTER

That a man should strive to know his own soul and its powers,
and to destroy the roots of sin

THERE is, nevertheless, one activity which is of great value
and, as I think, a highway to contemplation, in so far as any
human endeavour may be. It is for a man to enter into himself and come to the knowledge of his own soul and its
powers, its beauty, and its blemishes.[1] In this process you
will see the nobility and dignity which belong to the soul
naturally from its creation,[2] and the wretchedness and
misery which are the result of sin. And from the sight of this
there will come a great desire to recover again the dignity
and nobility which you have lost. The experience will fill
you with horror and detestation at yourself, and at the same
time with a strong determination to overcome yourself and
to destroy everything that comes between you and that dignity and joy. This is at first a difficult and painful spiritual
labour for those who give themselves to it earnestly. For it
is a striving in the soul against the root of all sins, great and
small, and this root is nothing else than a false, mis-guided,

[1] This I believe to be the activity to which he referred in chap. 40 (see
n. 2), and I do not believe that it is limited to the sort of considerations
which he gives in chap. 43. This coming to a knowledge of one's own
soul is a lengthy and gradual process and it goes hand in hand with the
reformation of the image of God in the soul. The soul turns progressively
from sin as it realizes progressively the extent of the roots of sin within
it. This entering into self is in fact nothing other than what he later calls
"seeking Jesus". In the next section (chaps. 46–54) he will describe how
God is to be sought within the soul itself, and in seeking Him there the
soul will find first the *image of sin*, its own sinfulness.

[2] When he speaks of "the nobility and dignity which belong to the soul
naturally from its creation", he is obviously referring to the soul of man
as it was first created by God, and there is nothing to suggest that this rec-
titude is "natural" to the soul in the sense that Baius was afterwards to
assert.

self-love. From this love, as St Augustine says,[3] come all
manner of mortal and venial sins. And indeed until the root
is dug up and laid bare, and, as it were, withered by the re-
jection of all love and anxiety springing from the flesh and
the world, the soul may never feel the ardent love of Jesus
Christ, nor enjoy the intimacy of His gracious presence; nor
will its understanding ever come to a clear view of spiritual
matters. By this labour a man must withdraw his heart and
his mind from the love of all earthly creatures, from vain
thoughts, and images of all sensible things, and from all self-
love, so that the soul may find no rest in these things. Then
since it cannot find rest in the love and sight of Jesus Christ
it must needs suffer pain. This labour is somewhat severe
and exacting, but, unless I am mistaken, it is the way that
Christ taught in the gospel to those who would be His perfect lovers. *Contendite intrare per angustam portam* (Luke
xiii. 24): *quam arcta est via quae ducit ad vitam et pauci in-
veniunt eam* (Matt. vii. 14). Strive therefore to enter by the
narrow gate for the way that leads to heaven is narrow and
few men find it. And how narrow the way is our Lord tells
in another place: *Si quis vult venire post me, abneget semetipsum,
et tollat crucem suam, et sequatur me* (Matt. xvi. 24). *Item qui
odit animam suam in hoc mundo, in vitam aeternam custodit eam*
(John xii. 25). That is to say: Whoever will come after me,
let him forsake himself and hate his own soul. That is, forsake
all carnal love and hate his own bodily life and the vain pleasure of his senses for love of Me; and let him take the cross,
that is suffer the pain of this world, for a time, and then follow Me in the contemplation of My humanity and My divinity. This is so narrow a way that nothing material may pass
through it, for it is a slaying of all sin; as St Paul says: *Morti-*

[3] The reference may be to *De Civitate Dei*, Lib. xiv, cap. 28 (P.L., xli,
col. 436), or to the *Sermons*, Serm. xcvi, n. 2 (P.L., xxxviii, col. 585);
Serm. cccxxx, n. 3 (P.L., xxxviii, col. 1457).

ficate membra vestra, quae sunt super terram; immunditiam, libi-dinem, concupiscentiam malam (Col. iii. 5). Slay your members on the earth; not the members of the body but of the soul, as impurity, lust, and unreasonable love of yourself and earthly things. Therefore as up till now your labour has been to withstand great external sins and open temptations of the enemy, as it were from without, now in this spiritual work you must destroy and break down the root of sin in yourself so far as you are able. And that you may the more readily bring it about, I shall give you what advice seems good to me.

THE FORTY-THIRD CHAPTER

That a man should know the excellence and the dignity that the soul first had from God, and the wretchedness and misery that it has fallen into through sin

THE soul of man is a life with three powers[1]—memory, understanding, and will—made in the image and likeness of the Blessed Trinity, whole, perfect, and righteous. The

---

[1] *The soul of man is a life.* This definition of the soul, though strictly inadequate, is sufficiently near to the scholastic definition of the soul as *primum principium vitae* (St Thom., *Summa*, Ia, q. LXXV, art. 1) for Hilton's purpose. Julian of Norwich (*Rev. of Divine Love*, chap. 53) uses the same expression, "He willeth we be aware that our Soul is a life."

With regard to the comparison of the three powers of the soul to the Trinity, many of the Fathers have made use of it, and the ultimate source seems to be St Augustine (*De Trinitate*, Bk. x). References to Hugh of St Victor and St Anselm on the point will be found in the notes to the French edition of *The Scale* (ad loc.). It may be added that St Augustine seems to have meant by *memoria* not so much a particular faculty of the soul as the source and principle of all conscious activity (cf. St Thom., *Summa*, Ia, q. LXXIX, art. 7 ad 1am), and it is in this sense that it could be said to be an image of the First Person of the Trinity. Hilton uses the word "mind", and in Middle English this could mean both "mind" and

memory has the likeness of the Father in as much as it was given power to retain His image, neither forgetting it nor being distracted by creatures. The understanding was made clear and bright without error or darkness, as perfect as it might be in a body not glorified; and so it has the likeness of the Son, who is eternal Wisdom. The will was made pure, springing up to God without love of the flesh or of creatures, by the sovereign goodness of the Holy Ghost, and so it has the likeness of the Holy Ghost, who is divine love. So man's soul, which may be called a created trinity, was perfected in the memory, sight, and love of the uncreated Blessed Trinity, which is God. This is the dignity and nobility which belong to man's soul naturally at its creation.[2] You possessed this state in Adam before man's first sin.[3] But when Adam sinned, choosing to squander his love on himself and creatures, and to take his pleasure in them, he lost all his nobility and dignity, and you also in him, and he fell from that blessed Trinity into a horrible, dark, wretched trinity; that is into forgetfulness and ignorance of God, and into a monstrous love of himself. It was an unreasonable act, for as David said in the psalter: *Homo, cum in honore esset, non intellexit; comparatus est jumentis insipientibus, et similis factus est illis* (Ps. xlviii. 13). Man knew not when he had nobility, and therefore he lost it and was made like a beast. See then the present misery of your soul.[4] Your memory was once

---

"memory"—although the N.E.D. only gives one example of the former meaning before 1400. To have kept "mind" would perhaps have given the sense of Augustine's *memoria* better, but I have used what has become the traditional terminology. The same problem arises in chap. 62 of *The Cloud*, where Dom Justin McCann has retained the word "mind" in his version. See his note on the point.

[2] See chap. 42, n. 2.

[3] In the sense that before Adam's sin human nature was in the state described.

[4] Hilton gives in this chapter certain considerations which are calcu-

64

stably fixed on God, but now it has forgotten Him and seeks
to find rest in creatures, now one, now another, and it can
never find full rest for it has lost Him in whom alone it may
be found. And so it is with the understanding. The will also,
once pure, with a taste and delight in spiritual things, is
turned now to an animal pleasure in itself and creatures; in
the senses through gluttony and sensuality, and in imagination through pride, vainglory, and covetousness. So far is this
the case that you can hardly do any good deed without being
defiled by vainglory. And you can hardly apply any of your
senses to a delectable object without your heart being seized
and inflamed with a vain lust and attraction for it, which
drives out any feeling and taste for the love of God from the
heart. Every spiritual man knows this well. It is the misery
of the soul and the harm caused by man's first sin, not to
mention all the other evil and sins that you have voluntarily
added. And be sure of this, even though you had never committed a venial or mortal sin, but had only incurred this
which is called original—for it is the first sin and is nothing
else than the loss of the justice in which you were created
—you would never have been saved, if our Lord Jesus Christ
by His precious passion had not redeemed and restored you
again.

---

lated to make a man wish to turn from sin and serve God. The realization
of the plight he is in is, of course, a necessary preliminary to the determination to reform himself, but, as I said in n. 1 to the last chapter, the
real acquirement of self-knowledge is a much deeper and more lengthy
process, only achieved in the process of seeking God. The kind of consideration which he devotes to the soul here is only a preamble designed
to make a man undertake the business of reforming his soul in the image
of God. How this is to be done and what it will involve forms the subject-
matter of the next section (46–54).

THE FORTY-FOURTH CHAPTER

*How every man may be saved by the passion of Christ, be he
never so sinful*

AND if you think that I have thus far made too great demands
of you, which you cannot meet, I will now come down as
low as you please, for my profit as well as for yours. For I say
that however miserable a wretch you are, however great
sins you have committed, turn away from yourself and all
your works, good and bad, humbly and trustfully ask for
mercy and salvation through the power of the precious passion of Christ, and without doubt you will obtain it. You
will be saved from original sin and from all others, and it is
as an anchoress that you will be saved. And not only you,
but all Christians who trust in the passion, and humble
themselves, who acknowledge their wretchedness and, asking mercy and forgiveness by the merits of the passion, submit themselves to the sacraments of Holy Church—though
they have been weighed down by sin all their lifetime and
never tasted spiritual favours or had any spiritual knowledge
of God—shall through their faith and good will by the merits
of the precious passion of our Lord Jesus Christ be saved and
come to the happiness of heaven. You know all this well and
yet it pleases me to say it. See the endless mercy of our Lord,
how He condescends to you and to me and to all sinful
wretches; ask mercy, then, and you will receive it. The
prophet said in the person of our Lord: *Omnis enim qui invo-
caverit nomen Domini, salvus erit* (Joel ii. 32). Let every man,
whatsoever he be, call upon the name of God, that is to say
ask salvation through Jesus and His passion, and he shall be
saved. Some men use this kindness of God well and are saved
by it, and some men, relying on this mercy and kindness and
thinking that they can call upon them when they will, remain in their sins. And then they fail to obtain them, for

they are taken before they know it, and so damn themselves.

But then you say:[1] If this is true, then I wonder greatly at what I find written in some holy men's books. Some say, I understand, that he who cannot love this blessed name Jesus, nor take any spiritual joy and pleasure in it in this life, shall be cut off from the joy and happiness of heaven, and shall never attain it. Indeed when I read these words, I am amazed and very much afraid for I hope that, as you say, many through the mercy of God shall be saved by keeping His commandments and true repentance for their past

[1] The long passage from here to the end of the chapter presents some textual difficulty. I am indebted to Miss Birts for the information that of the manuscripts she has seen, twenty-two contain it and thirteen omit it, while three of those which have it show an awareness that some copies were without it, and one of those omitting it has a marginal reference to the omission. She further drew my attention to the important point that in the text of chaps. 38–52 the manuscripts fall into two main groups, and this division cuts across the division into manuscripts with or without this passage. That is to say the passage is absent from a number of manuscripts in each group but not from all in either group. It would seem then that it must have been in the archetype of these two groups, whether or not that was Hilton's autograph. No explanation has yet been found of how it came to be dropped from some manuscripts of each group, and it is possible that it never will be. Miss Gardner (in *Medium Aevum*, 1936, p. 29) suggested that a leaf was originally lost by accident. This would account for some of the manuscripts in the group to which it belonged being without the passage, but we can only suppose that it was deliberately left out in the other group by a scribe who knew of the shorter version and was either lazy or in a hurry.

The French editors (*Scala Perfectionis*, Paris, 1923, p. 195 n.) expressed the view that it was a reference to Rolle's *Encomium Nominis Jesu* (Horstman, *Richard Rolle of Hampole and his followers* (London, 1895), vol. 1, p. 186), and it would seem that this may well have been the case. Hilton quotes the author he is criticizing as saying that he who cannot (1) love, and (2) find joy in the Holy Name shall be "alien" to the bliss of heaven. The *Encomium* says: "Also witte alle þat þe name of Ihesu is heleful, frutful, and glorious. þerfore quo sal haue hele þat lufs it noght? qua sal bere fruit before Crist þat has not þo floure? and Ioy sal he noght see þat Ioyande lufd noght þo name of Ihesu."

sins, who never felt spiritual sweetness nor inward relish in
the name of Jesus, nor in His love. And therefore I am the
more amazed that these books say the contrary as it seems.
And to this I reply that it seems to me that what they say, if
it is properly understood, is not contrary to what I have
said. For this name Jesus means no more in English than
health or healer. Now every man in this miserable life is
spiritually sick, for no man lives without sin, which is
spiritual sickness. As St John says of himself and other perfect
men: *Si dixerimus quia peccatum non habemus, ipsi nos seduci-*
mus, et veritas in nobis non est (1 John i. 8). If we say we have
no sin, we deceive ourselves and the truth is not in us. And
therefore no man may come to the joy of heaven until he is
cured of this spiritual sickness. But on the other hand no
man who has the use of his reason may have spiritual health,
unless he desires it, and loves it, and delights in it, and indeed hopes to get it. Now the name of Jesus is nothing else
than this spiritual health; and so it is true what they say, that
no man may be saved who does not love the name of Jesus,
for no man can be spiritually in health if he does not love
and desire it. Just as if a man were sick in body, no earthly
thing would be so dear to him, or so necessary and much
desired as bodily health; for if you gave him all the riches
and honour in the world and did not cure him, if it were in
your power, you would give him no satisfaction. It is so
with a man that is sick spiritually and suffers the pain of
spiritual sickness. Nothing is so dear or so necessary to him,
or so much to be desired as spiritual health, and that is Jesus,
without whom all the joys of heaven may not satisfy him.

And this is surely the reason why our Lord, when He became man for our salvation, would not be called by any
name that betokened His eternal being or His power, His
wisdom or His justice, but only by that which betokened
the cause of His coming, which was the salvation of man's

soul. And this salvation was most dear and most necessary
to man. And this name Jesus betokens this salvation. And so
it seems true that no man shall be saved, if he does not love
Jesus. For no man may be saved, if he does not love salvation, and hope to have it through the mercy of our Lord
Jesus and by the merits of His passion. And he who lives and
dies in the lowest degree of charity may have this love. But
on the other hand he who cannot love the blessed name of
Jesus with spiritual delight nor enjoy it with heavenly
melody in this life shall not experience in heaven the fullness
of joy that will belong to one who on earth was able to
delight in Jesus in the abundance of perfect charity. And so
this saying may be understood.

Nevertheless he who in this life has only the lowest degree
of charity by keeping God's commandments shall be saved
and have a full reward in the sight of God. For our Lord
Himself said: *In domo patris mei multae mansiones sunt* (John
xiv. 2). In My Father's house are many manions. Some are
for perfect souls, who in this life were filled with charity
and the grace of the Holy Ghost and sung the praises of God
in contemplation with great sweetness and heavenly relish.
These souls shall have the highest reward in the happiness of
heaven, for they had the greatest charity; they are God's
favourites. Other souls, who are not disposed to contemplation and who have not had the fullness of charity that the
apostles and martyrs had in the early days of the Church,
shall have lesser reward in the happiness of heaven; they are
God's friends. This is what our Lord in Holy Scripture calls
chosen souls, when He says: *Comedite, amici, et inebriamini,
carissimi* (Cant. v. 1). Eat ye, my friends, and be inebriated,
my beloved ones. As if He had said: You who are my friends,
because you kept my commandments and put my love before
the love of the world and loved me beyond any earthly
thing, shall be fed with the spiritual food of the bread of

life. But you who are my loved ones, who not only kept my commandments, but of your own free will carried out my counsels, and beyond that loved me exclusively and entirely with all your souls and burned in my love with spiritual delight—as did the apostles and martyrs and all other souls that by the grace of God come to perfection—you shall be made drunk with the finest wine of my cellar, that is the sovereign joy of love in the happiness of heaven.

THE FORTY-FIFTH CHAPTER

That a man should strive to recover the dignity of his soul, and reform again in himself the image of the Trinity

NEVERTHELESS, though this is the truth about the everlasting mercy of God to you and me and all men, we should not therefore, relying on this, be deliberately reckless in our lives. For the very reason that we now hope to be restored by the passion of our Lord to the dignity and happiness which we lost by Adam's sin we should be the more careful to please Him. And though we can never recover it entirely here, we should desire to recover a semblance of that dignity; that our soul may be restored by grace, as it were, to a shadow of that image of the Trinity, which it originally possessed and which it will have in its fullness in heaven. True contemplative life has its beginning here in this feeling of love, and in the spiritual knowledge of God which comes by the opening of the eyes of the soul. And this life shall never be lost or taken away, but it will be fulfilled in the happiness of heaven in another way.[1] Our Lord promised

[1] I take this to mean that there will be a difference of degree rather than of kind between the experience of the contemplative on earth and in heaven, and this is in accord with the view of contemplation as an awareness of the life of grace in the soul that Hilton will develop in the

this to Mary Magdalene, who was a contemplative, when He said of her : *Maria optimam partem elegit, quae non auferetur ab ea* (Luke x. 42). Mary has chosen the best part, that is the love of God in contemplation, for it shall never be taken from her. I do not say that you may recover, while you are living here, such complete and perfect purity and innocence, knowledge and love of God, as you had in the first place, or as you shall have hereafter. And I do not say that you can escape all the wretchedness and pains of sin, nor that living in your mortal flesh you may completely destroy a false, vain love of yourself, nor avoid all venial sins. And I do not say that these will not, unless they are stopped by fervent charity, keep rising up out of your heart as water from a fouled spring. But if you cannot entirely stop them, I would that you might somewhat abate them, and come as near as you can to purity of soul. For our Lord[2] said to the children of

---

second Book (cf. Bk. II, chap. 40, n. 4). I do not think that it is necessary to suppose that Hilton is committing himself one way or the other on the question as to whether the contemplative can fall from grace. It may be remembered that St John of the Cross was apparently of the opinion that the soul which had attained the so-called Transforming Union, or Spiritual Marriage, was confirmed in grace (*The Spiritual Canticle*, stanza XXII, n. 3. *Complete Works* translated and edited by E. Allison Peers (London, 1934), vol. II, p. 308), while St Teresa was much less willing to commit herself (*Interior Castle*, VII Mans., chap. 2. *Complete Works* translated and edited by E. Allison Peers (London, 1946), vol. II, p. 337). It would seem that theoretically there must still be a possibility of falling from grace, though in practice the soul which has reached this stage will be confirmed in it. It is of interest though to note that speaking of the third degree of contemplation in chap. 8 (Bk. I) Hilton says : "In this union a marriage is made between God and the soul which shall never be broken," which would seem to point to the fact that on this matter he held the view that was afterwards to be held by St John of the Cross.

[2] In modern usage we confine the term "our Lord" to Christ in His humanity. Hilton applies it equally to the Godhead, as indeed he does the Holy Name Jesus itself, and he defends himself for so doing in chap. 42 of the second Book. I have kept to his usage throughout Bk. I.

Israel, when He led them into the Promised Land, and figuratively to all Christians: *Omnis locus, quem calcaverit pes tuus tuus erit* (Deut. xi. 24). As much land as you may tread upon with the foot of true desire, so much shall you have in the Promised Land, that is in the happiness of heaven, when you attain to it.

THE FORTY-SIXTH CHAPTER

How Jesus shall be sought, desired, and found[1]

SEEK then what you have lost in order that you may find it. I am sure that anyone who had once a little insight into the dignity and beauty which belong to the soul by nature and which it may have again by grace, would hate and despise all the happiness and love and beauty of this world as he would a piece of carrion. And his only desire night and day—but for the frailty and the bare necessities of his bodily nature— would be to lament and seek by prayer how he might come to it again. But inasmuch as you have not yet seen fully what it is, because your spiritual eyes are not yet opened, I will

[1] It will be useful to give an outline of the content of this section (46–54) which really provides the key to the understanding of the whole of Hilton's doctrine. Further elucidation will be added in notes on the individual chapters.

chaps.

46 }	The foundation of this reform and of all holiness is the
47 }	desire for God, "seeking Jesus".
48 }	
49 }	He is to be found within us.
50	We cannot hear His voice because of the tumult of worldly cares.
51	The necessity for humility and charity.
52 }	
53 }	The effort to attain God—which is in fact prayer—will
54 }	result first in the discovery of our own sins.

give you one word which shall comprise all the object of your endeavours, for it contains all that you have lost. This word is Jesus. I do not mean Jesus as it may be painted on a wall, or written with letters in a book, or formed on the lips, or imagined inwardly by an effort of the mind, for in this way a man without charity may find Him. But I mean Jesus Christ, that Blessed Person, God and Man, son of the Virgin Mary, whom the name signifies; who is all goodness, endless wisdom, love, and sweetness; your joy, your dignity, and your everlasting happiness, your God, your Lord, and your salvation.

If, then, you feel a great desire in your heart for Jesus, whether prompted by the remembrance of His name, or in any other way, and this desire is so strong that it drives all other thoughts and desires of the world and the flesh, as it were by force, out of your heart, so that they find no place there, then you are truly seeking your Lord Jesus. And if you feel this desire of God, of Jesus—it is all the same[2]— helped and strengthened by spiritual power till it is turned into love and affection, into spiritual relish and sweetness, into light and knowledge of the truth, and if for the time being your mind dwells on no created thing and experiences no movement of vainglory, or of self-love, or of any other ill-regulated affection—for these things do not arise at such times—if your desire is entirely concentrated on Jesus, and

[2] Hilton is here making an explicit reference to what in fact he takes for granted throughout, namely the divinity of Christ. The fact that Christ was truly God and at the same time truly man is the mystery of the Incarnation, which theology came to express by saying that the divine and human natures were united in the Second Person of the Trinity, so that whatever can be predicated of either nature can be predicated of the Person. That Hilton should have taken all this for granted is, of course, perfectly natural, but the name Jesus is, however, usually confined to Christ in His human nature, to God Incarnate; Hilton applies it to the Godhead itself. See chap. 45, n. 2.

rests in Him with sweetness and unction, then you have found something of Jesus. Not Jesus as He is, but an image of Him. And the more you find of Him the more you will desire Him. That prayer or meditation or activity which brings you the strongest and purest desire of Him and the clearest sense of His presence is the one by which you seek and find Him best. And therefore, if you will, ask yourself what you have lost and what you seek, raise your mind and the desire of your heart to Jesus Christ, even though you are blind and can see nothing of His divinity, and say that it is He whom you have lost, and He whom you would have, and nothing else. Avow that your one desire is to be with Him where He is, and that you desire no joy or happiness in heaven or on earth apart from Him.[3] And even though by the grace of God you experience the feeling of His presence, do not rest in that as though you had fully found Him, but forget what you have found and always desire Him more and more so that you may find Him better, as though what you

[3] Hilton has no esoteric doctrine, no magic formula to conduct the soul to contemplation. What he demands is that it desire God. That is the burden of all this section and the particular theme of chaps. 46 and 47. He is careful to point out that it is not an emotional experience of God that the soul must seek (chap. 47, p. 75), and it is important to realize what this desire of God does in fact mean. It must mean that the soul desires to make contact with Him, to possess Him in the only way that it can, and that is by raising the mind and the will to Him, in other words it is prayer, and Hilton recognizes that for the recluse for whom he is writing this may be a very intense experience. "If you feel a great desire in your heart . . . and this desire is so strong that it drives all other thoughts and desires . . . out of your heart" etc. (p. 73). It is really contemplative prayer that he is referring to here, what he calls meditation (see chap. 34, n. 1), and it accounts for what he says in chap. 15 about its being by meditation that we discover the virtues of which we stand in need. It is by turning to God in a prayer which we should call today affective, and which may be truly contemplative, that we find Him within us—and also discover the roots of sin within us. See chap. 48, n. 2.

had already found was nothing. For be assured that the experience you have of Him, however great it is—yes, even if you were carried in ecstasy with St Paul into the third heaven—is not Jesus as He is in the happiness of heaven. He exceeds anything that you may know or feel of Him. And therefore if you would find Him as He is in the happiness of heaven, never give up your spiritual striving while you live.

THE FORTY-SEVENTH CHAPTER

What profit it is to have the desire of Jesus

INDEED I would rather have a true and pure desire of Jesus in my heart, though with very little spiritual enlightenment, than practise all the bodily mortification of all men living, enjoy visions and revelations of angels, or experience the most pleasing effects in my bodily senses, if they were without this desire. In a word, none of the joys of heaven or earth would tempt me, unless they contained the desire of Jesus. David the prophet felt this, as I understand him, when he said: *Quid enim mihi est in caelo? et a te quid volui super terram?* (Ps. lxxii. 25). Lord, what is there for me in heaven, or what would I on earth without thee? As though he had said: Lord Jesus, what heavenly joy can satisfy me, if I do not desire Thee while I am on earth, and love Thee when I come to heaven? As though he said: None at all! Then if you would have any experience of Him in body or soul, seek nothing but a true desire of His grace and His merciful presence, so that you feel your heart can find no rest but in Him. This was what David sought when he said: *Concupivit anima mea desiderare justificationes tuas in omni tempore* (Ps. cxviii. 20). Lord, my soul longed for the desire of thy righteousness. Seek then as David did desire by desire. And if by this means

75

you come to feel in your prayers and meditatio
mate presence of Jesus Christ in your soul, kee
and see that you do not lose it, so that, if you
away from Him, you may quickly find Him again

THE FORTY-EIGHTH CHAPT

Where and how Jesus shall be sought and

SEEK then Jesus whom you have lost. He wills t
and it follows that He can to some extent be fc
says Himself: *Omnis qui quaerit invenit* (Matt. v
man that seeks shall find. The seeking is labor
finding joyous. Follow therefore the counsel
Man if you would find Him: *Si quaesieris q*
sapientiam, et sicut thesauros effoderis illam;
timorem Domini, et scientiam Dei invenies (Prov
you seek wisdom, which is Jesus, as silver
digging deep for it, you will find it. It beho
deep in your heart, for He lies hidden there,
all love and attraction for earthly things, and
anxiety about them, and so you will find w
Jesus. Be like the woman in the gospel then
Lord said: *Quae mulier habens drachmas dece*
unam, nonne accendit lucernam, et everrit domum
diligenter donec inveniat eam? Et cum invenerit,
suos, dicens: Congratulamini mihi, quia inveni
perdideram (Luke xv. 8, 9). What woman is
lost a coin, who will not light a lamp and rai
and search till she find it? As much as to
when she has found it she calls her friends to
them: Rejoice with me because I have fou
I had lost. This coin is Jesus whom you have

had already found was nothing. For be assured that the experience you have of Him, however great it is—yes, even if you were carried in ecstasy with St Paul into the third heaven—is not Jesus as He is in the happiness of heaven. He exceeds anything that you may know or feel of Him. And therefore if you would find Him as He is in the happiness of heaven, never give up your spiritual striving while you live.

THE FORTY-SEVENTH CHAPTER

What profit it is to have the desire of Jesus

INDEED I would rather have a true and pure desire of Jesus in my heart, though with very little spiritual enlightenment, than practise all the bodily mortification of all men living, enjoy visions and revelations of angels, or experience the most pleasing effects in my bodily senses, if they were without this desire. In a word, none of the joys of heaven or earth would tempt me, unless they contained the desire of Jesus. David the prophet felt this, as I understand him, when he said: *Quid enim mihi est in caelo? et a te quid volui super terram?* (Ps. lxxii. 25). Lord, what is there for me in heaven, or what would I on earth without thee? As though he had said: Lord Jesus, what heavenly joy can satisfy, if I do not desire Thee while I am on earth, and love Thee when I come to heaven? As though he said: None at all! Then if you would have any experience of Him in body or soul, seek nothing but a true desire of His grace and His merciful presence, so that you feel your heart can find no rest but in Him. This was what David sought when he said: *Concupivit anima mea desiderare justificationes tuas in omni tempore* (Ps. cxviii. 20). Lord, my soul longed for the desire of thy righteousness. Seek then as David did desire by desire. And if by this means you come to feel in your prayers and meditations the intimate presence of Jesus Christ in your soul, keep it firmly and see that you do not lose it, so that, if you should fall away from Him, you may quickly find Him again.

THE FORTY-EIGHTH CHAPTER

Where and how Jesus shall be sought and found

SEEK then Jesus whom you have lost. He wills to be sought, and it follows that He can to some extent be found, for He says Himself: *Omnis qui quaerit invenit* (Matt. vii. 8). Every man that seeks shall find. The seeking is laborious but the finding joyous. Follow therefore the counsel of the Wise Man if you would find Him: *Si quaesieris quasi pecuniam sapientiam, et sicut thesauros effoderis illam; tunc intelliges timorem Domini, et scientiam Dei invenies* (Prov. ii. 4, 5). If you seek wisdom, which is Jesus, as silver and gold by digging deep for it, you will find it. It behoves you to dig deep in your heart, for He lies hidden there, and to cast out all love and attraction for earthly things, and all sorrow and anxiety about them, and so you will find wisdom, that is Jesus. Be like the woman in the gospel then, of whom our Lord said: *Quae mulier habens drachmas decem, si perdiderit unam, nonne accendit lucernam, et everrit domum suam et quaerit diligenter donec inveniat eam? Et cum invenerit, convocat amicos suos, dicens: Congratulamini mihi, quia inveni drachmam quam perdideram* (Luke xv. 8, 9). What woman is there who has lost a coin, who will not light a lamp and ransack her house and search till she find it? As much as to say: None. And when she has found it she calls her friends to her and says to them: Rejoice with me because I have found the coin that I had lost. This coin is Jesus whom you have lost; if you will

find Him, light a lamp, which is God's word as David says:
Lucerna pedibus meis verbum tuum (Ps. cxviii. 105). Lord, Thy
word is a lamp to my feet. By this lamp you will see where
He is and how you may come to Him; and if you wish, you
may light another lamp, which is your reason,[1] for our Lord
says also: *Lucerna corporis tui est oculus tuus* (Matt. vi. 22). The
lamp of your body is the eye. In just the same way it may be
said that the lamp of the soul is the reason, by whose aid the
soul may see all spiritual things. You may find Jesus by this
lamp, if you hold it up from underneath the bushel; as our
Lord says: *Nemo accendit lucernam et ponit eam sub modio, sed
super candelabrum* (Matt. v. 15). No man lights a lamp in
order to set it under a bushel, but on a lamp-stand; that is to
say that your mind must not be over-much occupied with
worldly matters, useless thoughts, and carnal affections, but
must rise up above all earthly things as far as possible to the
sight of Jesus Christ. And if you raise your mind in this way,
you will see all the dust and dirt, all the motes, in your
house, that is to say all the carnal loves and anxieties in your
soul.[2] And yet not all, for as David said: *Delicta quis intel-*

---

[1] For what he has to say about the use of reason in this and the next
chapter see chap. 52, n. 1.

[2] This passage, and indeed the whole chapter, is very important for the
understanding of Hilton's spirituality. He has established in the last two
chapters (46 and 47) that before all else the soul must desire God—or
Jesus. It must, then, seek to establish contact with Him, to find Him. But
where? Hilton is quite explicit that it is within his own self that a man will
find Him. "It behoves you to dig deep in your heart, for He lies hidden
there" (p. 76). But Hilton does not leave us with any vague metaphor. He
tells us in the very next words what the process involves. "It behoves
you . . . to cast out all love and attraction for earthly things, and all sorrow
and anxiety about them, and so you will find wisdom, that is Jesus"
(p. 76). As put thus far the process is negative, and it is in fact not possible merely to cast something out of the mind without putting anything
in its place. Accordingly he says that the mind "must rise up above all
earthly things as far as possible to the sight of Jesus Christ" (p. 77). In

ligit? (Ps. xviii. 13). Who may know all his sins? As much as to say: No man. And you shall cast all sins out of your heart, and sweep your soul with the broom of the fear of God and wash it with your tears, and so you shall find your coin, Jesus. He is a coin, He is a penny, He is your heritage. The finding of this coin is more easily described than performed. It is not the work of an hour or a day, but of many days and years with much labour of both body and soul. And if you do not relax, but search diligently, sorrow and sigh deeply, lament silently, and humble yourself till you weep for anguish, because you have lost your treasure Jesus, you will at the last in His good time find Him again. And if you find Him as I have said, that is if you are able in purity of conscience[3] to feel the intimate peaceful presence of the humanity of Christ, even though it is only a foreshadowing and a glint of His glory, then you may, if you will, call all

---

other words the immediate outcome of desiring Jesus is prayer, the raising of the mind and heart to God. "And," Hilton goes on, "if you raise your mind in this way, you will see all the dust and dirt, all the motes in your house, that is to say, all the carnal loves and anxieties in your soul" (p. 77). This last sentence is immensely significant for Hilton's teaching. In a sense, of course, it describes the experience of any one who has tried to pray. The effort is made to fix the mind on God and all our worldly preoccupations crowd in on us. But Hilton means more than just the ordinary experience of distractions. The point is that the soul does see all the dust and dirt in its house. The effort to raise the mind and the heart to God results first of all in knowledge of self. Hilton devotes the next chapter (49) to this very important idea and then takes it up again in chap. 52 where further comment will be made (n. 2).

[3] *Purity of conscience.* In Middle English the word *conscience* had both the particularized meaning it has today and also that of consciousness, inward thought, or mind. Hilton generally seems to use it in the latter sense but the word purity (cleanness) in conjunction with it here seems to suggest the meaning we attach to the word today, and I have accordingly translated it conscience. Either meaning might fit the sense. In chap. 53 the word clearly seems to have the meaning of mind.

your friends to you to rejoice because you have found your coin.

THE FORTY-NINTH CHAPTER

Where Jesus is lost and where, by His mercy, found again

SEE then the courtesy and the mercy of Jesus. You have lost Him. But where? Truly in your own house, that is, in your own soul. If you had lost the power of reason by original sin, you would never have found Him again. But he left you your reason, and so He is in your soul and shall never be lost out of it. Nevertheless you remain separated from Him till you have found Him. He is in you, although lost so far as you are concerned; but you are not in Him till you have found Him. He showed His mercy in this, that He would only allow Himself to be lost where He might be found. There is no need to go to Rome or to Jerusalem to look for Him, but turn your mind into your own soul, where He is hid, and seek Him there—as the prophet says: *Vere tu es Deus absconditus* (Isa. xlv. 15). Truly, Lord, Thou art a hidden God. He Himself says in the gospel: *Simile est regnum caelorum thesauro abscondito in agro; quem qui invenit homo, prae gaudio illius vadit, et vendit universa quae habet, et emit agrum illum* (Matt. xiii. 44). The kingdom of heaven is like to a treasure hidden in a field, which when a man finds, for joy he goes and sells all that he has and buys the field. Jesus is the treasure hidden in your soul. If you might find Him there and your soul in Him, surely you would gladly forgo pleasure in all earthly things to possess Him. Jesus sleeps spiritually in your heart, as He once did in the body when He was in the ship with His disciples. But they, fearing to perish, wakened Him and He quickly saved them from the storm. In the same way do you rouse Him by prayer and waken Him with the cry of your desire, and He will quickly arise and help you.

THE FIFTIETH CHAPTER

What hinders a man from hearing and seeing Jesus within himself [1]

NEVERTHELESS I think that you sleep to Him more often than He does to you. For He often calls you with His sweet secret voice, and quietly moves your heart to leave the tumult of worldly vanities in your soul and occupy yourself only with Him and listen only to Him. David said of our Lord: *Audi, filia, et vide, et inclina aurem tuam, et obliviscere populum tuum, et domum patris tui* (Ps. xliv. 11). Oh daughter, hear and see and incline your ear to me, and forget the people of your worldly thoughts and the house of your natural carnal affections. Lo, here you may see how our Lord calls you and all others who will hearken to Him. What hinders you then, that you can neither see nor hear Him? In truth there is so much noise and disturbance in your heart caused by useless thoughts and desires of the flesh that you can neither see Him nor hear Him. Therefore put away all unquiet disturbance and break the love of sin and of vanity and bring into your heart the love of virtues, and then you will hear your Lord speak to you.

[1] In this chapter Hilton is only saying in another way what he has already said in chap. 48. A man is unable to raise his mind and his heart to Jesus, to make contact with Him in prayer, because of the worldly interests and sinful desires which draw his attention. In chap. 48 he uses the metaphor of dust and dirt in a house, here of noise and tumult, to describe these preoccupations and evil tendencies which hinder the mind and will from turning to God.

THE FIFTY-FIRST CHAPTER

*That humility and charity are the special livery of Jesus, and
by these virtues the soul is reformed to His likeness*[1]

As long as He does not find His image reformed in you He is
a stranger and far removed from you. Strive therefore to be
arrayed in His likeness, that is in humility and charity,
which form His livery, and then He will know you intimately and show you His secrets. He Himself said to His disciples: *Qui diligit me, diligetur a patre meo, et manifestabo ei
meipsum* (John xiv. 21). Whoever loves me shall be loved by
my Father and I will show myself to him. No virtue or work
that you may do will make you like our Lord without humility and charity, for these two are specially God's livery.
And that appears clearly in the gospel where our Lord speaks
of humility: *Discite a me, quia mitis sum et humilis corde* (Matt.
xi. 29). Learn of me, He says, not to go barefoot, or to go
into the desert and fast for forty days, or to choose disciples,
but learn from me humility, for I am mild and meek of
heart. Of charity too He says: *Hoc est praeceptum meum: ut
diligatis invicem sicut dilexi vos. Item in hoc cognoscent homines
quia discipuli mei estis, si dilectionem habueritis ad invicem* (John
xiii. 34, 35). This is my commandment, that you love one
another as I have loved you; for in that shall men know you
for my disciples. Not because you work miracles, or cast out
devils, or teach, or preach, but because each of you loves
the others in charity. If you will be like Him, have humility
and charity. And charity means, as you know well, loving
your neighbour as yourself.

[1] Hilton has already treated of humility and charity in the second section, chaps. 16–23, and he will return to them again more than once in
the remaining chapters of the Book (chaps. 62 and 77). In laying so much
stress upon them he is, of course, in keeping with the whole of Catholic
tradition.

THE FIFTY-SECOND CHAPTER

How a man shall recognize the roots of sin within himself

You have heard something of what your soul is, what dignity it had, and how it lost it. And I have told you also that this dignity might by grace and assiduous labour to some extent be recovered and enjoyed again. Now I will tell you according to my poor ability how you may enter into yourself to see the roots of sin and destroy them as far as possible, and so recover in part the dignity of your soul. You must cease as far as may be for a time from all bodily works, from all external occupation. Then you must recollect your thought and withdraw it from the bodily senses, so that you pay no attention to what you hear or see or feel—your heart must not be fixed on these things. And after this, empty your mind as far as you can of all images of material things and all remembrance of your past actions and those of other men.[1]

[1] Does Hilton mean by this the sort of exercise that was advocated by the author of *The Cloud of Unknowing*? (see for example chaps. 5 and 7). This was a fixing of the mind upon the simplest possible idea of God and involved a deliberate exclusion of any images, even of the humanity of Christ (chap. 7). Hilton's language at first sight seems to suggest something of the sort, but I do not think that it is in fact what he intends. In chap. 54, where he resumes the idea, he says explicitly, "You must be careful to take the thought of Jesus Christ and dwell earnestly on His passion and His humility" (p. 85). In accordance with this is what he says in chaps. 48 and 49 about the use of the reason. In chap. 48, after quoting the Scripture text about the woman who had lost a coin, he says, "if you wish, you may light another lamp; which is your reason . . . your mind must not be overmuch occupied with earthly matters, useless thoughts and carnal affections, but must rise up above all earthly things as far as possible to the sight of Jesus Christ" (pp. 76 and 77). And again in chap. 49, "If you had lost the power of reason by original sin, you would never have found Him again, but He left you your reason" (p. 79). Now it was precisely the use of reason that the author of *The Cloud* deprecated in his spiritual exercise. The mind must rest on the simple idea of God as far as

This requires little effort when you feel devotion, but you must do it when you feel no devotion, for then it is very much harder. And make this your whole purpose, as if you would neither seek, nor feel, nor find anything except the grace and the spiritual presence of Jesus. This is laborious, for useless thoughts will press on you to draw your mind down to them. But through a determined remembrance of Jesus Christ you may withstand them, and, if you do so, you will find something; not Jesus whom you seek, but only the mere remembrance of His name. What more? In truth you will find nothing but an obscure and heavy image of your own soul, which has neither light to know God nor affection to love Him.[2] This image, if you examine it closely, is sur-

---

might be without any use of the discursive reason. That Hilton made no such demands is proved, I think, from the emphasis he lays on devotion to the humanity of Christ. In chap. 25, where he is treating explicitly of prayer, he says: "But through devout and persevering consideration of the humility of His precious humanity you may come to feel the goodness and grace of His divinity" (p. 37). And in chap. 15, "For be sure of this, that until your heart is cleansed from such sins through a firm grasp of the truth, and consideration of Christ's humanity, you cannot come to any true spiritual knowledge of God" (p. 22). In the same way Hilton in chap. 35 apparently welcomes mystical experiences which involve contemplation, or meditation as he calls it, of the humanity of Christ.

[2] In chap. 48 Hilton stated that the first result of trying to fix the mind on Jesus would be an awareness of our own sinfulness. Such an awareness is, of course, the necessary preliminary to any striving after perfection and Hilton will make it the basis of his teaching in the rest of this Book. The important question as to whether he advocates the sort of exercise that was demanded in *The Cloud of Unknowing* has been discussed in the previous note, but the point to observe here is that the effort to concentrate the mind on Jesus being at first, generally speaking, of little or no avail, the soul becomes aware of its own sinfulness, of what Hilton calls the image of sin in it. Psychologically this is so. The persevering effort to raise the mind and the heart to God in prayer will in fact result in a most surprising revelation of self. And when in chap. 55 Hilton speaks of this image of sin as the source from which flow the rivers of the seven deadly

rounded with foul black clothes of sin—pride, envy, anger,
sloth, covetousness, gluttony, and sensuality. This is not the
image of Jesus, but it is an image of sin; as St Paul calls it, a
body of sin and a body of death (Rom. vi. 6). This image and
this black shadow you bear about with you wherever you go.
Out of it spring many streams of sin, great and small. Just as
out of the image of Jesus, if it was reformed in you, there
would mount up to heaven spiritual desires, pure affections,
wise thoughts, and all the other virtues. So out of this image
spring movements of pride and envy and other vices, which
cast you down from the dignity of a man into the likeness of
a beast.

THE FIFTY-THIRD CHAPTER

What the image of sin is like and what it is in itself

Now perhaps you are wondering what this image is like.
And therefore that you should not consider long, I tell you
that it is like no material thing. What is it then? you say. In
truth it is nothing, and you may discover that if you will
make trial as I have said. Withdraw your thought from all
material things, and you will find nothing in which your soul
may rest. This nothing is only a darkness of mind, a lack
of love and light; as sin is nothing but a lack of God.[1] If
the roots of sin were withered in you and your soul was

sins he is not exaggerating or being unreal. Until we recognize that the
roots of all sins are within us, we can never attain to the humility which
we need to lay the foundations of the spiritual life securely.

[1] The French version has *une privation du bien*, though Underhill
and Orchard both have "God". As pointed out in a note to the French
version, St Anselm's definition of evil as *absentia debiti boni* is more theo-
logically correct—the absence of a good that ought to be there. The
absence of God might rather be described as a result of sin, inasmuch as
He is no longer present by grace.

truly reformed to the image of Jesus, when you recollected yourself, you would not find nothing, but you would find Jesus; not only the mere remembrance of His name, but Jesus Christ in your heart teaching you. Then you would find light of understanding and no darkness of ignorance; you would find love of Him and no painful bitterness and heaviness. But because you are not yet reformed, when your soul withdraws from all bodily things and finds nothing but darkness and heaviness, it seems a hundred years till it can be out again by some bodily pleasure or vain thought. And no wonder; for who would not soon run out of his house, if he came home and found nothing but a smoky fire and a scolding wife. So your soul, when it finds no comfort in you, but only the black smoke of spiritual blindness and the re-proaches of carnal thoughts whose crying takes away all peace, is indeed discontented till it can get out again. This is darkness of mind.

THE FIFTY-FOURTH CHAPTER

That he who will find Jesus must strive perseveringly to destroy the image of sin in spiritual darkness

NEVERTHELESS you must labour in this darkness of mind, that is you must withdraw your thought from all material things as far as possible. And then, when you find nothing but sorrow and pain and blindness in this darkness, you must put up with this and endure it for a time, if you will find Jesus. And here you must be careful to take the thought of Jesus Christ and dwell earnestly on His passion and His humility,[1] and by His power your thought will rise above this darkness with fervent desire to God. You must not fix

[1] See n. 1 on chap. 52.

your thought on this nothing, but on Jesus Christ whom you desire, as if you would overcome the nothingness and pass through it. You must dread and hate this darkness and this nothingness as though it were the devil of hell, and you must despise and destroy it. For within this nothing Jesus lies hidden in His joy, and all your searching will not find Him, unless you pass through this darkness of mind. This is the spiritual labour that I spoke of, and the cause of all this writing is to move you to undertake it, if you feel the grace. This darkness of mind and this nothing is the image of the first Adam. St Paul knew that well for he said: *Sicut portavimus imaginem terreni hominis, ita portemus imaginem iam et caelestis* (1 Cor. xv. 49). As we have before borne the image of an earthly man, that is the first Adam, so we may now bear the image of the heavenly man, who is Jesus, the second Adam. He often found the first image heavy indeed, for it was so burdensome to him that he cried out: *O quis me liberabit de corpore mortis?* (Rom. vii. 24). Ah, who shall deliver me from the body and the image of death? And then he comforted himself and others along with him, thus: *Gratia Dei per Jesum Christum* (Rom. vii. 25). The grace of God by Jesus Christ.

THE FIFTY-FIFTH CHAPTER

Of the image of sin and what comes from it

I HAVE told you a little of this image, how it is nothing. Nevertheless if you cannot understand how what I say is true, that nothing can be an image—for nothing after all is nothing—I will speak of it more plainly.

This image is a false, misguided, self-love. And all sorts of sins spring from this love by seven rivers, which are:

pride, envy, anger, *accidia*,[1] covetousness, gluttony, and lust. There is no difficulty in recognizing them. By one or other of these rivers comes all manner of sin, which, if it is mortal, quenches charity, and, if it is venial, lessens its fervour. And so you see that this image is not nothing but is a great evil, for it is a strong spring of self-love from which flow the seven rivers that I have mentioned. But now you say: How can this be? I have forsaken the world and am enclosed in a cell and have no dealings with men. I do not contend with any, I neither buy nor sell, nor have any secular business, but by the mercy of God I keep myself chaste and do not give way to carnal pleasures. And besides this I pray, keep vigils, work bodily and spiritually as well as I can, how then should this image be as great in me as you say? As to this I grant that you probably do all this and more, and I hope it is the truth. You make every effort to stop the rivers from flowing out, but perhaps you leave the spring within untouched. You are like a man who had in his garden a fouled well with many streams from it. He stopped the streams and left the spring alone and thought all had been safe. But the water sprang up at the bottom of the well and stagnated so long that it spoilt all the beauty of the garden, and yet the water did not flow out. It may be so with you, if by grace you have stopped the rivers of this image from flowing forth. That is good as far as it goes, but beware of the spring within. In truth, if you do not stop that up and cleanse it to the best of your ability, it will spoil all the flowers in the garden of

[1] *Accidia*. I have thought it best to leave the word in its Latin form. Although in Middle English—already in the *Ancren Riwle*—it came to be identified with sloth as the fourth deadly sin, it does not mean the same thing as sloth in modern English. St Thomas defined it as *tristitia de spirituali bono* (*Summa*, IIa IIae, q. xxxv, art. 2); it is a certain weariness and disgust in well-doing particularly associated with, and likely to attack, those leading the religious life. The word *accidie* was formed from it in Middle English but is now obsolete.

your soul, however beautiful they may appear outwardly in the sight of men. But now you ask how, if you set about this work, you may know whether you have succeeded. So I will tell you how you may judge by experience whether this image remains in you or to what extent, and by that you may know how far its polluted source is dried up in you. And since pride is the principal river, I shall speak of that first.

THE FIFTY-SIXTH CHAPTER

What pride is, and when it is sin

PRIDE is nothing else according to the learned than the love of one's own excellence,[1] that is of one's own renown. The more, therefore, you value your renown the greater is your pride, and the greater is this image [of sin] in you. If you feel a movement of pride; that you are holier, wiser, more virtuous than another, that God has given you grace to serve Him better than others; if you judge all others beneath you and that you are superior to them, and if you feel delight and self-complaisance in this feeling of superiority, it is a sign that you bear this dark image [of sin], and though it is hidden from the sight of men, it is manifest to God. But you say that you cannot escape such movements of pride, for you often feel them against your will, and therefore hold them as no sin, or if sin, only venial. I reply that the mere feeling of these movements of pride, whether they spring from this evil image in you or from the temptations of the devil, is not sin. That is a grace and privilege granted to all baptized

[1] This definition of pride is found in St Augustine (*De Genesi ad Litteram*, Bk. XI, chap. 15; P.L., t. XXXIV, col. 436–7) and was quoted by St Bernard (*De Gradibus Humilitatis*, chap. 4; P.L., t. CLXXXII, col. 949). It should be noted that for pride to be sinful the love of one's own excellence must be inordinate, as Hilton makes clear in the following chapter (57).

Christians by virtue of the passion of Jesus Christ; for indeed to Jews and Saracens, who do not believe in Christ, all such movements are mortal sins.[2] St Paul said: *Omne quod non est ex fide peccatum est* (Rom. xiv. 23). All that is done without belief in Christ is mortal sin. We Christians, of His mercy, have the privilege that such feelings are not sin, but they are the punishment of original sin. Nevertheless, when by negligence and lack of knowledge of yourself you carelessly entertain this movement in thought and take pleasure in it, then there is sin, more or less, according to the measure of charity; sometimes venial, sometimes mortal. When it is venial and when mortal I cannot completely tell you. Nevertheless I shall say something on the subject.

THE FIFTY-SEVENTH CHAPTER

When pride is mortal sin and how it is so in worldly-minded men

WHEN the movement of pride is received with pleasure, so that the heart chooses to rest and delight in it and seeks no other end but satisfaction in it, then it is mortal sin.[1] For a

---

[2] Hilton could have found this opinion in St Anselm (*Tract. de conc. praesc. Dei cum lib. arb.*, q. III, chap. 7; P.L., CLVIII, col. 530), and perhaps in St Augustine (*De Nuptiis et concupiscentia*, Bk. I, chaps. 25–6; P.L., XLIV, col. 429–30, and *Contra duas Epistolas Pelag.*, Bk. I chap. 13, n. 27; P.L., XLIV, col. 563). St Thomas formally rejected it (*Summa*, Ia IIae, q. LXXXIX, art. 5), and it is not admitted by theologians today. In any case the acts of the unbaptized, *ex hypothesi* without grace, cannot be meritorious of heaven.

[1] St Thomas states that pride *secundum genus suum* is a mortal sin because by it a man refuses the place allotted to him by the divine order of things. It is essentially a refusal to subject oneself to God and is therefore of its nature a serious sin, though it may not in fact always be so, and probably seldom is, because of imperfection in the act (*Summa*, IIa, IIae, q. CLXII,

man who acts thus chooses this pleasure as his God, not resisting it with reason or will, and therefore it is mortal sin.
But you say: What man is so foolish as to take pride for his
God? No man alive would do such a thing. To this I reply
that I cannot and will not tell you in particular who sins
mortally by pride, but in general I say that there are two
sorts of pride, bodily and spiritual.

Bodily pride belongs to worldly minded men, spiritual to
hypocrites and heretics. These three sin mortally in pride.
I refer to such worldly-minded men as St Paul speaks of: *Si
secundum carnem vixeritis, moriemini* (Rom. viii. 13). If you
live according to the flesh you shall die. I say that a worldly
man who loves and seeks his own honour and chooses it as
his final happiness sins mortally. But you object: Who would
choose the love of his own honour instead of God? I reply,
Any one who loves it so much as to seek to pass as greater or
better than another. One who labours for this end sins mortally, if he is prepared to go to the length of breaking God's
commandments or losing his charity for his neighbour,
either in act or in intention, rather than forbear his honour.
And this applies equally if it is only a question of carrying
out his own will. Such a one prefers his own credit to the
love of God and his neighbour. And yet a man who sinned

---

art. 5). Hilton is speaking rhetorically in describing a man as taking pride
for his God, but he is giving expression to the fundamental idea of sin as
an aversion from God and in truth a substitution of self-will for God's
will. When he comes to answer the question more specifically later on
in this same chapter, "Who would choose the love of his own honour instead of God?"—and thereby commit a mortal sin of pride—his answer
is not satisfactory. He states that pride may be a mortal sin, if it leads a
man to commit another mortal sin. It might, for example, cause a man to
steal, but in that case the sin would be one of theft, for, in scholastic
language, sins are differentiated specifically according to their objects
(*Summa*, Ia IIae, q. LXXII, art. 1). Hilton was no doubt right in drawing
attention to the practical importance of discovering the real causes of sin.

mortally in this way would say that he did not choose pride for his God; but he deceives himself, for he chooses it by his actions. But a worldly man who does not love and seek his own honour to the extent of committing a mortal sin or losing his charity for his neighbour in order to preserve it, does not sin mortally but only venially—to a greater or lesser extent according to the degree of his charity and other circumstances.

THE FIFTY-EIGHTH CHAPTER

How pride in heretics is mortal sin

A HERETIC sins mortally by pride for he chooses to adhere to and take pleasure in his own opinion, thinking it to be true, when it is opposed to God and Holy Church.[1] He will not give up his opinion but clings to it as the truth, and so he makes it his god. But he is deceived, for God and Holy Church are so united that whoever acts against one acts against the other. And therefore he lies who says that he loves God and keeps His commandments, and at the same

[1] In considering Hilton's remarks about heretics it is necessary to remember the time at which he lived. What was the first popular heresy in the history of the Church in England broke out near the end of his life. Wyclif was condemned in 1382 and Hilton died in 1395. The tone of his remarks here and elsewhere (chap. 20, and Bk. II, chap. 3) would suggest that *The Scale* was written between these two dates, and what external evidence there is there seems to confirm this (see "Walter Hilton and the Mystical Tradition in England", H. L. Gardner, *Essays and Studies of the English Association* (1936), vol. XXII, p. 113). For him they were all formal heretics who had revolted against the Church to which they belonged. In fact, Hilton is not very happy in seeking to put all pride in certain classes of men, heretics or hypocrites, as necessarily mortal sin. It is certainly true that heretics or hypocrites might be guilty of the most serious pride, but the judgement of the individual must be left to God, as Hilton is willing to do in the case of hypocrites, but not apparently of heretics.

time despises the Church and disregards the ordinances made by the head of it for the governing of all Christians. He does not choose God, but he chooses the love of himself in opposition to the love of God, and so he sins mortally. And in the very point in which he thinks most to please God he most displeases Him; for he is blind and will not see. The Wise Man speaks of this blindness and this false adherence of heretics to their own opinion thus: *Est via quae videtur homini recta; et novissima ejus deducunt ad mortem* (Prov. xiv. 12). There is a way which to man seems right and the end of it leads to everlasting death. This way is especially heresy, for carnal sinners who sin mortally and remain in their sins generally come to repentance after a time and are stricken in their conscience that they are not in the right way. But a heretic always thinks that he acts well and teaches well, and no man better. And so he thinks that he is in the right way, and he feels no remorse of conscience or humility of heart. And in truth unless God in His mercy sends him humility while he lives, he will in the end go to hell. And yet he thinks he has done well and earned the happiness of heaven for his teaching.

THE FIFTY-NINTH CHAPTER

How pride in hypocrites is mortal sin

THE hypocrite also sins mortally by pride. A hypocrite is one who makes self-satisfaction his end and chief delight. It happens in this way; a man does many good works, corporal and spiritual, and the enemy puts it into his mind to consider how good and how holy he is, how worthy in the estimation of men, and how high in God's sight above other men. He perceives this thought and assents to it, because, in so far as it is true, he thinks it good and from God—for he does in fact do all these good works better than other men. But as the result of this assent there arises such self-love and complaisance in his heart, he thinks he is so good and so holy and has so much grace, that it takes all other thoughts, both spiritual and worldly, out of his mind for the time being and causes his heart to rest in this vain self-satisfaction. The pleasure caused by this spiritual pride is very great, and so a man keeps it and nourishes it as much as he can. He will pray, keep vigils, fast, wear a hair-shirt, and otherwise afflict himself and think little of it for the sake of this self-love and the empty pleasure he takes in it. At times he praises and thanks God vocally and at times he squeezes a tear from his eye, and then he thinks that all is well. But in fact the cause of all this is the love of his own praise, which he takes for love and joy in God. And that is where the sin lies. He does not choose sin as sin, but he chooses this pleasure that he feels as a good and an end in itself, and makes no effort to set his will against it, for he thinks he is taking pleasure in God. But it is not so, and therefore he sins mortally. Job said of the hypocrite: *Gaudium hypocritae ad instar puncti. Si ascenderit in caelum superbia ejus, et caput ejus nubes tetigerit, quasi sterquilinium in fine perdetur* (Job xx. 5–7). The joy of a hypocrite is no more than a flash; if he rise into heaven with the swelling of his heart and his head touch the skies, at the end he is cast down as a dung-heap. The joy of a hypocrite is but a flash; for however much he delights in himself all his lifetime and decks himself out with good works to be seen and praised by the world, in the end he has nothing but sorrow and pain. But, you answer, there are few or none so blind that they would take empty joy in themselves to be joy in God. I can make no comment on that, and would not if I could; but one thing I can tell you, that there are many hypocrites and yet they think that they are no such thing, and there are many who are afraid of being hypocrites, and in fact they are not. Which is one and which is the other God knows, and none but He. He who has a humble fear shall not be deceived, and he who thinks himself safe may easily fall. For St Paul says: *Qui existimat se aliquid esse, cum nihil sit, ipse se seducit* (Gal. vi. 3). He who thinks himself something, when in truth he is nothing, deludes himself.

THE SIXTIETH CHAPTER

How movements of pride and vainglory in good men are only venial sins

BUT it is otherwise with those who give themselves to the contemplative life and who renounce their own wills, and give themselves wholly to God with the general intention of not sinning deliberately by pride, and who seek only to please God. Such as these, who have fully offered their wills to God, do not commit more than venial sin, even when they feel many movements of vainglory and take momentary pleasure in them but without full deliberation. And this is particularly the case if, when they become aware of such vainglory, they correct themselves and set their wills against it, asking mercy and help from God. Our Lord in His mercy is quick to forgive the sinful pleasure then, and to reward their efforts in rejecting it. That is the kindness of our Lord to His special servants and the members of His household, that is to those who for His love renounce all sins of the world and the flesh with determination and give themselves up body and soul to His service, as do enclosed anchoresses and true religious, who for the love of God and the salvation of their souls enter an order approved by Holy Church.[1]

[1] Hilton is here referring to what is known as a virtual intention, that

And even those who entered religion in the first place for a worldly reason—as for their bodily maintenance—if they change their minds and come to live their lives for spiritual motives, are true religious as long as they persevere with their good intention as far as their frailty will allow. And that is true of all—whatever be their status in the Church, priests, clerics, or laymen, married women, or maids—who for the love of God and the salvation of their souls sincerely abandon all worldly honours and pleasure and reduce their worldly activities to the bare minimum. These are in a special way God's servants in the Church, if they devote themselves entirely to Him by devout prayer and holy thoughts and other good works, bodily and spiritual, and persevere in this intention. And through this good will, that by the grace of God is theirs, they will increase in grace and charity while they are here on earth and have a special reward in the happiness of heaven. They will be counted above those of the elect who did not consecrate themselves body and soul, either publicly or privately, to God's service. All these, God's servants, the members of His household as I have called them, though through frailty or ignorance they take momentary pleasure in such movements of vainglory, commit no mortal sin, because their reason and will are blinded by the pleasure they feel, so that they do not recognize the temptation. For the general intention which they have to please God and forsake sin is their safeguard in these movements, and in all others that are the result of frailty, and it will remain so as long as they persevere in it.

---

is a general intention, in this case to serve God to the best of one's ability, which persists, even when not consciously adverted to, until it is revoked by an act of the will. When it is a case of indeliberate acts a man acts in view of the end which he has previously proposed. Hilton is speaking of religious who have consecrated their lives to God.

THE SIXTY-FIRST CHAPTER

How different states in the Church will have different rewards in heaven, and of two sorts of reward in particular

FOR your consolation and that of all other enclosed anchoresses, and indeed for that of all those who by the grace of God have entered a religious Order approved by Holy Church, I will go further and say that all such, who by the mercy of God save their souls, will by reason of their state of life have a special reward and honour in the happiness of heaven, which other souls, however holy, will not share. This honour is without comparison greater than all the honour of the world, and, if you could see it, you would not for all earthly glory—though you could have it without sin—change your state of anchoress or of religious, or diminish that special reward in heaven. It is called an accidental reward, and that its nature may not be misunderstood I shall speak more plainly about it. You must know that in heaven there are two rewards which God gives to the elect. One is essential. It consists in the love and knowledge of God, and is granted according to the degree of charity which God gives to the soul while it is still in a mortal body. This is the best and greatest reward for it is God Himself, and it is given, to a greater or lesser degree, according to their measure of charity, to all souls that are saved, whatever their state in the Church may have been. He who loves God with the greatest charity in this life will have the greatest reward in heaven, for he will have the most perfect love and knowledge of God, and that is the highest reward. And as far as this reward is concerned, it may happen that some man or woman of the world, lord or lady, knight or squire, merchant or ploughman, will have a greater reward than some priest or friar, monk or canon, or enclosed anchoress. And why? Most certainly because of his greater charity. The other reward, which is secondary, God gives for particular good works which a man does voluntarily beyond what he is bound to do. The doctors of the Church mention three: martyrdom, preaching, and virginity. Because these surpass all others in excellence they will have a special recompense called an aureole, which is a special honour and sign established by God for those who have performed this work. It is given to them apart from the essential reward of the love of God which is given to all. It is the same with other good works of a particular nature, which, if done sincerely, are specially acceptable in the sight of God and are highly approved of by the Church, for example embracing the state of an anchoress or other approved religious. The stricter the order the more excellent is the work in the Church's judgement.[1] After these, but on a lower plane, comes the taking of priest's orders, whether to work for souls, or to administer the sacraments of the Church, or merely for private devotion to please God and benefit one's neighbour by the sacrifice of the precious Body of our Lord Jesus Christ. These are indeed special and holy works in the judgement of the Church and in the eyes of God. When they are done sincerely for Him they earn a special reward in heaven varying for each man according to his degree. The state of a bishop and a prelate receives a higher accidental

[1] This was the popular view which found open expression in the *Epistle* of the Abbot Robert in the early twelfth century during the controversy between the monks and the Augustinian Canons. *In sancta Ecclesia quanto quisque ordo est arctior, tanto est et altior* (P.L., CLXX, col. 665). St Thomas with his usual lucidity pointed out that the strictness of the exercises carried out by a particular religious order was not in itself the principal matter for commendation, but that they must be judged by their suitability to attain the end of all religious life, namely the perfection of charity (*Summa*, IIa IIae, q. CLXXXVIII, art. 6, ad 3am). The discipline of the Church, which allows transference to an order of stricter life but not the reverse, is no doubt a practical acknowledgement of the weakness of human nature.

reward than any other. The truth of this appears from Scripture in the prophet Daniel, where he says: *Tu autem, vade ad praefinitum tempus, et requiesces, et stabis in sorte tua in finem dierum* (Dan. xii. 13). That is to say, the angel when he had shown Daniel the secrets of God said: Depart to the rest of your bodily death, and you shall take your appointed place as a prophet at the last day. And indeed as Daniel will appear as a prophet at the day of judgement and have the honour due to a prophet apart from the supreme reward of the love and sight of God, so you shall take your place as an anchoress, and a religious as a religious, and both will have a special honour above all other men at the day of judgement.

THE SIXTY-SECOND CHAPTER

A short exhortation to humility and charity

IF you accept what I have said, you may find matter for consolation and also for humility in your manner of life. For although, if you are saved, you will have this special reward for your way of life, nevertheless there may be many a married woman, or woman living in the world, who is nearer to God than you are, and who will have a greater love and knowledge of God hereafter than you, for all your state. And you have reason for shame, if you do not strive to attain as high a degree of love and charity as a person living in the world. For if by the gift of God you have as much charity as one occupied in worldly affairs, you will have as great an essential reward. And beyond that you will have the special reward appropriate to your state, which he will not have. If you will make good progress then, forget about your state, for in truth it is nothing in itself, and concentrate all your longing and all your efforts on obtaining charity and humility and other spiritual virtues—for that is all that matters.

THE SIXTY-THIRD CHAPTER

How a man may know how much pride is in him

I HAVE almost forgotten about this image, but now I will return to it. If you wish to know how much pride there is in you, you may test yourself in this way. Consider candidly whether praise, or blame, or the favour of worldly men, is acceptable to you and brings you idle pleasure and self-satisfaction. Do you think secretly that men ought to praise your life and pay more attention to what you say than to any one else? And on the other hand, if men correct you and make no account of you, thinking you no more than a fool and a hypocrite, or if they slander or calumniate you, or trouble you in any other way without cause, and you feel in your heart great bitterness against them and a great repugnance to suffer shame or injury in the eyes of the world, it is a sign that there is great pride in this dark image, however holy you may appear in the eyes of men. For though these movements are only slight and venial, nevertheless they are a sure indication that there is great pride still lurking in your heart, like a fox in its earth. These movements and many others arise from this image. So far is this the case that you can hardly perform a good act without some mixture of pride and self-satisfaction, and all your good deeds are marred and made displeasing in the sight of God. I do not say that they are completely spoiled by this pride, but they are not so pleasing in the sight of God as they would be if they sprang from true humility. And so if you would attain the love of God with a pure heart, you must avoid vainglory by refusing not only deliberate assent to pride but also care-less pleasure in it without consent of the will; you must ex-clude involuntary movements of it as far as possible. But you cannot do that unless you are alert to guard your heart, as I will tell you later.

THE SIXTY-FOURTH CHAPTER

Of anger and envy and their branches

EXAMINE this image thoroughly and you will find two limbs belonging to it, envy and anger, from which spring many branches, and these hamper the love and charity you should have for your neighbour. The branches of anger and envy are these: hatred, suspicion, rash judgement, bitter criticism, disdain, slander, unjust accusation, unkindness, defamation, dislike, anger and sadness against those who despise or speak ill of you, joy at their misfortune, bitter zeal against sinners or those who do not act as you think they should, with a strong desire, under colour of righteousness, that they should be punished for their sins. These movements appear good, but if you examine them well, you will find them directed more against the person than the sin. The man must be loved however sinful he is, and the sin must be hated in whomsoever it is found. Many are deceived in this, for they take the bitter instead of the sweet, and darkness instead of light, as the prophet says: *Vae vobis, qui dicitis malum bonum, et bonum malum; ponentes lucem tenebras et amarum in dulce* (Isa. v. 20). Woe to them that say evil is good and good evil, and take light for darkness and bitter for sweet. This is what all those do, who, when they should hate the sin of their fellow-Christians and love the person, hate the person instead of the sin and think that they hate the sin. This is an art in itself for those who can practise it well.

THE SIXTY-FIFTH CHAPTER

*That is it a great achievement to love men and hate
their sin*

IT is no great achievement to watch and fast till your head
aches and your body grows weak, nor to go to Rome and
Jerusalem barefoot, nor to set about preaching as though you
would convert all men; and it is no great achievement to
build churches and chapels, to feed the poor and build hospitals. But it is a great achievement for a man to be able to
love his neighbour in charity; to show wisdom in hating the
sin and loving the man. For though all the works that I mentioned are good in themselves, nevertheless they are common to good men and bad, for every man might do them, if
he wished and had the means, and so I hold it no great
achievement to do what every man may do. But to love his
neighbour in charity and hate his sin may only be done by a
good man through the gift of God, and not through his own
efforts. As St Paul says: *Caritas Dei diffusa est in cordibus nos-
tris per Spiritum Sanctum, qui datus est nobis* (Rom. v. 5).
Charity is diffused in your hearts by the Holy Ghost who
dwells in you, and this is the reason it is so precious and so
hard to come by. Without this all other good works do not
make a man good or worthy of the happiness of heaven; this
alone makes him good and his deeds meritorious.[1] All other
gifts of God and works of man are common to good and bad,
to the elect and the reprobate, but the gift of charity belongs
only to the good and the elect.

[1] See Bk. I, chap. 66, n. 2.

THE SIXTY-SIXTH CHAPTER

That for the same works different men will be differently recompensed

A GOOD man for the love of God fasts, watches, goes on pilgrimages, renounces the pleasures of the world, sincerely and without pretence. He will have his reward in heaven. A hypocrite does the same works out of vainglory and receives his reward here. In the same way a true preacher of God's word, filled with charity and humility, sent by God and approved by the Church,[1] will have a special reward, the aureole, for his preaching. But a hypocrite or a heretic, who has neither humility nor charity, and is not sent by God or the Church, will have his reward for his preaching only here. So a good man living in the world builds churches, chapels, abbeys, hospitals, and does other good works of mercy for the love of God. He will have his reward in heaven; not for the works in themselves, but for the good will and charity that by God's grace inspired them. Another man out of vanity, for the love and praise of the world, and to gain a reputation, performs the same good works—and he has his reward here. The reason in all these cases is that one has charity and the other not.[2] Which is one and which the other God knows, and none but He.

[1] It may be well to remember that at the time this was written the Lollards were sending out their "poor priests" who were emphatically not approved by the Church.

[2] Hilton is here speaking of charity as a theological virtue, and in order to understand what he says it is necessary to keep in mind the whole scheme of the divine economy. The true end of man, the vision of God in heaven, is supernatural, and it is for this reason that no purely human action, however good in itself, can merit it. We must be raised to a supernatural state by sanctifying grace for our actions to become meritorious of the happiness of heaven. The infusion of this grace brings with it the theological virtue of charity by which the soul is moved to love

THE SIXTY-SEVENTH CHAPTER

That the actions of all men should be considered good if they appear so outwardly, except those of manifest heretics and the excommunicated

AND therefore we should love and honour all men in our hearts and approve all their actions that appear good, although the men may in fact be evil in God's sight. But an exception must be made in the case of the open heretic and of a man who has been publicly excommunicated. We should avoid intercourse with both of these and we should condemn their actions, however good they appear, as long as they are rebels to God and Holy Church. So if a layman who is excommunicated builds a church, or gives food to a poor man, you may safely hold these acts as worthless.[1] And if an open heretic, who is a rebel to the Church, preaches and in-

---

God as its last end, and other things in so far as they conduce to this. Charity is thus the directive of all the other virtues, and is loosely identified with sanctifying grace as being its principal effect in the powers of the soul. Hilton himself identifies them in chap. 68. Hence, as for Hilton the hypocrite and the heretic are *ex hypothesi* not in a state of grace (cf. chap. 58, n. 1) their actions are not performed under the influence of the theological virtue of charity and cannot be meritorious of the happiness of heaven—they are not raised to the supernatural plane at all. So, in his second case, the good actions of a Christian are supernaturally meritorious if he is in a state of grace, but not otherwise.

[1] In order to understand Hilton's remarks in this chapter it is necessary to recall what was said about grace and charity in n. 2 on the previous chapter. As we have seen, the heretic is for him a formal heretic, who has sinned against the light and is not in a state of grace. So the excommunicated man is a public and unrepentant sinner. We should perhaps be more chary of judging the conscience even of such a man, but granted that that is his position, then lacking grace his acts are not supernaturally meritorious, and this is the sense in which Hilton means they are worthless, "nought" as he says.

structs, though he converts a hundred thousand souls, reckon that he himself gains nothing by it. For these men are openly out of charity, and without charity no man's actions are of value.

THE SIXTY-EIGHTH CHAPTER

That no good action can assure salvation without charity, and only the humble can feel charity

AND so I say that it is a great achievement for a man to be able to love his neighbour with charity, as can be proved from the words of St Paul: *Si linguis hominum loquar et ange-lorum, caritatem non habuero, nihil sum; et si habuero omnem fidem, ita ut montes transferam, caritatem non habeam, nihil sum. Et si noverim mysteria omnia, nihil sum; et si distribuero omnes facultates meas in cibos pauperum, et tradidero corpus meum ita ut ardeam, caritatem autem non habuero, nihil mihi prodest* (1 Cor. xiii. 1–3). It was in praise of charity that St Paul said: If I speak the language of all men and of angels and have not charity, I am nothing. And if I have such great faith that I can move mountains and carry them away and have not charity, I am nothing. If I know all the secrets (of God), without charity I am nothing. And if I give all my possessions to the poor and my body to the fire to be burnt and have no charity, it is of no profit to me. Here it appears from St Paul's words that a man may do all corporal good works and yet be without charity, and that charity is nothing else than the love of God and one's neighbour. How then should any poor wretch living on earth, whatever he may be, take pleasure or feel any confidence in himself by reason of what he can do by his bodily powers or his natural reason, since it will be of no avail without charity to his neighbour?[1] And this charity

[1] When he speaks about good works being of no use without charity to

may not be obtained by any action of his own, for it is the free gift of God granted to humble souls, as St Paul says. Who then may be bold enough to say, "I have charity", or "I am in charity"? Indeed no man may say it with assurance but he who is perfectly and sincerely humble.[2] Other men hope and believe by various signs that they are in charity,[3] but he who is perfectly humble is aware of his charity and so may truthfully say, "I am in charity". St Paul was humble in this way for he said of himself: *Quis separabit nos a caritate Dei? tribulatio? an angustia? etc.* (Rom. viii. 35). Who shall separate me from the charity of God? Tribulation, or anguish? And he answers himself, and says that no creature shall separate him from the charity of God which he has in Christ Jesus. Many do acts of charity and have no charity, as I have said; for to reprove a sinner opportunely in order to

---

one's neighbour, it is important to realize that Hilton is not referring to a mere feeling of goodwill to other men. That he does in fact mean the theological virtue of charity is evident from what he goes on to say about it: that it may not be obtained by any action of our own, but is the free gift of God.

[2] Only the truly humble can have assurance that they are in charity, or grace. It should be observed that such an assurance can only be a moral certainty. No man could know absolutely that he is in grace without a divine revelation.

It may be recalled that in chap. 16 he speaks of humbling oneself by reason, and in chap. 18 refers to the perfection of humility (see chap. 18, n. 1). Perfect humility in fact, he will say in the second Book, can only come from the gift of the Holy Spirit and will accompany the essential contemplative experience, which he describes in the second Book as an awareness of grace. The two are interlocked. Only the perfectly humble has an awareness of grace (or charity), and only one who has received this experience can be perfectly humble. The teaching is sound enough, but it brings no assurance to the beginner, as Hilton is aware, and his answer will be treated in n. 4.

[3] Hilton is using charity here as the equivalent of sanctifying grace. See chap. 66, n. 2.

make him amend is an act of charity, but to hate the sinner instead of the sin is against charity. The truly humble man can distinguish one from the other, but no one else. A man with all the moral virtues of the philosophers could not do it. He could hate the sin in other men, for he hates it in himself, but he could not love the man in charity for all his philosophy. And if a man has never so much learning and theology and is not truly humble, he will fall into error and confound these two hatreds. But humility merits a gift from God, and it is something which cannot be learnt from man.

But perhaps I have alarmed you by saying that charity may not be acquired by any work that you can perform. What are you to do then? I say it is true that there is nothing so hard to get with your own efforts as charity, and on the other hand there is no gift of God so easily obtained, for God gives no gift so freely and gladly and commonly as He does charity. How then shall I get it, you say? Be meek and humble interiorly and you will receive it. [4] And what is easier than to be humble? Indeed nothing. Then it appears that there is nothing that may be so easily had as charity, and therefore you are not to be alarmed. Be humble and it will be yours. As St James the apostle says: *Deus superbis resistit, humilibus dat gratiam* (Jas. iv. 6). God, he says, withstands proud men, but to humble men He gives His grace. And this grace is in truth charity, for you will have charity according to the measure of your humility. If your humility is imperfect, in your will only and not in your feelings, then your charity

[4] Charity is obtained by being humble. Clearly he is not referring to the perfect humility he has just been talking about, which can only come with charity. It must be to the humility which we can attain by reason, which he described in chap. 16, that he is referring. It should be noted that no action of man can in itself merit grace, which is a free gift of God, but Hilton is no doubt right in inculcating humility as the fitting attitude of mind in which to approach God, and going on the principle *facientibus quod in se est Deus non denegat gratiam*.

will be imperfect. This is good, for it is sufficient for salva-tion, as David says: *Imperfectum meum viderunt oculi tui* (Ps. cxxxviii. 16). Lord, in Your mercy, You see my imperfec-tion. But if your humility is perfect, you will have perfect charity, and that is best. The first (imperfect) we must needs have, if we will be saved, and we should desire it. If you ask me who has perfect humility, I will only say now that he is humble who really knows himself as he is.

THE SIXTY-NINTH CHAPTER

How a man may recognize how much anger and envy is hidden in his heart

Look again at this image if you will discover how much anger and envy is hidden in your heart without your being aware of it. Take careful note of yourself when such move-ments arise in you. The more swelling of anger there is, and the more melancholy bitterness or ill-will you feel, the greater is this image. For the more you complain with im-patience, either against God, because of trouble or sickness or bodily discomfort which He sends you, or against your neighbour, the less is the image of Jesus reformed in you. I do not say that such complaints and irritation, which come from the weakness of human nature, are mortal sins, but I do say that they prevent purity of heart and peace of conscience, so that you cannot attain perfect charity, which should lead you to the contemplative life. For the purpose of all I say is that you should not only cleanse your heart from mortal sins, but also as far as possible from venial, so that by the grace of Jesus Christ the roots of sin may to some extent be re-moved.

THE SEVENTIETH CHAPTER

How you may know whether you love your enemy, and the example you should find in Christ

ALTHOUGH for a time you may feel no ill-will to your neighbour, yet you cannot be sure that the flame of anger is extinguished in you; you have not yet mastered the virtue of charity. Only let an angry or a shrewd word come home to you and then see if your heart is confirmed in charity. The more your ill-will is roused against anybody the further you are from perfect charity to your neighbour, the less it is roused the nearer you are to possessing charity. Take note whether you are moved by anger and outward signs of disapproval, or by a secret hate in your heart, to despise or humiliate or consider him as nothing. But if, on the contrary, the more harm he does to you in word or deed the more pity and compassion you have for him, as it might be for a man that was out of his mind; if you feel that you cannot find it in your heart to hate him, because love appears to you so good in itself, but you are moved to pray for him and to help him and to desire his improvement, and this not only in word as hypocrites are able to do but with heartfelt feeling, then your charity to your neighbour is perfect. St Stephen had this perfect charity when he prayed for those who stoned him to death. Christ counselled it to all who would be His perfect followers when He said: *Diligite inimicos vestros, benefacite his qui oderunt vos, orate pro persequentibus et calumniantibus vos* (Matt. v. 44). Love your enemies and do good to those who hate you; pray for those who persecute and slander you. And so, if you will follow Christ, learn to imitate Him in this art. Learn to love those who are your enemies and who are sinners, for these it is who are your neighbours. Consider how Christ loved Judas, who was His mortal enemy and a sinful wretch. How good Christ was to him, how kind, how courteous and how humble to him whom He knew to be utterly worthy of condemnation. In spite of this He chose him to be an apostle and sent him to preach with the other apostles. He gave him power to work miracles, was as kind to him in word and manner as He was to the other apostles, washed his feet and fed him with His precious Body, and instructed him as He did the rest. He never openly exposed him nor abused him, never treated him with contempt nor spoke ill of him; and yet He might have done all these things with justice. On top of it all, at His capture Judas kissed Him and called Him his friend. And yet Christ showed all this charity to one whom He knew to be unworthy. There was no pretence or flattery in His action, but sincere love and charity. For though Judas on account of his wickedness was unworthy of any gift from God or any sign of love, nevertheless it was fitting that our Lord should act in accordance with His nature. He is love and goodness and so it becomes Him to show love and goodness to all His creatures as He did to Judas. (I do not say that He loved him for his sin, or that He loved him as one of His elect, as He did St Peter. But He loved him inasmuch as he was His creature, and gave him signs of His love, if he would but have used them for his amendment.) Follow this example if you can, for though your body is enclosed in a cell, nevertheless in your heart, which is the dwelling-place of love, you should be able to attain a measure of such love for your neighbour as I have described. He who thinks himself to be a perfect follower of Christ's teaching and example—and some think they are inasmuch as they preach and give instruction and are poor in the things of this world as Christ was—and cannot imitate Him in having charity towards all men, good and bad, friends and enemies, without pretence or flattery, without contempt, anger, or ill-tempered reproof, in truth deceives himself. The closer that he thinks himself to following this example the further he is from it; for Christ said to those who would be His disciples: *Hoc est praeceptum meum, ut diligatis invicem, sicut dilexi vos* (John xiii. 34).[1] This is my commandment that you love one another as I have loved you. For if you love as I loved, then you are my disciples. But now you ask how you are to love the bad as well as the good. I answer that you must love both good and bad with charity, but not for the same reason, as I shall explain to you. "You shall love your neighbour as yourself"(Matt. xxii. 39). Now you must love yourself only *in* God or *for* God. You love yourself in God, when by His grace you practise virtue, and you love yourself only for the virtue and goodness that God gives you. Then you love yourself in God, because you do not love yourself but God. You love yourself for God, when finding yourself in mortal sin you wish to recover the state of grace, for then you do not love yourself as you are, for you are in truth evil, but you love yourself as you would be. In just the same way you should love your fellow-men. If they are good and just, then you must love them, but in God by charity, for the sole reason that they are good and just. It is then truly the justice and goodness of God that you love; and you must love them more than if they were sinners. As for your enemies who hate you, or those whom you know not to be in a state of grace, you must love them not for what they are, nor as though they were virtuous, for they are not; but you must love them for God, that they may regain the state of grace. And in this way you will hate in them nothing but what is contrary to justice, and that is sin. This is, as I understand it, the teaching of St Augustine.[2] Only he who is humble, or truly desires to be, can love his neighbour.

[1] The Vulgate text has *Mandatum novum do vobis; ut diligatis invicem sicut dilexi vos*. The form of Hilton's quotation suggests that it was made from memory.

[2] *Sermo* IV, chap. 19 (P.L., XXXVIII, col. 43); *in Psalm.* CXXXVIII, n. 28 (P.L., XXXVII, col. 1801–2).

THE SEVENTY-FIRST CHAPTER

How to recognize the degree of covetousness that is still in your heart

EXAMINE this image well and you will find that covetousness and love of the things of this world comprise a large part of it; more than you think. You have left the riches and possessions that the world has to offer and are enclosed as a religious, but are you free from the love of these things? I do not think that you are as yet. It is easier to renounce worldly possessions than it is to renounce the love of them, and it may well be that you are still covetous, but for small things now rather than great, for a penny rather than a pound, a halfpenny instead of a silver piece. It is a poor exchange, and you are not much of a trader. I am giving childish examples I know, and yet they have significance. If you will not believe me, test yourself. Is the possession of such little things as you have a source of pleasure and satisfaction to you? Do you want to possess something that you have not got, and does the desire of it occupy your mind and distract you from the pursuit of virtue and of God? If so, it is a sign that there is covetousness in this image. If you want a further test, what is your attitude if anything you have is taken away by force, or borrowed, or otherwise lost to you? Are you vexed, annoyed, troubled, to be without something you want and cannot have, or against him who has it and will not give it back when he could? This is a sign that your heart is given to the things of this world, for it is the way men of the world act. They are upset and angry when they suffer loss of property or money, and they contend openly in word and action with those from whom they have suffered it. You secretly do the same in your heart, and yet it is not a secret from God. And in this you are more to blame than a man of the world, for you have outwardly given up the love of the things of this world, but he has not, and he is therefore perfectly justified in seeking to regain his possessions by lawful means. Perhaps you say that you must have such things as are necessary to your state of life, just as a layman must. Certainly I grant you that, but you should not be attached to them, nor take pleasure in the possession of them, nor sorrow at the loss of them. As St Gregory[1] says, the measure of your sadness at losing a thing is the measure of your attachment to it when you possessed it. And so if your heart was purified and you had a real desire for spiritual things, and had at the same time some slight insight into them, you would set no store by the things of this world. You would be altogether free of them. To have an attachment for and actually to possess more than you reasonably need is a great fault. To be attached to something of which you do have need is also a fault, but a lesser one, but to possess and make use of what you need without being attached to it is blameless. Many indeed who profess the state of poverty are in error on this point and it hampers their love of God. I bring no accusation against any particular man or any particular state, for there are good and bad in every condition of life. But to everyone, man or woman, religious or secular, who has undertaken the state of voluntary poverty, whatever his rank, I say that as long as his affection is attached to any earthly thing that he possesses or wants to possess, he cannot really have pure love of spiritual things or a clear view of them. As St Augustine[2] said, addressing God: Too little does any man love Thee, who loves some other thing together with Thee. For the more you love and desire earthly things, the less is the love of God in your heart. And although this love of earthly things does not extinguish charity, unless it is so strong that it completely strangles the

[1] St Gregory, *Moral. in Job*, Bk. I, chap. 5 (P.L., LXXV, col. 531); Bk. XXXI, chap. 13 (P.L., LXXVI, col. 585).
[2] St Augustine, *Confessions*, Bk. X, chap. 29 (P.L., XXXII, col. 796).

love of God and one's neighbour, it nevertheless lessens the fervour of charity, and also the special reward in heaven that belongs to perfect poverty. And that is a great loss for those who can recognize it. For he who can appreciate a spiritual reward at its true worth would not lessen the smallest reward that might be his in heaven for all the joy and all the possessions on earth, though he could have them without sin. My teaching outstrips my practice, but I beg of you by the grace of God do what I recommend, if you are able. And I would that others might. For it would be a consolation to me, that although I cannot have this virtue myself, I might have it, so to speak, in you or in others who have received more grace from God than I have. But since the mere roots of covetousness hinder a man so much from feeling the love of God in his soul, how much more must men in the world be hindered who devote all their energies night and day to getting riches and worldly possessions. They can find no pleasure in anything else, and they do not look for it. I will say no more about them now, for in this work I am not concerned with them. But this I do say, that if they realized what they are doing, they would not act so.

THE SEVENTY-SECOND CHAPTER

How a man may know when he sins by eating and drinking, and whether these sins are mortal or venial[1]

But in spite of the darkness of this image you may see yet more in it, namely a carnal love of self manifesting itself in gluttony, sloth, and impurity. These carnal desires reduce a

---

[1] It may be useful to relate Hilton's teaching in chaps. 72, 73, and 75. In chap. 72 he points out that since eating and drinking are necessities of nature they cannot be dispensed with, and the virtue of temperance is to

man to the level of a beast, and hinder him from the enjoyment of the love of God and the sight of spiritual things. You
may say that, since you must of necessity eat and drink and
sleep and cannot do these things without pleasure, it seems
there can be no sin in them. I reply that, if you are reasonably
moderate in eating and drinking and the other things necessary to your bodily welfare, and you take no more pleasure
in them than nature demands, and do this because of the
benefit it brings to your spiritual life, then certainly you
commit no sin. In that case you do indeed know how to regulate your diet. I myself am very far from having that knowledge and farther still from the practice of it. To eat is
natural to me, but to have the skill to regulate what I eat can
only come from grace. St Paul had this skill as he said himself: *Ubique et in omnibus institutus sum; et saturari, et esurire, et
abundare, et penuriam pati. Omnia possum in eo qui me confortat*
(Phil. iv. 12, 13). I am instructed in all things; to be hungry
and to eat, to abound and to suffer need. I can do all things in
Him who strengthens me. St Augustine, too, addressed God
thus: Thou hast taught me, Lord, to take my food as a medicine.[2] Hunger is a malady of my nature and food is its medicine, and so the pleasure that accompanies it, in so far as it
is natural and necessary, is no sin. But when the pleasure is
sought deliberately for itself, it is sinful. And it is there that

---

be practised in regulating what cannot be eliminated. This point was
made by Cassian (*Conferences*, v, 19–20). In chap. 73 he points out that
the gratification of lust is not a necessity and therefore every effort
should be made to eliminate it completely, but, he says, this may be done
by spiritual means only, not by physical. In chap. 74 he makes the point
that spiritual sins are in themselves more serious than carnal ones. Although, as he says, this is not the popular view, it is the one held by theologians, not in the sense that any spiritual sin is worse than any particular
carnal sin, but considering only this difference and *caeteris paribus* spiritual
sins are graver. cf. St Thom., *Summa*, Ia, IIae, q. LXXIII, art. 5.

[2] St Augustine, *Confessions*, Bk. x, chap. 31 (P.L., XXXII, col. 797).

the mastery lies; to have skill to distinguish necessity from deliberate pleasure. They are so joined together and one so accompanies the other that it is difficult to accept one as necessary and reject the other as deliberate indulgence, for it often appears as necessary. Nevertheless, since this sin is rooted in a necessity of nature which is not in itself a sin— for however holy a man is he needs to eat and drink and sleep —the pleasure that comes under the colour of this necessity and yet goes too far is a less serious sin. For it is not usual for a man to sin mortally by gluttony, unless he is burdened by other mortal sins that he has committed before. In that case gluttony may more easily be a mortal sin.[3] For there is no doubt that he sins mortally who puts his whole pleasure in the delights of the flesh, and of eating and drinking, to the extent of seeking no other happiness and wanting to live always in these carnal delights—for such a man puts the love of his body before that of God. A man who is burdened by a mortal sin of pride or of envy is blinded and so much in the devil's power that for the time being he has not got the proper use of his free will, and so he cannot resist the attractions of his lower nature but gives himself up to them like a beast to carrion. And since his will is not habitually directed primarily to God, because he is in a state of sin, therefore his gluttonous desires may easily be mortal sins, for he does not resist either habitually or on this particular occasion. But he who is in a state of grace has always an habitual intention[4] of serving God, whether he is asleep or awake, eating or drink-

[3] The French edition aptly quotes Billot. I translate: As long as the state of personal sin remains (the question is of mortal sin), there is a moral necessity that a man will fall repeatedly into new sins, because in this state his will is as it were bent back and turned to his own good, which for the sinner is his last end. *De Virtutibus Infusis*, ad Iam IIae, q. LXVIII, Rome (1921), p. 176.

[4] Cf. note on chap. 60. What I have here called an habitual intention is what is technically known as a *virtual* one.

ing, or whatever he may be doing, as long as it is not evil in itself, and by this intention he chooses God before all else, and would forgo all the pleasure of the world rather than displease God, so great is the love he feels for Him. This intention, although it is only habitual, is by the grace of God of such effect that, although he may fall by frailty into taking too much food or drink—either by eating too much, or too often, or too greedily, or with too much pleasure and too delicately, or before he ought to—still his intention saves him from mortal sin. And this is so as long as he is in a state of grace and keeps his habitual intention in all that he does; and especially it is true, if he acknowledges his own misery and begs for mercy and has the special intention of resisting all desires of the flesh. God is good and merciful, and He quickly forgives these venial sins of gluttony in a humble soul; for the movements of gluttony, inasmuch as they are the hardest of all sins to avoid, because of the requirements of nature, are the most excusable and the least dangerous. And for this reason you may not cut at the root of this sin as you must at that of all others. For the root of this sin is necessity, from which there is no escape, unless in desperation you kill it, as many foolish people do, when they ought rather to flee from the thief and spare the honest man, that is to say flee from unreasonable and voluntary pleasure and preserve their bodily nature. But against other sins you must take no half measures. You must destroy not only the mortal sins and more serious venial ones, but the root of them as far as you are able.

THE SEVENTY-THIRD CHAPTER

How the roots of lust are to be destroyed by spiritual rather than by bodily exercises

In accordance with what I have just been saying, note that, though you cannot live without food and drink, you can live without lust, if you have the determination, and be all the better for it. And so you must not only avoid the act, which is mortal sin, but also interior voluntary pleasure in it, which is venial and may be mortal. And beyond this you must attack the root of it in order to overcome all impulses of the flesh. But this attack on the root of lust must be spiritual, by prayer and spiritual virtues, and not bodily by way of bodily penance.[1] For be sure of this, that though you watch and fast and take the discipline and make every effort of which you are capable, you will never have purity and chastity but by the grace of God and His gift of humility. You might kill yourself before you would destroy all impulses of the flesh and temptations to impurity in mind and body by external mortification. But by the grace of God acting in a humble soul the root of it may be destroyed, the spring dried up. And then true chastity in body and mind will follow. The same might be said of pride and covetousness and similar sins, for you need not be proud or covetous in order to live; and therefore you must destroy all trace of them as far as you are able. But in gluttony you must cut away the excesses and leave the root untouched.

[1] Traditionally some degree of external mortification has always been considered a safeguard against such sins, but Hilton is surely right in saying that they cannot be overcome by a *tour-de-force*. This is in keeping with the advice that he gave about these sort of temptations in chap. 38, namely that a frontal attack on them, so to speak, is of little avail. They cannot be driven directly from the mind, but good, or at least indifferent, thoughts must be substituted.

THE SEVENTY-FOURTH CHAPTER

*That a man should strive to overcome all temptations to sin,
but especially to spiritual sin*

THUS he who strives to resist feelings of pleasure in food
and drink with more vigour than he does feelings of pride—
which because they are not so obviously undesirable are
more easily condoned—or feelings of anger, envy, covetousness or lust, has only a half view of spiritual truth.[1] For he
does not understand how displeasing pride or envy is in
God's sight. If he had the spiritual insight to see how displeasing they are and how opposed to God, he would have a
greater horror of the movements of pride and the pleasure
that may be taken in them, and he would dread envy or anger
against his neighbour more than the pleasure of gluttony or
lust. But not everyone is of this opinion. Generally men are
more afraid of a temptation to carnal sin and more sorry and
depressed by it than they are of temptations to vainglory or
similar sins. They are misguided in this, as they may learn if

---

[1] Hilton has a very involved sentence here. "And therefore he that
riseth against the feeling of fleshly liking in meat and drink, more felly and
more sharply than against the feelings and stirrings of pride, which for
they seem fair are not lightly reproved, or of envy, ire, covetize, or
lechery, I say that he is half blind." As the point of the chapter is that
spiritual sins are more serious than carnal ones, I take it that envy, ire,
and covetize are to be connected with pride, and the words in between
regarded as a parenthesis. It is difficult to see how lechery comes to be
associated with these spiritual sins and one would suspect textual corruption, but Miss Birts tells me that there is little sign of this in the manuscripts. She points out that the sentence is perhaps to be connected with
the last sentence of the previous chapter: "In gluttony you must cut away
the excesses but leave the root untouched." He is emphasizing this last
aspect of gluttony by which he distinguishes it from all other sins including lust, and passes on in the rest of the chapter to the idea that both
gluttony and lust are, as carnal sins, less serious than spiritual ones.

they will read the Scriptures and what the learned have to say on them.[2] But I will not quote them for you now.

I do not say that those who take pleasure in gluttony and impurity commit no sin, for I am well aware that the different species of them are sinful to a greater or lesser degree according to the amount of deliberate pleasure and other circumstances. But you ought to know and judge all sins as they are in reality, the greater as greater—that is all spiritual sins—and the lesser as less—that is all carnal sins. And you must detest and avoid all of them, spiritual and carnal, to the utmost of your power. For be sure of this, that the desires of the flesh and immoderate pleasure in food and drink, or any bodily pleasure that exceeds reasonable necessity, although they are not always great sins to a man in a state of grace, nevertheless they weigh down the spirit, and a soul that seeks holiness and the enjoyment of God must do all in its power to avoid them. For spiritual consolations cannot make themselves felt in the soul while carnal delectation is felt in the body.

THE SEVENTY-FIFTH CHAPTER

That hunger and bodily suffering are a great hindrance to the spiritual life

AND so, if you will arrive at purity of heart, you must resist irrational impulses of the flesh. But the root of them you should not attack,[1] as I said before, for this root is necessity, as for example natural hunger, which you must needs feel and attend to at the proper time. You must take the medi-

---

[2] Cf. St Gregory, *Moral. in Job*, Bk. XXXIII, chap. 12 (P.L., LXXVI, col. 688); also chap. 72, n. 1.

[1] He seems here to ignore the distinction he made between gluttony in chap. 72 and lust in chap. 73.

cine of food as you would take remedies for a bodily illness so that you may the better serve God both in body and spirit.

For know this, that anyone who wishes to give himself to the spiritual life will find himself much hampered by the pains of hunger voluntarily undertaken, or sickness, or headache, or any other sort of bodily suffering brought on by his own fault by excessive fasting, unless it is by the very special grace of God. For although bodily suffering—either produced by doing penance or by illness—or much work does not always interfere with the fervour of love felt in devotion, indeed often increases it, I hold that it hinders the fervour of love in contemplation. For this can only be felt in great repose of soul and body.[2]

THE SEVENTY-SIXTH CHAPTER

The remedies a man should use against indiscreet eating and drinking

THEREFORE lead a normal life and treat your body reasonably, and then let God send what he pleases, health or sickness. Receive it with joy and do not deliberately complain against God. Take your food as it comes, making reasonable provision for it if needs be, and accept it cheerfully as a necessity. But be on your guard against too great pleasure in it; avoid too much as well as too little. And if you should fall into either of these errors and feel remorse of conscience and are vexed and depressed over it, lift up your heart to our Lord and ask His forgiveness, acknowledging yourself

[2] For this discretion in matters of food and drink cf. *The Cloud of Unknowing*, chap. 42, Rolle, *The Form of Living* (*English Writings of Richard Rolle*, edit. H. E. Allen (Oxford, 1931), chap. i, p. 86), and *An Epistle of Discretion* (*The Cell of Self-Knowledge*, edit. Edmund Gardner (London, 1910), p. 95).

a brute. Tell Him that you will do better, and trust in His
mercy to forgive you. And when you have done this, and the
more briefly the better, trouble yourself no more about it,
and do not strive as though you would utterly destroy these
impulses in you, for it is not worth your while. You will
never succeed. But turn to some other occupation, bodily or
spiritual, as you feel disposed, so that you may advance in
other virtues such as humility and charity. For he who
desires and strives after none but these two, always seeking
how he may attain them, will in this way grow in all the
others—chastity and abstinence for example although he
pays little direct attention to them. He will make greater
progress in them in a year than he would in seven, if he
strove continually against gluttony and lust, and took the
discipline every day from morning till evening.

THE SEVENTY-SEVENTH CHAPTER

*That by desiring humility and charity and striving after them
a man comes more quickly to all other virtues*

GET humility and charity then, and if you will make serious
efforts to do so, you will have occupation enough. And if you
succeed in attaining them, they will regulate your food and
drink and all your bodily requirements without need of help
from anyone else[1] ; you will not be in doubt or anxiety, or
feel annoyance or depression or ill-regulated desires, but
you will enjoy the peace of a good conscience and great repose. I did not think to have said so much on this matter ;
carry out my advice if you can, and may God bless your

[1] "Without need of help from anyone else." I have thus translated "that
there shall no man wit it but if thou wilt". The translation fits the context
and might be held to be implied by the original. It is the interpretation
adopted by the French translation.

efforts. From what I have said you can see to some extent how this image of sin stands in your way. The Gospel relates how Abraham spoke to the rich man who was in hell: *Chaos magnum inter nos et vos firmatum est, ut hi qui volunt transire ad vos, non possint, neque inde huc transmeare* (Luke xvi. 26). There is a great gulf, that is to say, a thick darkness, between us, so that we cannot come to you nor you to us. This dark image, which is in your soul and mine also, may be called a great gulf, for it prevents us from coming to Abraham, that is Jesus, and it prevents Him from coming to us.

THE SEVENTY-EIGHTH CHAPTER
Of the five bodily senses

LIGHT your lantern then and you will see in this image five windows by which sin enters into your soul; as the prophet says: *Mors ingreditur per fenestras nostras* (Jer. ix. 21). Death comes in by our windows. These windows are the five senses by which your soul goes out and seeks its pleasure and its refreshment in earthly things contrary to its true nature. By the eye it seeks for strange and beautiful things, and by the ear wonderful and new tidings, and so with the rest; and by the deliberate immoderate indulgence of its senses on trivial things the soul is much hindered in the use of its special powers. So you must shut these windows and bar them, and only open them when necessity demands.

THE SEVENTY-NINTH CHAPTER

That the soul through lack of knowledge of itself goes out by these five windows to seek external pleasures

AND it would be no difficulty to you [to keep the windows of your soul closed], if you clearly understood the nature of your soul and the beauty that it would have if it were not overlaid by this black image. But because you do not know your own soul, you neglect your interior life and seek your refreshment in the external world like an irrational animal. God says to the Beloved in Scripture: *Si ignoras te, O pulcra inter mulieres, egredere et abi post vestigia gregum sodalium tuorum, et pasce haedos tuos* (Cant. i. 7). If you know not yourself, fairest among women, go forth and follow after the steps of the flock of your fellows and feed your kids. That is as much as to say: O soul, naturally beautiful, made in the likeness of God, frail as a woman in your body by reason of original sin, you do not know yourself and are unaware that your delight should be in the food of angels, and so you go out by your bodily senses and seek your nourishment and your pleasure like a beast of the flock—that is as one of the reprobate. The thoughts and affections which you foster are unclean as goats. It is a shame for you to act so.

THE EIGHTIETH CHAPTER

That the soul should seek what it needs from Jesus within itself and not from things without

AND therefore come home again to yourself and keep within and beg no more outside for the food of swine. If you will still be a beggar, beg within of your Lord Jesus, for He is rich enough, and readier to give than you to ask. Go out no more as a beast of the flock, as a worldly man who has no pleasure but in his bodily senses. And if you do this, your Lord Jesus will fulfil all your desires. He will take you to His wine cellar and make you taste of His best wines, for He has many casks. It is what the Beloved says of our Lord in Holy Scripture: *Introduxit me rex in cellam vinariam* (Cant. ii. 4). A king led me into a wine cellar. That is to say: inasmuch as I forsook the drunkenness of the lusts of the flesh, which are bitter as wormwood, the king of bliss, the Lord Jesus, led me in; first into myself, that I might see and know myself, and afterwards into His wine cellar, and He made me taste of His wine, that is of spiritual sweetness and heavenly joy. These are not my words, a sinful wretch, but they are the words of the Spouse in Holy Scripture. And I address them to you that you may draw in your soul from external things and imitate her as far as you are able.

THE EIGHTY-FIRST CHAPTER

That the window of the imagination needs to be closed as well as those of the senses

BUT you say that you already do this. You neither see nor hear of the doings of the world, and you use none of your bodily senses more than necessity demands. This is the reason of your enclosure. In that case you have shut a large window in this image. But still you are not safe, for you have not closed the secret opening of the imagination. You may not see me with the eye of your body, and yet you may see me with the eye of your soul in the imagination. And you may do the like with all material things. Then if your soul is voluntarily occupied in imagining vanities of the world and in desiring worldly things for your comfort and ease, though it may be within as far as the bodily senses are concerned, it is far outside in these vain imaginations. You may ask if it is any great sin for a soul to be occupied with these matters, either in the senses or in the imagination. To that I say that I would not have you ask such a question, for he who would love God truly does not ask whether one sin is greater than another. He is to consider anything that hinders his love of God a great sin, and nothing a sin but what is evil and interferes with this love. What is sin but the privation of God?[1] I do not say that such a hindrance will be as grievous to him as a mortal or, for that matter, a venial sin, and I do not deny that he knows mortal from venial and is more anxious to avoid the former.

THE EIGHTY-SECOND CHAPTER

When the use of the senses is mortal sin and when it is venial

NEVERTHELESS I shall say something more in answer to your question, for it leads me to say more than I thought to have said in the beginning. Our Lord said in the Gospel: *Homo quidam fecit cenam magnam et vocavit multos. Et misit servum suum hora cenae dicere invitatis ut venirent. Primus dixit: Villam emi; rogo te, habe me excusatum. Secundus dixit: Juga boum emi quinque, et eo probare illa. Et tertius dixit: Uxorem duxi, et ideo non possum venire* (Luke xiv. 16–20). A man made a great supper and invited many to it, and he sent his servant at suppertime to them that were invited. The first excused him-

---

[1] Hilton is talking here in a popular sense. The privation of God is more properly the effect of mortal sin than sin itself. What I think he means is that any imperfection which hinders the soul's union with God is to be avoided as though it were sin, even though in fact it is not, and the soul is aware that it is not.

self from coming, for he had bought a farm; the second also excused himself, because he had bought five yoke of oxen and he went to try them; the third, because he had married a wife. I say nothing of the first and last, but I will speak of him that bought the oxen. These five yoke of oxen signify the five senses, because they belong to animal nature. Now the man that was invited to the supper was not reproved because he had bought the oxen, but because he went to try them and so could not come. So in your case, to have your senses and to use them in necessity is no sin; but if you go to try them by taking vain pleasure in creatures, then there is sin. And if you choose that pleasure as the final end of your soul, so that you look for no further happiness, then the sin is mortal. For you make this pleasure into your God, and so you will be turned out of the supper. St Paul forbade this use of the senses when he said: *Non eatis post concupiscentias vestras.*[1] You shall not pursue your lusts or voluntarily taste pleasures. Anyone burdened with mortal sin will not escape mortal sin in this, even though he is not aware of it. I hope, however, that it does not concern you. Nevertheless, if by frailty you take pleasure in your senses, but remain in charity and do not choose the pleasure as an end in itself, desiring God above all things, the sin is venial, greater or less according to the circumstances. You will not be excluded from the supper in the happiness of heaven for these venial sins. But unless you use all your endeavours to avoid such sins, you will be deprived of the enjoyment of that banquet while you are living on earth. For although venial sins do not destroy charity, they hinder its fervour and the feeling of it in the spirit.

[1] It looks as though Hilton was trusting to his memory here. St Paul says *carnis curam ne feceritis in desideriis* (Rom. xiii. 14), which has much the same meaning as Hilton's text, but he may have had in mind a text from Ecclesiasticus, *Post concupiscentias tuas non eas* (xviii. 30), and wrongly attributed it to St Paul.

THE EIGHTY-THIRD CHAPTER

*How those who give themselves to the spiritual life should
behave to visitors*

You may say that you cannot help hearing of the world, for
various people, laymen and clerics, often come to speak
with you and tell you all sorts of frivolous stories. I reply that
intercourse with your fellow-men will do you little harm,
and may indeed help you, if you are prudent over it. For by
it you may test the measure of your charity to your neighbour, whether it is great or small. You are bound, like every
other man and woman, to love your neighbour in intention
and also to prove your love for him by action, when there is
reasonable cause, according to your ability and knowledge.
Certainly, as an enclosed religious you are not to go abroad
to seek occasions of helping other men by works of mercy,
nevertheless you are bound to have charity towards them all
in your heart and to show outward signs of it to those who
come to you. And therefore, when somebody comes to speak
to you, and you have no idea who he is or why he comes, be
ready to find out what he wants. Do not keep aloof or allow
him to wait a long time for you. How ready and happy you
would be if an angel from heaven came to speak to you. Be
as ready and willing to speak to your fellow-men when they
visit you. For till you have spoken to your visitor you do not
know who he is, or why he comes, or what his need may be.
And if you are at your prayers and are unwilling to be interrupted, because you think you should not leave God for conversation with a man, I think in this case you are mistaken.
For if you act wisely you will not leave God, but you will
find Him; you will possess and see Him as much in your
neighbour as in your prayers, although in another manner.

If you have the right sort of love for your fellow-men, it
should not be a hindrance to your spiritual life to talk with

them discreetly. I suggest this as a guide to your discretion.
When somebody comes to you, ask him modestly what he
wants. If he comes to tell you some trouble and to be consoled by you, listen to him gladly and let him say what he
wishes for the easing of his heart. When he has finished give
him any comfort you can in all charity, but not at too great
length. If he starts telling idle tales of what other men are
doing, answer him little and give him no encouragement;
he will soon become bored and take his leave. If an ecclesi-
astic comes to give you instruction, hear him humbly out of
respect for his state. If what he says consoles you, question
him further, but do not offer to instruct him. It is not for
you to instruct a priest except in necessity. If what he says is
no consolation to you, answer little, and he will soon depart.
If somebody comes to bring you an alms or to listen to you
and be instructed by you, speak kindly and humbly to them.
Do not reprove anybody for his faults. It is not your business,
unless by chance if it is somebody you know very well and
you are sure that he will take it from you. In short, say what
you think will be for the spiritual profit of your neighbour—
as much as you can give and he will take. Otherwise keep
silence as much as possible, and in a short time you will not
be much troubled. That is my opinion; do better if you
can.

THE EIGHTY-FOURTH CHAPTER

The dark image of sin and its clothing

FROM what I have said you may get some idea of the darkness of this image; not that I have described it fully as it
is, for that is beyond my powers. Nevertheless more will
appear, if you look closely, even in the little that I have said.
You may ask how I know that you bear about such an image

as I have spoken of, and I answer you by a word from the prophet: *Inveni idolum mihi* (Osee xii. 8). I have found in myself a false image that men call an idol, foully disfigured and deformed by the malice of the sins which I have described. And by these sins I am turned from purity of heart and the practice of spiritual virtues to carnal delights and worldly vanities, more than I can say. And that state causes me great sorrow, and to beg for mercy. By this misery that I feel in myself to a far greater extent than I have said I am the better able to tell you of your own image. For we are all descended from Adam and Eve who were clothed in animal skins, as Scripture says: *Fecit Dominus Adae et uxori ejus tunicas pelliceas* (Gen. iii. 21). God made for Adam and his wife clothes of skins to signify that for his sin he was deformed like a beast, and we are born in these garments of skin with our true form obscured and disfigured.

THE EIGHTY-FIFTH CHAPTER

The members of this image of sin

THIS image is ugly to look at. The head is pride, for pride is the first and principal sin as the Wise Man says: *Initium omnis peccati superbia* (Ecclus. x. 15). The beginning of all sin is pride. The back part of it is covetousness; as St Paul says: *Quae retro sunt obliviscens, in anteriora me extendo* (Phil. iii. 13). I shall forget all worldly things that are behind and stretch forward to everlasting things. The breast, in which is the heart, is envy, for it is not a carnal sin but it is of the devil; as the Wise Man says: *Invidia diaboli mors introivit in orbem terrarum. Imitantur illum omnes qui ex parte ejus sunt* (Wisdom ii. 23, 25). Death came into the world through the devil's envy, and all who are of his party follow him in this sin. The arms of this image are anger, for a man wreaks his vengeance by his arms—against the commandment of Christ in the Gospel: *Si quis percusserit te in unam maxillam, praebe illi sibi et alteram* (Matt. v. 39). If a man strikes you with his hand on one cheek, you shall not strike him again, but offer him the other. The belly is gluttony as St Paul says: *Esca ventri et venter escis; Deus hunc et has destruet* (1 Cor. vi. 13). Food for the belly and the belly for food; but God will destroy both the belly and the food. That will be at the very end, at the full restoration of His elect and the judgement of the reprobate. The legs are impurity of which St Paul says: *Non exhibeatis membra vestra arma iniquitatis ad peccatum* (Rom. vi. 13). You shall not give your members, especially your private members, to be members of sin. The feet of this image are *accidia*, and therefore the Wise Man says to the soul to stir it to good works: *Discurre, festina, suscita amicum tuum* (Prov. vi. 3). Run quickly about good works, make haste, for the time passes, and raise up your friend, who is Jesus, by devout prayer and meditation. These are the members of this image.

THE EIGHTY-SIXTH CHAPTER

Of what constitutes the image of Jesus and the image of sin

THIS is not the image of Jesus but resembles rather an image of the devil; for the image of Jesus consists in virtues, humility, love, charity. But this image with all its members is that of a false carnal love of self. You bear this image and so does every other man, whoever he may be, until it is to some extent broken down and destroyed by the grace of God. So David in the psalter: *Verumtamen in imagine pertransit homo; sed et frustra conturbatur* (Ps. xxxviii. 7). Though in the beginning man was made stable and firm in the image of God, nevertheless because of sin he lives in this world clothed in the image of sin, and thereby is become unstable and troubled. St Paul speaks of this image thus: *Sicut portavimus imaginem terreni hominis sic portemus imaginem caelestis* (1 Cor. xv. 49). As we have first borne the image of the earthly man, Adam, that is the image of sin, now we must bear the image of the heavenly man, Jesus, the image of virtues, if we would come to the love of God.

THE EIGHTY-SEVENTH CHAPTER

How the image of sin should be crucified and the image of Jesus made to live

WHAT then is to be done with this image? I answer with the words of the Jews to Pilate about Christ: *Tolle, tolle, crucifige eum* (John xix. 15). Take this body of sin and crucify it; that is, break down this image and slay the love of sin in yourself. As Christ's body was slain for our offences, so, if you will be like Christ, you must put to death bodily pleasure and the lust of the flesh. As St Paul says: *Qui autem Christi sunt, carnem suam crucifixerunt cum vitiis et concupiscentiis* (Gal. v. 24). Those who are followers of Christ have crucified and mortified their flesh, that is the image of sin, with all its lusts and irrational desires. Slay pride then and break it down and raise up humility; break down anger and envy and raise up love and charity to your neighbour; instead of covetousness cultivate poverty of spirit, instead of *accidia*, fervent devotion and promptness to all good works, and instead of gluttony and impurity, temperance and chastity in body and soul. This was St Paul's advice when he said: *Deponentes veterem hominem cum suis actibus, qui corrumpitur secundum desideria erroris; et induite novum hominem, qui secun-*

dum Deum creatus est in sanctitate et justitia (Eph. iv. 22, 24).
Put off the old man, that is the image of sin of the old Adam
with all its members, for it is corrupted in the desire of error,
and put on the new man, which is the image of God, by holiness and justice and the fullness of virtues. Who will help
you to break down this image? Truly the Lord Jesus. In His
power and in His name you shall break down this idol of sin.
Pray to Him assiduously and He will help you.

THE EIGHTY-EIGHTH CHAPTER

*The value of guarding the heart, and how much the soul is
identified with what it loves*

COLLECT then your scattered heart and act according to the
advice of the Wise Man when he says: *Omni custodia serva cor
tuum, quia ex ipso procedit vita* (Prov. iv. 23). With all your
endeavour keep your heart, for out of it comes life. And that
is indeed the fact when it is well kept, for then wise thoughts,
pure affections, and a burning desire of virtue and charity
and of the happiness of heaven come out of it, and make the
soul live a blessed life. On the other hand, if it is not guarded,
then, as our Lord said in the Gospel: *De corde exeunt cogita-
tiones malae, quae coinquinant hominem* (Matt. xv. 19, 20).
Evil thoughts and impure desires come from the heart and
these are what defile a man. They slay the soul, if they are
mortal, or weaken and sicken it, if they are venial. For what
is a man but his thoughts and his loves? It is these alone which
make a man bad or good. The more you love and know God
and the more you love your neighbour the greater is your
soul, and if your love of God is small, then your soul will be
so too, and if you have no love, your soul is worth nothing
as far as goodness is concerned, but its power for sin is great.

If you want to know what it is you love, examine your thoughts; for where your love is there will be your eye, and the thought will dwell where the heart takes pleasure. If you love God much, you will like to think much of Him, and if you love Him little your thought will be little upon Him. Regulate your thoughts and your affections well, and then you will be virtuous.

THE EIGHTY-NINTH CHAPTER

How the image of sin is to be destroyed

BEGIN then to break down this image. Consider yourself and your misery, as I said. But if it comes to your mind how proud, vain, envious, melancholy, and covetous, how carnal-minded and how full of corruption you are; how little knowledge or experience of God you have, and on the other hand how knowledgeable and prompt you are about earthly things and what pleasure you take in them; in short if you think yourself as full of sins as a hide is full of flesh, do not be disquieted. When you have done all this, raise up your heart to your Lord Jesus and ask His help. Beg of Him most earnestly that He will help you to bear the heavy burden of this image or else that He will break it. Think how shameful it is for you to satiate yourself with the food of swine, which is what carnal pleasures are, you who should look for spiritual pleasures in the joy of heaven. If you make this effort, you will be attacking the roots of sin in yourself, and the experience may bring you pain and sorrow, for you will begin to see that every soul must be in pain, if it cannot rest and take pleasure either in its creator or in creatures. Then when you feel a strong desire to experience the presence of Jesus and to forsake the love of all earthly things and no longer to find satisfaction in bodily feelings, you will feel as though weighed down by self. All creatures will seem to turn against you, and all the things that you took pleasure in before will turn to pain. You will have forsaken yourself and be unable to find consolation in God, and this is bound to be a cause of suffering. Nevertheless put up with it for a time, hold firmly to the bare thought of Jesus, seek nothing but your Lord, do not easily be dissuaded from your purpose, and do not seek consolation in external things while the trial lasts. It will not last long, for our Lord is near and will soon bring you relief. He will help you to put up with your body and its corruption, and the merciful power of His gracious presence will break down the false image of love in you. This will not happen all at once but gradually, until you are to some extent reformed in His likeness.

THE NINETIETH CHAPTER

How to deal with movements of pride and other vices

AFTER you have attacked the roots of sin in yourself in this way and when the struggle is over, you will be able to control yourself with more discretion and facility, and to guard your thoughts and affections more closely, and to know whether they are legitimate or not. And then if you feel a movement of any sort of pride, be on your guard and do not neglect to pay attention to it; look squarely at it and despise it as far as you are able. Have no mercy on it and give no credence to it however specious it may appear. Be assured that it is false even if it seems true. As the prophet says: *Popule meus, qui te beatum dicunt, ipsi te seducunt, et in errorem mittunt* (Isa. iii. 12). O, my people, those who say you are blessed and holy deceive you and lead you into error. And if you often do this earnestly, you will by the grace of God in a short time largely dry up the spring of pride in you and much reduce the pleasure you take in it, so that you will hardly feel it, and when you do feel it, it will be so weak that it will do you little harm. And then you will get some spiritual insight into the goodness and beauty of humility, and you will seek it and love it for its own sake. You will be glad to be considered such as in fact you are, and if need be to suffer contempt and reproof for the love of justice. In the same way when you feel a movement of anger, or melancholy, or ill-will towards your neighbour, although reason, and even charity, seem to justify it, be on your guard and be ready to restrain it lest it turn to passion. Resist it and, if possible, do not act on it either in word or deed, but whenever it arises drive it down again. Slay it with the sword of the fear of God and it will not hurt you. Remember in all these movements of pride, vainglory, envy, and the like, that if you resist them with your will and your reason as soon as you perceive them, you will kill them even though they remain involuntarily in your mind and you cannot easily get rid of them. Have no fear of them. They take away peace from your soul, but they do not defile it. You must act in the same way towards evil movements of covetousness, *accidia*, gluttony, and lust. Be always ready to withstand and despise them by reason and will.

THE NINETY-FIRST CHAPTER

What enables a man to know and acquire what he needs, and what most effectively destroys sin in him

AND you will be able to do that better and more easily if you will set your heart on one thing. And that thing is nothing else than [our Lord Jesus Christ, that Blessed Person, God and man. You must put Him as the one object of your desire, the light of your heart, having a reverent fear of displeasing

Him and a great] desire to please God; to love, know, see, and possess Him here by grace and to be united to Him fully in the happiness of heaven.[1] If you foster this desire of Jesus Christ, it will enable you to distinguish what is sinful from what is not, and between two good actions, which is the more perfect. If you will keep it always before you, it will teach you all that you need to know and obtain for you all that you want. And therefore if you would attack the roots of sin in general or any special sin in particular, keep this desire always before you and fix your mind rather on Jesus Christ whom you desire than on the sin which you seek to overcome. If you do this, then Jesus Christ will fight for you and will destroy your sin. You will achieve your purpose much sooner, if you will put this humble desire of God before all else, than if you devote your efforts only to suppressing the movements of sin, as though you would eradicate them simply by mastering yourself. You will never be able to do it in that way.

[1] The portion in square brackets is one of the "christo-centric" portions of which Miss Underhill speaks in the Introduction to her edition, and which are incorporated in the text of some manuscripts and missing in others. The discussion of the genuineness or otherwise of these passages must wait for the appearance of a full critical text, but it may be noted that, as Miss Gardner has pointed out (*Medium Aevum*, Feb. 1936, p. 23) their significance from the point of view of the subject matter is not very great, many of them being very short and the work being essentially christo-centric in any case. This passage is perhaps the most interesting of them, as it certainly looks as though it might be an interpolation which has been imperfectly incorporated into the text. The passage makes sense without it, but if the passage in square brackets is read there is a transference from "Jesus Christ" to "God" which is awkward syntactically—not that that would exclude the possibility of Hilton having written it. The interpolated passage, if it is an interpolation, certainly does introduce a christo-centric emphasis which is otherwise absent, and is in this respect the most significant of these passages. In other cases I have incorporated them in my translation without comment.

THE NINETY-SECOND CHAPTER

How a man should be conformed to the image of Jesus and Jesus formed in him

Do as I have said, and better if you can, and I hope that by the grace of Jesus you will put the devil to shame and suppress all these evil movements so that they will do you little harm. In this way you may break down and destroy this image of sin which disfigures the fair image of Christ in you. By humility and charity you will be conformed again to the Image of Christ in His humanity and this will lead you to be conformed to the image of Christ in His divinity. You will only attain a shadow of it here in contemplation, but in the happiness of heaven you will receive the fullness. St Paul says of this conformity to the likeness of Christ: *Filioli, quos iterum parturio, donec Christus formetur in vobis* (Gal. iv. 19). My dear children, whom I bear as a woman bears her child, until Christ is formed in you again. You have conceived Christ by faith, and He is living in you inasmuch as you have good will, and desire to serve and please Him. But He is not yet fully formed in you, nor you in Him, by the perfection of charity. And therefore St Paul bears you and me, and others too, with pain as a woman bears her child, until Christ is fully formed in us and we in Him. Whoever thinks to come to the full experience of contemplation in any other way, that is without the persevering remembrance of the humanity and passion of Christ and the practice of virtue, does not come in by the door and so will be cast out like a thief.[1] I do not deny that by the grace of God a man may

[1] This passage is reminiscent of *The Epistle of Privy Counsel* (chap. 9) (printed in *The Cloud of Unknowing and other treatises*, edited by Dom Justin McCann (London, 1952)). While the author of the *Epistle*—who was in all probability also the author of *The Cloud*—was very insistent that in the actual time of "the work", as he called it, that is of contem-

sometimes have a taste and foreshadowing of contemplation, even in an early stage of his spiritual life, but he will not have a constant experience of it. For Christ is the door and the porter, and no man may come in unless he partakes of His life and is marked by His sign, as He Himself said: *Nemo venit ad Patrem nisi per me* (John xiv. 6). No man comes to the Father but by me. That is to say no man may come to the contemplation of the Godhead, unless he is first reformed by humility and charity to the likeness of Jesus in His humanity.

THE NINETY-THIRD CHAPTER

The reason why this book was written, and how she for whom it was written should make use of it

WELL, I have told you something of the contemplative life in itself, as I conceive it, and then of the ways which by God's grace lead to it. Not that I can experience it and practise it in the way that I talk about it. But by my words, such as they are, I would first of all stir my own negligence to do better than I have done in the past, and then my purpose is to urge you, or anyone else who has undertaken the contemplative life, to strive more earnestly and more humbly in it by such simple words as God has given me grace to use. And so if anything I have said inspires you more to the love of God or gives you greater consolation it in, thank God, for it is His gift and not the result of anything I could say. And

---

plative prayer, as we should say, there must be no use of the imagination or reason even on the humanity of Christ, he was equally insistent that at other times such considerations must be made use of. See especially chap. 9 where he has the same references to the door and the thief. As I have said earlier (chap. 52, n. 1), I do not think that Hilton advocated any exercise which demanded the exclusion of the thought of Christ's humanity.

if it is no consolation to you, or does not appeal to you, do not dwell on it too long. Put it aside till another time, and give yourself to prayer or some other occupation. Take it as you find you can use it, and not all at once. Do not take anything that I have written too literally, but where you think after careful consideration that it falls short either through the inadequacy of my English or because the thought is not clear, correct it, but only where there is need. Further, what I have said does not apply to anyone leading an active life, but to you or any other contemplative. The grace of our Lord Jesus Christ be with you. Amen.

BOOK II

THE FIRST CHAPTER

How the soul of every just man is the image of God[1]

SINCE you wish to hear more of an image which I have before partly described to you, I will with pleasure, and at the same time with some misgivings, comply with your request, and with the help of our Lord Jesus Christ in Whom I put all my trust, I will say something more about it. In the first place, if you wish to know in a word what I mean by it, I mean nothing else than your soul; for your soul, and mine, and every rational soul, is an image, and no less than the image of God, as the Apostle says: *Vir est imago Dei* (1 Cor. xi. 7). Man is the image of God made in His likeness, and this likeness is not in his outward bodily appearance but in his inner powers. As Holy Scripture says: *Formavit Deus hominem ad imaginem et similitudinem suam* (Gen. i. 27). That is, God made the soul of man to His own image and likeness. It was of this that I spoke. Created in the image of God the soul had great beauty and splendour, burning with love and shining with spiritual light. But through the sin of Adam it was disfigured and transformed into another likeness, as I have said before. For it fell from the enjoyment of spiritual light and heavenly nourishment into a distressing darkness and a lust for this miserable life. It became an exile and an outcast from the heritage of heaven that would have belonged to it, if it had remained firm, and fell first into the

[1] Hilton in these first three chapters is describing the plight in which man finds himself owing to the Fall. He describes how man was originally made in the image of God, and how this likeness was lost through sin, and restored by our Lord. He had treated the subject in chaps. 43 and 44 of Bk. 1, but here he goes at greater length into the "fittingness" of Redemption through the passion and death of Christ.

misery of this earth, and then into the prison of hell for all eternity. And it would never have been able to return from this prison to its heavenly home, if it had not been refashioned to the form it first possessed. But the reformation[2] could not be brought about by any earthly man. For every man was overwhelmed by the same misfortune, and none was able to help himself, much less any other man. And therefore it had to be done by one who was more than man, that is by God. And it was only fitting that, if man was to be saved, He should reform him and restore him to happiness, Who in His goodness first created him for it. By the grace of God I will tell you, then, how the soul is to be reformed in the likeness of Him who first created it, and that is indeed the whole purpose of my writing.

THE SECOND CHAPTER

How the justice of God demands that sin should not be forgiven unless satisfaction is made[1]

THE justice of God demands that sin should not be forgiven unless satisfaction is made for it as far as this may be possible. Now the whole of mankind in the person of the first man, Adam, sinned against God so seriously, when it transgressed His special commandment and consented to the temptation of the devil, that it justly deserved to be separated from Him and condemned to hell for all eternity. And indeed, accord-

---

[2] Hilton habitually uses the word "reformation" to express this idea of the restoration of the soul to the image of God, and it seems best to keep the word as a technical term.

[1] The argument in this chapter is more or less closely based on that of St Anselm in the *Cur Deus Homo*, see especially Bk. I, chap. 20 (P.L., CLVIII, col. 392–3), Bk. II, chap. 8 (P.L., CLVIII, col. 405–6), and Bk. II, chap. 11 (P.L., CLVIII, col. 410–12).

ing to the strict justice of God, it could not obtain His pardon, unless full satisfaction were first made. But no mere man descended from Adam could make this satisfaction, because the sin and the offence to God were infinite, and therefore it exceeded the power of man to make satisfaction for it. And it did so also for this reason: one who has sinned, and who would make amends, ought to give to him that he has sinned against everything that might be due from him, even though he had not sinned, in addition to what he owes only on account of his sin. But mankind had nothing to offer to God in expiation for its sin beyond what it owed Him already. Whatever good act a man might perform, physical or spiritual, it was but his debt. For as the Gospel says, every man has an obligation to love God with his whole heart and soul and all his strength (Luke x. 27), and more than that he cannot do. Nevertheless this was not sufficient for the reformation of mankind, and even this man could not do without being himself first reformed. So if man's soul was to be reformed and the wrong made good, it was necessary that God Himself should reform this image and make satisfaction for the sin, since no man could do it. But God could not do that in His divinity, for He could not make satisfaction by suffering pain in His divine nature, nor was He called upon to do so. Therefore it was necessary for Him to take human nature that had sinned, and to become man. But again, it was impossible for Him to do that by way of ordinary generation, for God's Son might not be born of a woman known by man. Therefore he had to become man of a pure virgin, full of grace, our Lady St Mary, through a supernatural generation by the power of the Holy Ghost. And so it was done. For our Lord Jesus Christ, the Son of God, became man and through His precious death made satisfaction to the heavenly Father for man's guilt. And He was able to do that because He was God, and because [as

man]¹ He owed nothing on His own behalf, except in so far
as He was born of the race of Adam who first sinned. And so,
though He owed nothing for Himself, because He could not
sin, nevertheless by His own free will He took upon Himself the debt owing for the sin of mankind. In His mercy He
took the nature of man for man's salvation. For it is the
simple truth that there was never any man who could give
God anything that he did not already owe to Him save our
Blessed Lord, Jesus. For He could give God one thing that
was in no way due from Him, and only one thing, and that
was His life, and He did this by voluntarily taking death on
Himself from love of truth. There was no obligation on Him
to do this. In His life on earth He was bound to pay honour
to God, but He was in no way bound to accept death out of
love of justice. He had to accomplish justice, but He did not
have to die. For death is a penalty inflicted on man for sin,
but our Lord never sinned and could not sin, and therefore
He was not subject to death. And since He yet chose voluntarily to die, He gave to God more than He owed. And
since that was the human act of greatest worth ever performed, it was fitting that the sin of mankind should be forgiven in virtue of it. For in Jesus mankind found one of the
same race, free from the stain of sin, who was able to make
satisfaction for sin, and who could give to God all that was
due to Him and more. Our Lord Jesus, God and man, dying
thus for our salvation, it was but right that sins should be forgiven, and man's soul, created in the image of God, be restored to His likeness and to the happiness of heaven.

The passion and precious death of our Lord are the cause
of the reformation of our souls, and without them man's soul

¹ *As man.* The words are not in Hilton's text, but they are necessary to
make the meaning clear. Christ did not owe anything for Himself, because His human nature was without sin, but He had nevertheless taken
a human nature which had come under the dominion of sin.

would never have been reformed or come to the happiness of heaven. Blessed may He be in all His works. Now, through the power of the passion the flaming sword of the Cherubim who drove Adam out of paradise is laid aside, and the gates of heaven opened to every man who will enter. For the Person of Jesus is God, and even now, in the happiness of the Father, King of heaven; and as man He is porter at the gate ready to receive every soul that will be reformed to His likeness here in this life. For now every soul that wishes may be reformed to the likeness of God, since sin is forgiven and satisfaction made for the original guilt through Jesus. But although this is true, all souls do not profit by this precious passion and not all are reformed in His likeness.

THE THIRD CHAPTER

How there are two sorts of men who are not reformed by the passion of our Lord Jesus Christ

THERE are two sorts of men who are not reformed by virtue of the passion; those who do not believe in it, and those who do not love it. Jews and pagans do not benefit by the passion, because Jews do not believe that Jesus, the son of Mary, is the Son of God, and pagans do not believe that the sovereign wisdom of God would become man and in His humanity suffer the pains of death. And so to the Jews the preaching of the cross and the passion of Christ was a scandal and a blasphemy, and to the pagans fantasy and folly. But to true Christians it was a manifestation of the sovereign wisdom of God and His power. St Paul said: *Praedicamus vobis Christum crucifixum, Judaeis quidem scandalum, gentibus autem stultitiam: ipsis autem vocatis Judaeis atque Graecis, Christum Dei virtutem etc.* (1 Cor. i. 23–4). That is, we preach to you what we

believe, that Jesus Christ, who was crucified and who was
the son of Mary, is the Son of God, His sovereign power and
wisdom. And this Jesus is a scandal and a folly to the Jews
and pagans who do not believe in Him. By their unbelief
they prevent the reformation of their souls, and if they persist in unbelief they will never be saved or come to the happiness of heaven. For from the beginning to the end of the
world no man was ever saved, or ever shall be, unless through
faith, either explicit or implicit, in Jesus Christ to come or
already come. The elect who lived under the Old Testament
before the Incarnation had faith in Christ and believed that
He would come and reform man's soul. They believed it
either explicitly as the prophets and other holy men, or else
with an implicit and general faith, as did children and the
simple and imperfect, who had no special knowledge of the
mystery of the Incarnation. In the same way the elect under
the New Testament have faith in Christ already come. In the
case of spiritual and learned men their faith is explicit and
conscious, and in the case of children who die baptized, and
simple and ignorant people who are brought up in the bosom
of Holy Church, it is general and implicit. Since this is so, in
my opinion, they fall into a great and serious error who say
that Jews and Saracens may be saved by keeping their own
law, though they do not believe in Jesus Christ as the Church
believes. For it is held that they will be saved, since they
think their own beliefs good and safe and sufficient for salvation, and in that conviction perform what appear to be
many good acts, and since, perhaps, if they knew that the
Christian faith was better than theirs, they would renounce
their own and embrace it. But that is not enough.[1] For

[1] It is certain that any who are saved, that is, attain the supernatural
vision of God in heaven, do so through the merits of Christ, and the
ordinary means established by Him for participating in these merits we
know. We cannot say whether those who, through no fault of their own,

Christ, God and man, is both the way and the end. He is the mediator between God and man, and but by Him no man can be reconciled with God or come to the happiness of heaven. And therefore those who do not believe that He is both God and man can never be saved or come to heaven. There are others who do not love Christ or His passion, and whose souls are not reformed in His image. These are bad Christians who have not charity, and who live and die in mortal sin. These men believe, it seems, that Jesus is the Son of God and that His passion suffices for salvation, and they believe also all the other articles of the faith, but their faith is unformed[2] and dead, for they do not love Him, and they do not want the fruits of His passion. They remain in their sin and in the false love of this world until their last hour. And so they are not reformed to the likeness of God, but suffer the pains of hell for all eternity like Jews and Saracens. And they suffer much greater pains, inasmuch as they had the faith and did not keep it. For that was a greater sin than if they had never had it.

If you wish to know, then, which souls are reformed here in this life to the image of God by virtue of the passion of

---

are unaware of the Christian Faith can obtain grace in any other way—by a private revelation, or merely by acting according to their lights—but many today would hold as at least extremely probable the view which Hilton condemns. It is of interest to note that it is to be found in Piers Plowman (B Text, ll. 284 ff). Langland was an exact contemporary, but whether Hilton had read the poem or whether the view was current in theological circles and he had come across it elsewhere we have no means of knowing. Men were evidently more exercised about this point in the Middle Ages than we are sometimes inclined to think. Dante, for example, accepted Limbo (which is the fringe of hell) as the abode of the good pagan, but it seems was aware of the view afterwards put forward by Langland. See R. W. Chambers, "Long Will, Dante, and the Righteous Heathen", Essays and Studies of the English Association, IX (1924), p. 66. I have not found the view among the professional theologians.

[2] Fides informis. The technical term for faith without charity.

Christ, it is only those who believe in Him and love Him. In these souls the image of God, that through sin was distorted, as it were, into the image of a beast, is restored to its original form and to the worth and honour that it first had. And unless it is so restored no soul will be saved or come to the happiness of heaven.

THE FOURTH CHAPTER

Of two ways in which the image may be restored, one in fullness and one in faith

Now you ask, perhaps, how it may be that the image of God, that is man's soul, may be reformed to His likeness here in this life. It would seem that it cannot be, for if it were, it would have a clear intellectual apprehension of Him and a pure ardent love, as it did before the Fall. But no creature has these in this life, as you know; and as far as you yourself are concerned you can say truly that you feel yourself far from such a state. Your memory, your reason, and your power of loving, are so occupied with the things of this earth, that you have very little appreciation of spiritual things. You do not feel yourself reformed, but on the contrary, in spite of all your efforts, you feel yourself so enveloped in this dark image of sin, that, turn which way you will, you feel yourself defiled and besmirched by the carnal movements that arise in you. There seems to be no evidence, either in the powers of your soul or in your bodily reactions, that the spirit is conquering the flesh. And so it seems to you that this image can in no way be reformed, or if it can, you ask how it may be done. To this I answer that there are two ways in which this image of God, the soul, may be reformed —fully or in part.[1] Complete reform cannot be attained in

[1] It can be fully reformed only in heaven. In the next chapter he will

this life, but is reserved for the happiness of heaven. There man's soul will be reformed not to its original state, nor to the state which it might have attained if it had never fallen, but, through the great mercy and goodness of God, to much greater happiness and to a higher joy. For then the soul will find all its powers fully satisfied by God, and it will have no attraction for anything else. It will see humanity in the Person of Jesus united to God above all the angels. Jesus, God and man, will be all in all, and He alone and none other, as the prophet said: *Dominus solus exaltabitur in illa die* (Isa. ii. 11). In that, the everlasting day, our Lord Jesus will be exalted, and He alone.[2] And man's body will be glorified too, for it will receive the rich gift of immortailty and all that goes with it. The soul united to the body will possess all this and more that I cannot describe—but that will be in the happiness of heaven, and not in this life. For though our Lord's passion is the cause of this complete reformation of man's soul, nevertheless He did not will to grant it immediately after His passion to all the elect who were living on earth, but He reserved it until the Last Day—and for this reason. In His mercy He has predestined a certain number of souls to salvation, and at the time of His passion this number was not complete. Therefore a certain period of time was needed for it to be completed through successive generations of men. But if immediately after the death of our Lord

---

make a further distinction in the partial reform. It may be "in faith" or "in feeling", and he will develop this distinction in the chapters which follow.

[2] Hilton habitually uses Jesus, the name of God Incarnate, when he is referring apparently to the Godhead itself. Here he interprets *Dominus* of Isaias's text as referring to Jesus Christ, God Incarnate. In this Book his emphasis on our Lord, the Second Person, is less marked, and I have accordingly availed myself of the liberty he claims for himself in chap. 42 (Bk. II) and adopted the customary usage in most cases.

every soul that believed in Him had been glorified[3] and completely reformed forthwith, every man then alive would have wished to receive the faith in order to be glorified. Then generation would have ceased, and we who are living now, and others to come after us, the elect, would never have been born, and our Lord would not have been able to make up the full number of His elect. [4] But that might not be. And so God in delaying the complete reform of man's soul till the Last Day made a wiser dispensation, as St Paul says: *Deo pro nobis melius providente, ut non sine nobis consummarentur* (Heb. xi. 40). Our Lord provided better for us in putting off our reformation than by granting it then, for this reason; that the elect who preceded us should not come to the consummation of their destiny before us. [5] Another reason is

[3] Hilton says "blessed", but I take it that he is referring to the complete state of blessedness that he has described above, which includes the glorification of the body, though in this case the word "soul" is inappropriate. It would seem that he is using it in a wide sense, as we do colloquially, for the complete man, body and soul. I take it this was his meaning, because it is hard to see how the results of faith could have been so manifest to those who remained on earth, unless they had seen the effect in the bodies of the Just. In fact St Anselm, whom he seems to be following in all this (*De Conc. Praesc. Dei cum lib. arbit.*, cap. ix, P.L., CLVIII, col. 531-2) speaks of the faithful passing *in incorruptionem*.

[4] Generation would have ceased, presumably, because all men would have embraced the faith and passed to heaven, where there is no generation. We, and other souls whom Christ foreknew, would not have been born. God's plan, as it exists, would not have been, there would have been another plan. Hilton does not make it clear why the question of the glorification of the Just immediately after the passion should ever have arisen. St Anselm (loc. cit.) gives it: *Cur in hac vita perseveret in nobis poena peccati, deleto peccato*.

[5] "Should not make a full end." This would imply that he is referring to the glorification of the complete man, body and soul, and that this would have happened at once (cf. n. 1). There is nothing in the chapter to suggest that he is implying the view put forward by John XXII in the first half of the fourteenth century, that the souls of the Just could not enjoy

that, since man at his creation was endowed with free-will and could choose whether he would accept God or not, it was reasonable, since he would not choose God in the first instance but miserably fell away from Him, that if he should afterwards be reformed, he should be given the same free choice that he had originally. It was for him to decide whether he would profit by the reformation or not. And this may be a reason why man's soul was not fully reformed immediately after the passion of our Lord Jesus Christ.

THE FIFTH CHAPTER

The partial reform of the soul may be either in faith or in feeling

THE soul may also be partially reformed, and this experience it may have here on earth, and, indeed, unless it does attain partial reform in this life, it can never attain it at all and can never come to salvation. Partial reform may be of two kinds; one in faith only, the other in faith and feeling.[1] The first, re-

---

the Beatific Vision before the resurrection of the body. He only says that in fact the complete and final beatitude of man will include glorification of the body, as it will.

[1] *One in faith only, the other in faith and feeling.* These are Hilton's terms and they will occur frequently later in this Book, where he will enlarge upon their meaning. In chap. 17 in particular he points the contrast between them. It may, however, be useful to summarize the distinction between them at this point. Reform, we have already seen (cf. Bk. I, chaps. 45 and 51), means the re-formation of the soul in the image of God, and this is achieved essentially by the infusion of sanctifying grace at baptism. When this process takes place (as it generally does) with no further knowledge of God than that which is to be had through faith, Hilton calls it *reform in faith*. But when the restoration of the image of God in us has advanced so far as to be accompanied by some sort of experimental knowledge of God beyond that of faith, he calls it *reform in feeling*,

form in faith only, is sufficient for salvation; the second merits a great reward in the happiness of heaven. The first may easily be had and in a short time, the second only after a long time and with great spiritual labour. The first is not incompatible with a consciousness of the image of sin in us, for though a man should feel nothing but movements of sin and carnal desires, yet if he does not consent to them, he may be reformed in faith to the likeness of God. But the second sort of reform frees the soul from the attraction of movements of sensuality and the desire of worldly pleasures, and allows no such blemishes to exist in it. The first kind of reform belongs only to beginners and those who are making progress in the spiritual life,[2] and to men leading the active life. The second is for the perfect and contemplatives. By the first reform the image of sin is not destroyed and remains capable of making itself felt. But the second reform takes away the consciousness of this image of sin, and by the power of the Holy Ghost makes the soul aware of the workings of grace in it. The first is good, the second better, but the third, that which is attained only in the happiness of heaven, is the best of all. We will begin by speaking of the first and second and so come to the third.

---

or in *faith and feeling* (cf. note on Bk. II, chap. 31). This is, of course, a purely mystical state in which the soul achieves the highest degree of contemplation (cf. Bk. I, chap. 8). It has seemed best to retain Hilton's expressions as technical terms.

[2] For the classification of three states of soul, *incipientes*, *proficientes*, and *perfecti*, see *The Epistle to the Brethren of Mont Dieu* by William of St Thierry, chap. 5, translated by Walter Shewring and edited by Dom Justin McCann (London, 1930). Since "proficients" in modern English generally implies perfection, it is not a satisfactory translation of *proficientes*, and I have thought it better to paraphrase. Hilton refers to this classification elsewhere, e.g. Bk. II, chap. 10.

THE SIXTH CHAPTER

How a soul may lose its original likeness to God through two sorts of sin, original and actual

TWO sorts of sin cause a soul to lose its likeness to God; original, that is the first sin, and actual, that is sin which we deliberately commit. Both of these sorts of sin debar a soul from the happiness of heaven and condemn it to eternal suffering in hell, unless by the grace of God it is reformed to His likeness before it leaves this world. Nevertheless, there are two remedies for these two sins by which a deformed soul may be restored. In the case of original sin it is the sacrament of Baptism, and in the case of actual sin the sacrament of Penance. The soul of an unbaptized child has no likeness to God, because of original sin; it is nothing but an image of Satan and a brand of hell.[1] But by baptism, through the faith of the Church, it is immediately reformed from the likeness

---

[1] Man has been given a supernatural end, the immediate vision of God, and it follows that, since the end is supernatural, it cannot be attained without grace. It is the teaching of the Church that, since the infant that dies unbaptized has had no means of acquiring grace, it cannot enjoy the Beatific Vision, and thus suffers at any rate the pain of loss (*poena damni*). But it is the general opinion of theologians today, and has been from the twelfth century, that it does not suffer any pain of sense (*poena sensus*). The extent to which it may enjoy a certain natural happiness is disputed. It should be remembered that the vision of God is not something to which man has a natural right, and it cannot be held that an injustice has been done in not conferring an undue privilege.

When Hilton says that the soul of the unbaptized infant has no likeness to God, he is speaking rhetorically, as he is in the next chapter, where he says that the soul in mortal sin is deformed to the likeness of the devil. It does not become an image of the devil in the way in which the soul of the first man was created in the image of God. Even the unregenerate soul does in fact retain something of the divine image, inasmuch as it has a certain natural aptitude for knowing and loving God. See St Thom., *Summa*, Ia, q. XCIII, art. 4.

of the devil to the image of God, and is made like an angel of heaven. The same is true of Jews or Saracens, who before they are baptized are nothing but slaves of hell. But when they renounce their errors and humbly receive the truth of Christ and are baptized in water and the Holy Ghost, they are immediately reformed to the likeness of God. This transformation is so complete, as the Church believes, that, if they were to die immediately after baptism, they would go straight to heaven without more delay and never feel the pains of hell or purgatory, however much they had sinned before they came to the faith. And it is through the merits of the passion of Christ that they would have this privilege.

THE SEVENTH CHAPTER

How a soul that has lost the likeness of Christ through mortal sin may yet through the sacrament of Penance be restored to His image and likeness

WHEN a Christian has lost the likeness of God through mortal sin, he must, if he is to attain salvation, by the grace of God sincerely renounce his sins with sorrow and contrition of heart and have a firm intention of amending his life and turning to God. And he must then receive the sacrament of Penance, if he is able, or at least have the intention of doing so. When all this is done, there is no doubt that a soul, which before was deformed through mortal sin to the likeness of the devil, [1] becomes by the sacrament of Penance reformed to the image of God. To forgive all sorts of sin so easily and at once to fill with grace the soul of the sinner who asks mercy is a great act of kindness on our Lord's part. He does not wait till great penance has been performed or great

[1] See note to preceding chapter.

pain suffered in the body before He forgives. What He asks
is that the soul should hate its sin and determine for His love
to leave it and turn to Him. This is what He asks, for this is
what He enables the soul to do. When He finds these dispositions He forgives the sin forthwith and reforms the soul
to His likeness. The sin is forgiven and the soul escapes
damnation. Nevertheless the punishment due for the sin is
not fully remitted, unless there is a very high degree of sorrow and love. And therefore the penitent must make his
confession to his spiritual father, receive the penance en-
joined him and carry it out with goodwill. Then both the
sin and the punishment due to it are effaced before he leaves
this world.[2] It is a reasonable commandment of the Church,
and one that is very much to the advantage of man's soul,
that, though the sin is forgiven by virtue of contrition, a
man shall nevertheless, as an expression of humility and to
make complete satisfaction, confess fully to a priest, if he
has the opportunity. He obtains a sign and a guarantee of
forgiveness, and this is fitting. For just as a man who had
been condemned to death by an earthly king and then been
reprieved would need a written pardon as a sign and guarantee to other men in order to be completely safe, so in the
spiritual sphere a man who has merited death through having
offended the King of Heaven by mortal sin would not have
full security, if his sin were only forgiven by contrition be-

[2] For Hilton's views on the sacrament of Penance in general see the
next note. Here he seems to imply that the sacrament makes complete
satisfaction for sin, but such has never been the teaching of the Church.
The guilt and the eternal punishment are forgiven by the sacrament of
Penance, but a debt of temporal punishment may remain. This is pre-
supposed by the doctrine of Purgatory, to which Hilton refers as a matter
of course. See Bk. I, chaps. 34 and 38, Bk. II, chaps 6 and 28. It may be
noted that in Bk. I, chap. 34, he seems to imply that mental suffering
borne here on earth may make full satisfaction, and it is of course possible
to satisfy completely for sin in this life.

tween God and himself. He must have a document granted
by the Church, if he can obtain it, and the sacrament of
Penance is his document and sign of forgiveness. For since
he has sinned both against God and the Church, it is fitting
that he should have forgiveness from the one and a guarantee
from the other. That is one reason why confession is necessary. There is another; this reform of the soul is in faith only
and not in feeling, and so a rough, worldly-minded man,
who could only judge easily of external matters, would never
believe that his sins were forgiven, if he did not have some
outward sign. And that sign is confession, through which
he is assured of forgiveness if he does what lies within his
power. This is the belief of the Church, as I understand it.[3]

[3] One wonders whether Hilton had doubts about his view. In fact it
was only held by a limited number of theologians, though it had great
names behind it, and it has since been condemned. It will be worth
examining it somewhat closely. He says that when God finds the right
dispositions in a soul, contrition, a purpose of amendment, and the intention of confessing, He forgives the sin forthwith, but though the sin is
forgiven, it must nevertheless be confessed to a priest when the opportunity occurs. Now this means that the penitent must have had in the first
place what is called today "perfect" contrition, that is sorrow from sin
arising purely from the love of God. Such sorrow does in itself take away
the guilt of sin, though there remains the obligation of confessing it.
Hilton evidently takes it for granted that this will always be the state of
the penitent coming to confession. The sin has been forgiven but confession is necessary as an expression of humility, to make complete satisfaction (see previous note), and as a sign or guarantee, particularly necessary in the case of the *rudes*, the uncultured. That he held no other view of
confession seems certain from Bk. II, chap. 10, where he says that sorrow
for sin because we have deserved hell is not sufficient when we go to the
sacrament of Penance. In holding these opinions he was following a view
put forward by Peter Lombard (*Sent*. IV, dist. xviii, cap. 6; P.L., CXCII,
col. 887) and followed by St Bonaventure and many of the Franciscan
school, which regarded perfect contrition as a necessary requisite for the
sacrament of Penance, thus making the priestly absolution merely declarative (see Pohle-Preuss, *The Sacraments*, III (Herder, 1918), pp. 145ff).
The view was never held by St Thomas and was afterwards condemned by

And another reason is this. Although forgiveness depends primarily upon contrition and renouncing sin, and not upon confession, nevertheless I fancy there is many a soul that would never have had contrition nor left its sin, if it had not been for confession. For it often happens that in confession the grace of compunction touches a soul that was never touched by it before, but was always cold and dry. And because confession is so valuable for the majority of Christians, the Church has ordained that all should confess their sins at least once a year to their spiritual father, and that no matter how much contrition they may have felt for them. And yet if everybody took as much care to avoid sin and had the sense of God's presence that some men have, the Church would have no need to make confession a necessary duty. But all men are not so perfect, and perhaps much the greater part of Christians are very imperfect, and therefore the Church has imposed the general obligation of confession to all Christians who acknowledge her as their mother and give her their obedience. If this is so, as I believe, then whoever says that confession of sins to a priest is not necessary or even desirable, and that no man is bound to it, is greatly mistaken. What I have said shows that it is both necessary and helpful to all souls that are defiled by sin in this miserable life, and especially to those who through mortal sin are distorted from the likeness of God. For these there is no way of reformation except through the sacrament of Penance; and this consists principally in contrition and sorrow, and

---

the Council of Trent, which states explicitly that, while perfect contrition itself causes sin to be forgiven, though the obligation of confession remains, imperfect contrition, that is, sorrow for sins because by them we have deserved hell, is sufficient in the sacrament of Penance. The view that the priestly absolution is merely declarative is not compatible with the true view of a sacrament as an external sign of internal grace; it must effect that which it signifies.

secondarily in oral confession if there is opportunity. In this way a soul in sin is reformed to the image and likeness of God.

THE EIGHTH CHAPTER

How in the sacraments of Baptism and Penance the secret operation of the Holy Ghost reforms the image of God in the soul without the soul being aware of it

BUT this is what I have called reform in faith and not in feeling. As it is the property of faith to believe what is not seen, so it is its property to believe what is not felt. But he whose soul is reformed to the image of God by the sacrament of Penance is not conscious of any change, either in his body or in his soul. He feels as he did before, the same movements of sin, the same carnal desires, and the same attraction to the world. Nevertheless, in spite of this he must believe that he is reformed by grace to the likeness of God, though he neither feels it nor sees it. He may indeed, if he has the grace and watches over himself, feel sorrow for his sin, and that his will has turned away from it. But he does not see or experience in any way the reforming of his soul, how it is in a wonderful, but imperceptible, way changed from the hideousness of a devil to the beauty of an angel, through the mysterious power of God. He cannot see that, but he must believe it; and if he believes it, then his soul is indeed reformed. The Church holds that the sacrament of Baptism regularly administered reforms the soul of a Jew, or Saracen, or newly-born baby to the likeness of God through the secret imperceptible operation of the Holy Ghost, in spite of all the sensual movements of the body which will be felt after baptism just as much as before. In the same way, by the sacrament of Penance humbly and truly received, the soul of a bad Christian who has been all his life in mortal sin is reformed without his being conscious of anything except that his will is changed through the secret power of the Holy Ghost. His gracious operation suddenly takes effect and in a moment transforms an obstinate soul. From being spiritually hideous it becomes beautiful with an invisible beauty, from a slave of the devil it becomes heir to the inheritance of heaven, in spite of the carnal movements of this image of sin in its body. For you must know that the sacraments of Baptism and Penance have not the power to take away completely all movements of sensuality and disordered passions so that the soul never feels any rising of them. For if this were so, the soul would be fully reformed here to the dignity it had at its creation, but that condition it may never reach fully in this life. But these sacraments have the power to cleanse the soul from all the sins which it has committed; if it has left the body, to save it from hell; if it is still in the body, to give it grace to withstand the movements of sin. And they have the power, too, of maintaining it in grace, so that no movements of lust or the passions, however grievously they afflict it, may harm it or separate it from God so long as it does not voluntarily consent to them. This is what St Paul meant when he said: *Nihil damnationis est iis qui sunt in Christo, qui non secundum carnem ambulant*, etc. (Rom. viii. 1). That is, those souls that are reformed to the image of God in faith through the sacraments of Baptism or Penance will not be condemned for feeling this image of sin so long as they do not carry out the inclinations of the flesh in action.

THE NINTH CHAPTER

That we should believe that we have this grace of reforming, if our conscience witnesses that we have renounced sin and our will is directed to leading a good life

ST PAUL says of this reforming in faith: *Justus ex fide vivit* (Heb. x. 38). The just man lives by faith. That is, he who is justified by baptism or the sacrament of Penance lives by faith, and this is all that is necessary for salvation and to attain the peace of heaven. As he says again: *Justificati ex fide, pacem habeamus ad Deum* (Rom. v. 1). That is, we who are justified and reformed through faith in Christ have made our peace with God and are reconciled to Him, in spite of the evil inclinations that we find within us. It is true that this reforming is secret and may not be recognized in this life, but nevertheless whoever believes in it firmly and acts accordingly, and does not turn again to mortal sin, when the hour of death comes and the soul leaves the body, will find that I speak the truth. St John said for the comfort of the elect who live here in faith but suffer under this image of sin: *Carissimi, et nunc sumus filii Dei, sed nondum apparuit quid erimus. Scimus quoniam cum Christus apparuerit, tunc apparebimus cum eo, similes ei in gloria* (1 John iii. 2). Beloved, we are now, while we live on earth, sons of God, for we are reformed in His likeness by faith in Christ, though what we are is not yet manifest and remains hidden. Nevertheless we know well that when our Lord appears at the Last Day we shall appear with Him, and like Him, in eternal happiness. If you wish to know, then, whether your soul is reformed to the image of God or not, you may go by what I have said. Examine your conscience and see where your will is fixed, for everything depends on that. If it is turned away from every kind of mortal sin, so that you would not for the whole world knowingly and willingly break the Commandments of God; if you have humbly confessed the sins you have committed against His Law with the firm intention of renouncing them, and with sorrow for having committed them, then I say with assurance that your soul is reformed in faith to the likeness of God.

THE TENTH CHAPTER

That souls who live humbly in the faith of Holy Church and whose faith is animated by love and charity are reformed by the sacrament of Penance, even though they do not feel the gift of devotion or of spiritual consolation

THE majority of God's elect lead their lives in this state, reformed only in faith. They set their wills firmly against every sort of mortal sin; they keep themselves in love and charity towards their neighbour, and observe the commandments of God in so far as they know them. When evil inclinations arise in their hearts, to pride, or envy, or anger, or lust, or any other capital sin, they resist them and strive not to give way to them. And if it should happen that they sin venially, as it were against their will, through frailty or lack of knowledge, their conscience pricks them so grievously that they cannot rest until they have been to confession and received forgiveness. All who live in this manner are reformed in faith to the image of God. And if they live their lives in this state and are found in it at the hour of their death, they will be saved and will be fully reformed in the happiness of heaven, even though they may never have felt any spiritual consolation or received any special grace of devotion all their lives. If no soul were to be saved that had not been reformed in feeling and granted the devotion and spiritual consolation that are the lot of some, there would be few saved in comparison with the multitude lost.

But it is not to be believed that our Lord Jesus should have taken a human nature and gone through the bitter sufferings of death only for those who receive the grace of devotion and spiritual consolation. It would have been a poor result, if He had come so far and condescended so low for so few souls. No, His mercy extends wider than that. But on the other hand, if you think that the passion of our Lord is so precious and His mercy so great that no Christian soul will be lost, however much it sins, as some foolish people think, in truth you are greatly mistaken.[1] Take the middle course, therefore, and believe what the Church believes. Namely, that, if the greatest sinner on earth by the grace of God turns his will from mortal sin to repent truly and serve God, his soul is reformed, and if he dies in that state he will be saved. God promised this by His prophet, saying: *In quacumque hora conversus peccator et ingemuerit, vita vivet et non morietur* (Ezech. xviii. 21). Whenever the sinner turns to God from sin and repents, he shall live and not suffer eternal death. On the other hand, whoever remains in mortal sin and will not renounce it and receive the sacrament of Penance is not reformed to the likeness of God. And that is true also, if he does not receive the sacrament sincerely from the love of God, that is from love of virtue and purity, but only out of worldly shame, or for fear of the pains of hell.[2] If he dies in that state, he will not be saved. His faith will not save him, for his faith is dead and without charity and is therefore of no avail to him. But those whose faith is informed by even the least degree of charity are reformed to the likeness of God. Simple people are in this state, who have no special gift of devotion and who have not

[1] Cf. St Augustine *in Psalm.*, LXXX, n. 20 (P.L., XXXVII, col. 1043).
[2] See Bk. II, chap. 7, n. 3.

the knowledge of God that spiritual men have, but who believe in general what the Church believes without fully knowing what that is. In that faith, in so far as they can, they keep themselves in love and charity to their neighbour, flee all mortal sins, and perform works of mercy. They can be assured of the happiness of heaven, for it is written in the Apocalypse: *Qui timetis Deum, pusilli et magni, laudate eum* (Apoc. xix. 5). You that fear God, both little and great, give thanks to Him.

The great are those who have made progress or else are perfect in the love of God and are reformed in feeling. The little ones are imperfect souls, people living in the world, all those who have only a child's knowledge of God and very little realization of Him; they are carried in the bosom of the Church and nourished with the sacraments, as children are with milk. All such as these love God and give Him thanks that in His everlasting mercy and goodness He has saved their souls. For the Church, who is their mother and dearly loves her spiritual children, prays for them all to her spouse, Jesus, and obtains the healing of their souls through the virtue of His passion. And she prays specially for those who cannot express their own needs in prayer. Thus in the Gospel the Canaanite woman asked our Lord to heal her daughter who was possessed by a devil. He at first refused, because she was of another race. But she did not cease to beg until our Lord had granted her request and said to her: O woman, great is your faith; be it done to you according to your will (Matt. xv. 28). And her daughter was cured at that moment. This woman represents the Church who asks our Lord to help simple, ignorant souls, who are labouring under the temptations of the world and who cannot speak to God with fervent devotion or in the burning love of contemplation. It seems at first that our Lord refuses to hear, because these souls are, as it were, strangers to Him, but in the end, because of the great faith and the merits of the Church, He grants her all that she asks. And so these simple souls, who believe firmly what the Church believes, putting themselves entirely in God's hands and submitting humbly to the sacraments and the laws of the Church, are saved through the prayer and faith of their spiritual mother.

THE ELEVENTH CHAPTER

How even souls that have been reformed to the image of God have always need to strive against temptations to sin, and how they may know whether they give consent or not

THIS reforming in faith is easily come by, but it is not so easily retained. And so whoever is truly reformed to the likeness of God must labour much, if he will keep this image whole and pure and not let it through weakness of will degenerate into the image of sin. He dare not be idle or careless, for the image of sin inheres in him so closely that it constantly urges him to sin, and if he is not careful, he may easily give his consent. And therefore he must make a continual effort lest he should comply with the evil suggestions of this image, become reconciled to it, and obey its unreasonable demands. If he does so, he deceives himself. But as long as he struggles he need have little fear of consenting, for the effort will prevent him from being lulled into a false peace. A man should be at peace with everything except the devil and this image of sin. Against these he must always strive mentally and physically, until he has overcome them, and he will never do that fully in this life, where he bears this image about with him and is constantly aware of it. Certainly a soul may by the grace of God gain control over it to the extent of not consenting to its suggestions, but in this life no man can be completely delivered from it, so as not to feel any suggestion, or commotion in his bodily desires, or any vain thoughts.

A soul that is reformed in feeling and carried out of itself by love into the contemplation of God may, it is true, be free from sensuality and vain imaginations, and be so far delivered from movements of the flesh for a time that it is conscious of nothing except God. But that state does not last continually. And so every man must strive against this image of sin, and especially one who is reformed only in faith, for he may very easily be deceived by it. It is in the person of such a man that St Paul says: *Caro concupiscit adversus spiritum et spiritus adversus carnem* (Gal. v. 17). A soul reformed to the likeness of God fights against the sensual movements of this image of sin, and the image fights against the soul. St Paul was conscious of the conflict between these two when he said: *Inveni legem in membris meis, repugnantem legi mentis meae, et captivum me ducentem in legem peccati* (Rom. vii. 23). I have found two laws in myself, one in my soul, and another in my body. The second fights against the first and often leads me prisoner to the law of sin. These two laws in the soul I take to be these two images. The law of the spirit is the law of reason, when it is reformed to the image of God; the law of the flesh is sensuality, the image of sin. A reformed soul leads its life under these two laws. As St Paul says: *Mente enim servio legi Dei, carne autem legi peccati* (Rom. vii. 25). In my soul, that is in my will and reason, I serve the law of God. But in my body, that is in my carnal appetites, I serve the law of sin. But that a reformed soul should not despair, though it feels the uprising of sensuality against the will because of the corruption of human nature, St Paul excuses it in his own person, saying: *Non enim quod volo bonum hoc ago; sed malum quod odi, hoc facio. Si autem malum quod odi, hoc facio, non ego operor illud, sed quod habitat in me, peccatum* (Rom. vii. 19, 20). I do not perform the good that I wish; I would feel no movement of the flesh but I cannot achieve this state. And the evil that I hate, I do, that is the evil movements of my flesh. I hate them, and yet I cannot escape them. But since I hate these evil inclinations, although I feel them, and often take pleasure in them against my will, they are not imputed to me to my condemnation as though I were the author of them. And why? It is this corrupt image of sin that performs them and not I. Here St Paul in his own person comforts all souls that by the grace of God are reformed in faith, so that they should not too much fear the burden of this image with its irrational movements as long as they do not deliberately consent to them. Nevertheless, many souls that are truly reformed are often much and needlessly troubled on this point. For example, when they have felt carnal movements of pride, or envy, or covetousness, or lust, or any other capital sin, they sometimes do not know whether they have consented or not. And that is not surprising, for in the time of temptation the mind of weak man is so troubled and clouded that he cannot understand clearly, and he is not really a free agent. He is often attracted by pleasure before he knows it, and dwells on it long enough before he becomes aware of the fact. And for this reason some people cannot decide whether they have sinned in the time of temptation or not, and are worried over the matter.

With regard to this, I think a man may know in this way whether he has consented or not. He may be tempted to sin, and the sensual attraction is so great that it clouds his reason and seems to exercise an overpowering attraction. If, however, he refrains from evil actions, and has no wish to commit them, even though he could; if the attraction that he feels is itself distressing to him, and he would, if possible, put it away; and if, when the agitation is passed, he is glad to be free of it, then he may conclude that in spite of everything he has not given his consent, and that there has been no sin; at any rate no mortal sin. But the safest thing for simple souls that are perplexed and uncertain is that they should not be over confident. They should not be too sure that these movements of sensuality with the pleasure that accompanies them are not sins; for in this way they can slip into carelessness and a false security. On the other hand they must not be so anxious and simple-minded as to think them all mortal sins or even serious venial sins, for neither view is true.[1] They should hold them all as sins or imperfections and be sorry for them, but not concern themselves with judging whether they are mortal or venial. But if they become a weight upon the conscience such movements should be confessed at once, either in general or particular, and especially any inclination that is beginning to take root in the heart and to take possession of it so as to draw it down to sin and worldly preoccupations. And when they have thus been confessed in general or in particular, a man should believe firmly that they are forgiven and discuss no more whether they are mortal or venial. Let him occupy himself with trying to avoid future sins.

But some people are so unspiritual and so unwise that they would feel, or hear, or see the forgiveness of their sins in the same way that they would feel, or hear, or see a corporeal object, and, because this is impossible, they fall into doubt and can never rest. But that is foolish, for faith comes before feeling. Our Lord said to a man whom He healed of the palsy: *Confide fili, dimittuntur tibi peccata tua* (Mark ii. 5). Son, believe firmly that your sins are forgiven. He did not

[1] There is either mortal sin, or venial sin, or no sin at all, according to the measure of consent, but Hilton gives wise advice in saying that the well-disposed soul should not make itself anxious in trying to decide the exact culpability of sins in doubtful cases, but that if the conscience remains troubled they should be confessed.

say "see", or "feel", that your sins are forgiven, for sins are
forgiven spiritually and invisibly by the power of the Holy
Ghost, but He said "believe" it. In just the same way, if a man
will achieve peace of conscience, he must first, having done
what he can, believe in the forgiveness of his sins without
any spiritual feeling. If he does this, he will by the grace of
God afterwards come to feel it and understand that it is so.
The Apostle said: *Nisi credideritis, non intelligetis*.[2] That is, if
you do not first believe, you cannot understand. Belief comes
first and understanding follows. This understanding, or
sight of God, when it is the effect of grace, a soul may only
have if it is very pure, as our Lord said: *Beati mundo corde,
quoniam ipsi Deum videbunt* (Matt. v. 8). Blessed are the clean
of heart for they shall see God. That is, they will see Him,
not with their bodily eye, but with their inner eye, that is
with the understanding purified and illumined through the
power of the Holy Ghost to see truth. A soul cannot come to
this purity unless it has first a firm faith. As the Apostle said:
Fide mundans corda eorum (Acts xv. 9). Our Lord purifies the
hearts of His elect through faith. So a man must believe that
he is reformed through the sacrament of Penance, even
though he does not see it, and then he must endeavour to
live justly and virtuously as his faith demands so that he may
afterwards come to be reformed in feeling.

[2] The quotation is in fact from the *Itala* text of Isaias (vii. 9). The
French edition of *The Scale* gives references to quotations of this text in
Richard of St Victor, St Anselm, and St Augustine, but in no case is it
applied to the feeling of sin having been forgiven.

THE TWELFTH CHAPTER

In this life, even after the soul has been reformed, this image is at once beautiful and ugly: and of differences between the secret movements of souls that have been reformed and those that have not

A MAN's soul is at once beautiful and ugly. It is beautiful in so far as it is reformed in faith to the likeness of God. But it is ugly in so far as it still feels the evil inclinations and ill-regulated movements of this image of sin. In one aspect it is ugly as a beast, in another it is beautiful as an angel; it is ugly in so far as it is subject to sensuality, beautiful for the power of the reason to attain truth; ugly because of its carnal appetites, beautiful for the goodness of its will. So the soul of the elect is both beautiful and ugly, according to the saying of Holy Scripture: *Nigra sum, sed formosa, filiae Jerusalem, sicut tabernacula Cedar et sicut pelles Salomonis* (Cant. i. 4). I am black, but I am beautiful, daughters of Jerusalem, as the tabernacles of Cedar, as the skin of Solomon.[1] That is: You angels of heaven, daughters of the Jerusalem that is on high, do not despise me because I am black, for though I appear black as the tents of Cedar because of my union with the body, within I am as beautiful as the skin of Solomon, for I am reformed to the likeness of God. By Cedar is meant blackness, that is the devil. By a tent of Cedar is meant a reprobate soul, which is a dwelling-place of the devil. By Solomon, which means peace, is meant our Lord Jesus, for He is peace, and peace belongs to Him. By the skin of Solomon is meant a blessed angel, in whom our Lord dwells and is

---

[1] *Pelles*, literally skins, meaning tents. St Bernard applied the text to the Church in two of his *Sermons on the Canticles*, xxv and xxvii, where he points out (Sermon xxv, P.L. clxxxiii, col. 900) that this is the meaning. Hilton takes it literally in the sense of skin, in the singular.

hidden, as life is hidden in the skin of a living body. That is why an angel is likened to a skin. Then with humble trust in God and gladness of heart the soul of the elect may say: Though because of my body of sin I am black as a reprobate soul, that is a dwelling-place of the devil, nevertheless within, through faith and an upright will, I have the beauty of an angel of heaven. For Scripture says in another place: *Nolite considerare me quod fusca sim, quia decoloravit me sol* (Cant. i. 5). Do not consider my blackness, for the sun has blackened me. The sun blackens only the outside of an object, and the blackened surface is the image of bodily life. And therefore the soul says: Do not rebuke me because I am black, for my blackness is all external, the result of touching and bearing this image of sin, but it is not within. And though an elect soul reformed in faith dwells in this body of sin, feels the same carnal movements, and often does the same material acts as a reprobate soul, so that men cannot distinguish the one from the other, nevertheless there is a great difference in the sight of God. But the ability to recognize which is which belongs only to God, for it passes the judgement and experience of man, and therefore he should not condemn his fellow for acts that may be good or evil. For a man whose soul is not reformed is so completely occupied with the love of the world and so dominated by the pleasures of the flesh and of sensuality that he makes them the only object of his desire, and in his secret heart he wants nothing else but to enjoy them always. He feels no unction of grace moving him to hate the life of the flesh or to desire the happiness of heaven. It might be said that such a man does not so much bear the image of sin as be borne by it, like a sick man on a litter. In the same way a sinful man is so weak and powerless through lack of grace, that he can move neither hand nor foot to do a good action, nor can he set his will against the least temptation when it comes, but he falls on it like a beast on carrion. But a man whose soul is reformed, though he makes use of his senses and feels the stirrings of sensuality, hates these things in his heart and would rather do anything than rest in them. He draws back from taking pleasure in them as he would from the bite of an adder, and he would find his rest and fix the love of his heart in God if it were possible. Sometimes his desire stretches out to this, and the pleasures of this life grow wearisome for love of the life everlasting. Such a man is not carried by the image of sin like a sick man, but he nevertheless bears it about with him. But grace enables him to put up with his body with all its evil movements without being injured or defiled by them; he does not love, nor carry out, nor consent to things which are in themselves mortal sins.

This was literally fulfilled in the Gospel story of the paralytic. Being too weak to walk he was carried in a litter to our Lord, who, when He saw his plight, said to him in His goodness: *Surge et tolle grabatum tuum, et vade in domum tuam* (John v. 8). Rise up, and take up your bed, and go into your house. And he did so and was made whole. And just as this man, when he was cured, carried on his back the bed which before carried him, so it might be said spiritually, that a soul reformed in faith bears this image of sin which previously bore him.[2] And so do not be too anxious about the stains you contract from this image of sin which you carry. Do not fear them, in spite of the shame you feel at seeing them in yourself and in spite of the taunts of your spiritual enemies saying in your heart, "Where is your Lord Jesus? What is it that you are seeking? Where is this beauty that you speak of? What do you feel except blindness and sin? Where is that image of God that you say is reformed in you?" Comfort yourself by faith, as I have said before, and, if you do so, this faith will enable you to overcome all the temptations of your enemies.

[2] cf. St Gregory, *in Ezechiel*, Bk. 1, hom. xii (P.L., LXXVI, col. 922).

St Paul said: *Accipe scutum fidei, in quo tela hostis nequissima poteris extinguere* (Eph. vi. 16). Let a strong faith be your shield through which you may extinguish all the burning darts of the enemy.

THE THIRTEENTH CHAPTER

Three sorts of men; those who are not reformed, those who are reformed in faith only, and those reformed in faith and feeling

FROM what I have said it appears that men may be classed in various categories according to the various states of the soul. Some are not reformed to the likeness of God, and some are reformed only in faith, and some are reformed in faith and feeling.

For you must understand that the soul has (as it were) two parts.[1] One is the sensitive, that is the faculty of apprehension by the senses, which man has in common with the animals. It is from this, when it is not controlled by reason, that the image of sin springs, as I pointed out before. For if reason does not govern the use of the senses there is sin. The other part is called reason, and this is itself divided into two, the higher and the lower reason.[2] The higher may be considered as masculine, for it should rule and have dominion. In it the image of God is properly found, for it is by this

[1] In fact the soul, being spiritual, has no parts. It is a question of powers, ways of acting.

[2] The division goes back a long way. It is already found in St Augustine, but he is careful to point out that the higher and lower reason are not in fact two separate powers (*De Trinitate*, Bk. XII, chap. 4, P.L., XLII, col. 1000). The distinction is only applied to the reason as it is concerned with eternal or with temporal things. See St Thom., *Summa*, Ia, q. LXXIX, art. 9.

power that the soul knows and loves Him. The lower reason may be considered as feminine, for it should obey the higher reason as woman obeys man. Its function is to know and control the things of earth, to use them with discretion when they are necessary and to reject them when they are unnecessary. It must always act with reference to the higher reason and follow it. Now a soul that lives according to the desires and lusts of the flesh like an irrational animal, having no knowledge of God, or desire of virtue and the good life, but blinded by pride, fretted by envy, overlaid by covetousness, and defiled by lust and other great sins, is not reformed to the likeness of God. It is wholly occupied by the image of sin in its lower nature. But a soul that fears God, rejects the movements of sensuality, and leads a life well regulated in external conduct with the intention of pleasing God in its outward actions is reformed to the likeness of God in faith. It may feel the same sinful inclinations as the other soul, but it will suffer no harm from them, because it does not acquiesce in them. But a soul which by the grace of God avoids not only movements of sensuality that are mortal sins, but avoids venial sins as well, and does not even have the inclination to sin, is reformed in feeling. It apprehends God and spiritual truths in the higher parts of its reason, as I will explain later.

THE FOURTEENTH CHAPTER

How sinners are distorted into the likeness of various beasts; and they are called the lovers of the world

THAT man, then, is in a wretched state who does not appreciate the worth of his soul and does not even wish to do so. Is it not the most noble creature of God with the exception of the angels, whom it resembles? It is far above all corporeal beings, and it can only find its true rest in God. For this reason it should love nothing but Him, and it should seek only to be reformed to His likeness. But because he does not know this, man seeks to find his rest and his pleasure in bodily creatures that are lower than himself. That man acts unnaturally and unreasonably who forsakes God, the sovereign Good, eternal Life, and who does not seek Him and love Him, know Him or worship Him, but chooses to find his rest and his happiness in the transitory joys of earth. But this is what they do who love this world and find their happiness in this wretched life. Some find it in pride and vain glory, so that having lost the fear of God their one endeavour is to obtain the honour and praise of the world. They do not care what happens so long as they obtain it and surpass all other men in learning or skill, renown or fame, wealth or respect, power or authority, or in high estate. Some men take their pleasure in riches and the extravagant possession of earthly goods and make this the end of their lives. They set their hearts on this end so completely that they seek nothing else. For others happiness consists in the satisfaction of the desires of the flesh, in gluttony or lust. Some find it in one thing, some in another. In this miserable manner they turn themselves from the dignity of men into the likeness of beasts.

The proud man is like a lion, for he wishes to be feared and reverenced by all men and that nobody should hinder the carrying out of his will by word or act. If his will is thwarted he becomes angry and will take vengeance as a lion does on a smaller animal. A man who acts in this way is not acting as a man at all, for he is acting contrary to human nature; he is transformed into a lion. Anger and envy turn men into dogs. They bark at their neighbours, and bite them by evil words; they wound those who have done no harm,

injuring them in body and soul, contrary to the commandment of God. Men who are sluggish in God's service and unwilling to help their neighbours are like asses. They are
ready enough to go as far as Rome for wealth, or honour, or
to please men. But if it is a question of a spiritual end, of
helping their own souls, or of the honour of God, they are
soon tired. They do not desire these things, and, if they
move at all, it is only a step, and even that they take with a
bad grace. Some men are so wrong-headed and so animal in
their behaviour that they are like swine. They have no fear
of God, but follow only the lusts of the flesh, caring nothing for the dignity of man, which demands that they govern themselves by reason and restrain the irrational movements of their lower nature. As soon as they feel a temptation of the flesh they indulge it. Covetous men, who through
domination and oppression rob their neighbours of their
worldly goods, are like wolves that live by devouring other
creatures. False and deceitful men, who live by treachery and
guile, are like foxes.

These men, and others like them, who have no fear of
God, but break His Commandments and destroy His image
in their souls, make themselves like beasts, and indeed
worse, like the devils of hell. Men who live in this manner
and are not reformed when the hour of death comes will
have a rude awakening in that hour, and will meet retribu-
tion for the evil of their lives. Because the image of God was
in no way reformed in them through the sacrament of
Penance in this life, they will be cast out from the face of
their Creator and condemned to the depths of hell with the
devils for all eternity. St John says in the Apocalypse:
Timidis et incredulis, et execratis et homicidis, fornicatoribus,
veneficis, idololatris et omnibus mendacibus, pars illorum erit in
stagno ardenti igne et sulphure (Apoc. xxi. 8). The proud and
the unbelieving and the accursed, murderers, the lustful and

the covetous, poisoners and idolaters, all shall have their lot with devils in the pit burning with fire and brimstone. If the lovers of the world would often call to mind its transitory nature and how all inordinate love will be severely punished, they would soon come to hate the worldly pleasures in which they put all their happiness. They would raise their hearts to God and would make every effort to be reformed to His likeness before they left this world.

THE FIFTEENTH CHAPTER

How lovers of this world hinder the reforming of their souls in various ways

BUT some say, "I would readily love God and lead a good life and renounce the love of the world, if I could, but I have not the grace. If I had the grace given to a good man, I would act in the same way. But since I have not that grace, I cannot do so, and it is not for me to discover the way; I am excused." Certainly it is as they say; they have not the grace and so they remain in their sin and are unable to arise from it. But that does not excuse them in the eyes of God, for it is their own fault. In various ways they make it impossible for the light of grace to shine in their hearts. Some are so perverse that they do not wish to have grace or to lead good lives, for they know that then they must renounce the pleasure they take in the things of this world, and that they are unwilling to do, because this pleasure appeals to them so strongly that they will not forgo it. And they would also have to undertake works of penance such as fasting, watching, praying, in order to bring their bodies into subjection and to curb their sensual appetites. But they cannot do that, for it appears so abhorrent to them that they hate to think of it, and so in this cowardly and miserable manner they remain in their sin.

Some, it seems, would have grace and begin to prepare themselves for it. But their wills are strangely weak, for as soon as any temptation comes they succumb to it, though they know it is against the commandments of God. Their frequent falls have induced such a habit of sin, that it seems to them impossible to withstand temptation, and the imagined difficulty of the act weakens their will and breaks it.

Some, indeed, are stirred by grace, and their conscience urges them to give up their evil lives, but they find the idea so distressing and unpleasant that they will not entertain it. They flee from it and forget it, if they can, and seek their pleasure and comfort in creatures, in order that they may not feel the pricking of conscience in their souls.

Beyond this some are so blind and worldly-minded that they think there is no other life than this, and that man's soul is no more than that of an animal, and dies with the body as an animal's does. And so they say, "Let us eat and drink and make merry, for we are certain of this life. We see no other heaven." There are indeed some who say this in their hearts, even though they do not say it with their mouths. Of them the prophet said: *Dixit insipiens in corde suo: Non est Deus* (Ps. xiii. 1). The foolish man said in his heart, there is no God.

Every wretch who loves sin and chooses the love of this world as the end of his soul is the foolish man. He does not say there is no God with his mouth, for when things go well with him he will say "Blessed be God" with apparent reverence, and when he quarrels or is angry with God or his neighbour he will swear by God's blessed Body or any of His members. But in thought he denies God, because he thinks that God does not see his sin, or will not punish it as severely as Holy Scripture says, or that God will forgive his sin even though he does not leave it. Or else he thinks that no Christian will be damned however wicked he may be, or that if he fasts on our Lady's feasts, or says a certain prayer every day, or hears two or three masses, or performs some outward act under the pretext of honouring God, he will never go to hell, however much he sins and remains in his sin. Such a man says in his heart that there is no God, but he is foolish, as the prophet says. He will find to his cost that He whom he forgot and disregarded in his worldly prosperity is in truth God. As the prophet says: *Sola vexatio dabit intellectum auditui* (Is. xxviii. 19). Only suffering will give understanding. The man that does not know this in this life, and refuses to know it, will know it well enough when he is in [eternal] suffering.

THE SIXTEENTH CHAPTER

Advice to lovers of this world on what they should do if they wish their souls to be reformed before death

THESE men, though they are well aware that they are not in a state of grace and are in mortal sin, are in no way worried or sorry on account of this. They do not give it a thought. They abandon themselves to the pleasures of the senses and the joys of the world, and the further they are from grace the more they let themselves go. Perhaps some are glad to have no grace, that they may, as it were, give themselves more completely to sensual pleasures—as though God were asleep and could not see them. There are few sins so great. And by their perverseness they prevent the light of grace from reaching their soul, so that it remains in darkness. For grace is open to all spiritual beings, ready to enter where it will be received, as the sun shines on all corporeal beings where it is not prevented. Thus St John says in the gospel: *Lux in tenebris lucet, et tenebrae eam non comprehenderunt* (John i.

5). The light of grace shines in the darkness, that is on men's hearts that are dark through sin, but the darkness does not receive it. That is, the blinded hearts of men do not receive the light of grace or profit by it. Just as a blind man is surrounded by sunlight when he stands in it, and yet is not aware of it and cannot see his way by it, so in the spiritual sphere a soul blinded by mortal sin is surrounded by spiritual light, but he is none the better off, for he is blind and will not recognize his blindness. Few things hinder grace more than the refusal of a man to acknowledge his own blindness because of pride, or if he does recognize it, to take no heed and to bury himself in pleasures, as though there were no danger.

I advise all who are blind in this way, and bound with the love of this world, and fallen away from the beauty that properly belongs to man, to consider their souls, and prepare them to receive grace as far as they are able. And they may do so in this way if they like. When they are conscious that they are out of the state of grace and oppressed with mortal sin, they should consider that their state of being separated from God is one of great danger, as indeed it is. All that keeps them from falling into hell is the single thread of this bodily life on which they hang. How easily a single thread may be broken! Their breathing has only to stop, as may easily happen, and their soul would depart and be in hell for ever. If they would think of this, they would be in terror of the just judgements of God and the severe punishment for sin. It would bring them to sorrow and contrition for their sin and their lack of grace, and they would beg earnestly that they might have grace, and if they did so beg, then without doubt it would be given to them. It would drive out all the darkness and hardness from their hearts, and all their weakness of will, and they would have strength to renounce all the false love of this world in so far as it involves mortal sin. For there is no soul—I am speaking of those still united to the body—far removed though it may be from God through the malice of its will in mortal sin, that cannot be brought back by grace to a pure life. All that is needed is that the soul should submit its will with humility to God, that it should amend its life and sincerely ask grace and pardon from God, putting all the responsibility for its misery on itself and not on Him. Holy Scripture says: *Nolo mortem peccatoris, sed magis ut convertatur et vivat* (Ezech. xxxiii. 11). I will not the death of a sinner, but rather that he should be converted to me and live. For it is the will of our Lord that the most perverse man alive, who is disfigured by sin, should be reformed to His likeness, if he will show a change of will and ask grace.

THE SEVENTEENTH CHAPTER

That reform in feeling and in faith cannot be acquired in a moment but only at the end of a long time by means of grace and much bodily and spiritual labour

THIS reform in faith, as I said before, is easily attained. But reform in faith and feeling is not so easily come by. It requires much labour and perseverance. For all the elect are reformed in faith, even though they are in the lowest degree of charity. But reform in feeling is for those who reach the state of perfection, and it cannot be attained in a moment. It implies great grace and long spiritual exercises. A soul must first be cured of its spiritual sickness; the bitterness of the passions, the concupiscence of the flesh, and all the movements of the old man must be burned out with the fire of desire, and new feelings, the fruits of grace, introduced with burning love and spiritual light. Then is the soul approaching perfection and reform in feeling.

Such a soul is like a man who has been brought near to

death through illness. He may obtain a remedy which cures him and saves his life, but he cannot at once get up and go to work like a man in full health. The weakness of his body keeps him prostrate, and he must wait some time, make use of medicines, and follow the regime laid down by the doctor before he fully recovers his bodily health. In the same way spiritually; the man who is spiritually dead through mortal sin, though he may be restored to life by the medicine of the sacrament of Penance so that he is saved from damnation, is not at once free from his passions and sensual desires nor able to arrive at contemplation. He must wait a long time and take good care of himself and regulate his life wisely in order to recover health of soul. He will be weak for long enough before he is completely cured. But if he takes the remedies of a good doctor and makes use of them with discretion, he will much more quickly be restored to spiritual strength and come to reform in feeling.

Reform in faith is the lowest state of elect souls, below which they cannot well be, and reform in feeling is the highest state that a soul can come to in this life. But a soul cannot suddenly jump from the lowest to the highest, any more than a man who will climb a high ladder and puts his foot on the lowest rung can at the next moment be on the top one. He must go up them in order till he comes to the highest. So it is spiritually. No man suddenly receives the highest graces, but he may attain them through long exercises wisely regulated, when He helps and teaches in Whom all grace is found. For without His special help and interior teaching no soul can reach perfection.

THE EIGHTEENTH CHAPTER

The reason why relatively so few souls attain this reform in faith and feeling

BUT now you may say that since our Lord is so generous in the exercise of His goodness and so liberal with His gifts, it is strange that so few souls come to be reformed in feeling in comparison with the many who fail to do so. It would seem as though He were estranged from man, and that is not true; or else that He paid no attention to those who by faith have become His servants. In reply to that I would say that one cause [of so few being reformed in feeling] seems to me to be this. Many who are reformed in faith make no effort to advance in grace or to lead better lives through the serious cultivation of prayer and meditation[1] and other bodily and spiritual exercises. They think it is enough to keep themselves out of mortal sin and to remain in the condition in which they are. They say that it is enough for them to be saved, and to have the lowest rank in heaven; they desire nothing further.

It may be that some of the elect, who lead an active life in the world, act in this way, and it is not surprising, for they are so busy with worldly occupations that must be attended to that they cannot really give their attention to advancing in the spiritual life. But they are in a dangerous state, for they are constantly falling and rising again, and can never reach any stability in the practice of virtue. Nevertheless, there is some excuse for them in the conditions of their lives. But others, who need not occupy themselves with worldly affairs and are assured of their livelihood without worldly

[1] Hilton here uses the word "thinking" of which the equivalent in modern usage would be meditation. Wherever the word meditation occurs throughout the rest of this book it translates "thinking".

activity, as for example religious who bind themselves to the state of perfection in a religious order, could arrive at a high degree of grace, if they would put themselves in the right dispositions. And that is true also of others who are living in the world and who have the necessary aptitude and intelligence. Such people are more to be blamed, for they remain inert and idle, and do not care to advance in grace or to come to the love and knowledge of God.

And a soul that is reformed only in faith and will make no effort to advance is indeed in a dangerous condition. It may so easily lose what it has and fall into mortal sin again. For the soul cannot remain in one state while it is in the body; it must either advance in grace or fall back into sin. Its condition is like that of a man who has been pulled out of a pit, and who, when he has been brought up, refuses to move away from the brink. He acts very foolishly, for a puff of wind or one unguarded movement may send him down into it again in a worse plight than he was before. If he moves well away from the edge on to firm ground, then he will be safe even in a great storm. So in the spiritual sphere, he is very unwise who, after being rescued from the abyss of sin through reforming in faith, thinks that it is enough if he is not in mortal sin, and that he need make no advance, but may remain where he is on the brink of hell. At the least temptation from the devil or the flesh such a man falls into sin again. But if he flees from the abyss, that is, if he determines to reach a higher state of grace, and takes steps to acquire it by prayer, and meditation, and other good works, he will not easily fall again into mortal sin, even though he suffers great temptations.

And it is indeed strange to me, seeing that grace is so great a good, that a man, when he has so little of it that he could scarcely have less, should say, "I will no more of this, for I have enough." I never hear a man of the world, though he has more possessions than he needs, say "I have enough, I have no wish for more." He will always desire more and more, and use all his intelligence and all his power to increase his possessions, and there is no end to his covetousness. Much more then should the soul of the elect desire spiritual riches, for these never perish, and in them the soul finds its true happiness. A wise man will never cease to desire more grace, however much he has, for he who desires most will obtain most, and will indeed make great advances.

THE NINETEENTH CHAPTER

Another reason why reform in faith and feeling is so rare, and how voluntary but indiscreet attachment to exterior practices sometimes hinders souls from receiving more grace

ANOTHER reason [why so few are reformed in feeling] is this. Some who are reformed in faith, take up a certain programme, whether of exterior or interior exercises, at the beginning of their conversion, and think that they must always keep to it and never make a change, even though grace inspires them to a better. They think that they should always keep to the same practices, and by custom they become so attached to them that, when they have carried them out, they feel enormously gratified and think they have done a great thing for God. And if it happens that something interferes with their custom, though for a perfectly reasonable cause, they are upset and angry and troubled in conscience, as though they had committed a great sin. Such men put up an obstacle to greater grace, because they make perfection consist in something external. They set up their goal in the middle instead of at the end of their course.

The external practices used by beginners are good, but

they are only means leading to perfection, and therefore anyone who makes his perfection consist in them, and will go no further, but always persists in the same course, limits his own development. It is a simple craft that an apprentice can make no progress in, and of which he knows as much on the first day as he does twenty years later. Or if the craft is skilled, he must be very unintelligent or very unwilling to learn who makes no advance in it. But there is no craft that requires such skill as the service of God. It is the highest and the most difficult in which to attain mastery. And by the same token it is the most profitable and rewarding to him who can properly exercise it. And so it would seem that apprentices who never make any progress in it are either unintelligent or ill-willed.

I do not condemn those practices that beginners make use of, either exterior or interior, for they are good and useful. But I would have them used only as a preparation for higher things, as a convenient means until better can be found, so that even while they are being used, something better should be sought. Then, when the soul feels moved to make use of more spiritual exercises in which the body, the senses, and the imagination play less part, the earlier ones should be given up in their favour, provided that this will not give scandal to other people. If the two practices do not conflict, then both may be kept if it is so desired. I am not speaking here of practices that are demanded by the law of the Church or the rule of an order, or that are undertaken for penance, but of those which are undertaken voluntarily out of devotion. The prophet says in the Psalter: *Etenim benedictionem dabit legislator, ibunt de virtute in virtutem, videbitur Deus deorum in Sion* (Ps. lxxxiii. 8). The lawgiver will give his blessing, they will go from virtue to virtue, and the God of Gods will be seen in Sion. The lawgiver, that is our Lord Jesus Christ, will give His blessing; that is, He will give His gift of grace to the elect, withdrawing them from sin and transforming them into His likeness through their good works. By this grace they will advance and grow from virtue to virtue till they come to Sion, that is to contemplation, in which they will see the God of Gods. They will understand that there is only one God, and that there is none beside Him.

THE TWENTIETH CHAPTER

How without great bodily and spiritual effort, and without great grace and humility, it is impossible for the soul to be reformed in feeling and to maintain itself in that state

Now you may say that, since there is this danger of falling again for those who are reformed in faith alone, and since reform in feeling is so high and so sure a way for whoever can travel it, then you would like to know what are the best means to enable a man to find it, or if there is anything in special that he ought to do. I reply that you know very well that anyone who wishes to attain purity of heart and the experimental knowledge of God must strive vigorously and perseveringly against all the capital sins; not only against pride and envy, but against all the others, and their branches, that I described in the first Book, because the passions and sensual desires are a great obstacle to purity of heart and peace of conscience. And it is necessary also to acquire virtues, not only chastity and temperance, but also patience and mildness, charity and humility, and all the rest. And there is no one way of achieving this, but it can be done in many different ways according to the different dispositions found in men. Prayer, meditation, the performance of works of charity, may all contribute to it, and a man may give proof of it in various ways, in suffering hunger and thirst and cold, shame and contempt, for the love of virtue and of truth. You know this well, for you will find it in every book on the spiritual life, and hear it from every preacher who seeks to stir men's souls. It seems there is no special work that will certainly lead a soul to grace. It must come through the gift of our Lord Jesus and through much labour, which at the best will be little enough.

One reason [why there is no one way to reform in faith and feeling] may be this; our Lord Jesus Himself is in a special way the master of this craft and the physician of spiritual ills, for without Him nothing can be achieved, and so it is not unreasonable to demand that a man should carry out His teaching and inspirations. But the master who can only teach his pupil one lesson is not impressive, and the physician who only has one remedy for all ills cannot claim to be learned. And so our Lord Jesus, who is so wise and so good, shows His wisdom and His goodness by adapting His teaching to the learning of His disciples, and by varying His remedies according to the degree of their sickness.

A further reason is this: if there were any one act by which a man might infallibly come to the perfect love of God, he might easily think that he could come to it through his own unaided efforts, as a merchant acquires his riches by his own effort. But it is not so in the spiritual life. The love of God is not attained in that way. The man who wishes to serve God wisely and come to the perfect love of Him must desire no other reward apart from Him. But no creature can merit the possession of God by its own efforts. If a man were to perform all the works, bodily and spiritual, of all creation he could not merit God as his reward. For God is supreme happiness and infinite goodness, and surpasses without any comparison the deserts of all men, and so He can be obtained by no work of man, as a bodily reward may. God is free and gives Himself to whom He wills and when He wills, not for any particular work or at any particular time. Though a soul does all in its power for a lifetime, it will never have perfect love of Jesus till He freely gives it. On the other hand, surely God will not give such a grace except to a man who, for his part, does all that is in his power, and would do still more if he knew how.

And so it would seem that it is neither grace alone without the full co-operation of the soul, nor man's efforts alone without grace, that brings a soul to reform in feeling, a reform which consists in perfect love and charity. But together, grace and man's effort bring a soul to the blessed experience of perfect love. And furthermore this grace is only given to a humble soul that is filled with the fear of God. And so I say that one who is not humble and does not do what lies within his power cannot come to this reform in feeling. And he is not truly humble who does not know himself for what he is. He may perform every sort of good work that is in his power, fasting, watching, wearing a hair-shirt, and every other sort of bodily mortification; he may perform all the external works of mercy, or all interior acts of piety such as praying, weeping, sighing, and meditating, but if he rests in these acts, and relies on them, and considers them so highly that he presumes on his own merits, thinking himself rich and good, holy and virtuous, he has not attained true humility. And even if he says and thinks that everything he does is God's gift, he still has not true humility, for he does not really strip himself of all his good actions nor become truly poor in spirit and feel himself to be nothing as in fact he is. And indeed, until a soul can through grace feel that it is nothing and strip itself even of its good actions through the vision of the truth of Jesus, it is not perfectly humble.

For indeed what is humility but truth? And therefore he is humble, who by the grace of God sees that Jesus does everything, and that he himself does nothing but allow Jesus

to work in him as He pleases. For a man who judges everything by human reason and has no other standard it is difficult, and seems to be impossible and unreasonable, to perform good works and then to attribute them all to Jesus and
take no credit to himself. But to one who can see truth with
the eyes of the spirit it appears to be a true and reasonable
way of acting. And indeed he who has this vision will never
do otherwise, but will be moved to greater and more determined bodily and spiritual efforts. And this may well be one
reason why some who make the greatest bodily exertions
and practise the severest penance all their lives, and say endless prayers and psalters, never come to experience the love of
God as others seem to do in a short time with much less effort.
The reason is that they have not the humility that I spoke of.

On the other hand the man who does not play his part
cannot come to feel grace. Such a man argues thus: "Why
should I exert myself? Why should I pray or meditate, watch
or fast, or perform any other bodily mortifications in order
to attain such a grace, since it cannot be obtained except by
the free gift of Jesus? I will continue to rule my life by
human standards, and perform none of these bodily or
spiritual works until He gives me the grace. For if it is dependent on His gift, then no effort is demanded on my part.
Whether I do much or little it will be given to me. And if
He does not wish to give it, however much I do, I shall never
arrive at it." A man who argues in this way can never come
to be reformed in soul. He turns voluntarily to worldly idleness and makes it impossible for himself to receive the gift
of grace, inasmuch as he declines both the interior effort,
which consists in a constant persevering desire for Jesus,
and also the exterior effort, which consists in the performance of outward bodily actions. Such a man cannot come
to be reformed.

To sum up; he who has not true humility and who does

not exert himself, either interiorly only, by great fervour and constant desire and assiduous prayer and meditation, or else by both interior and exterior exercises, cannot be reformed in soul to the image of God.

THE TWENTY-FIRST CHAPTER

That a man who will come to Jerusalem, that is the City of Peace, which is Contemplation, must have great humility and faith and suffer much hardship in body and soul

SINCE you desire to know some way by which you can come nearer to reform in feeling, with the help of God I will tell you what seems to me to be the shortest and easiest way, and I will do so by taking the example of a pilgrim. [1]

A man wished to go to Jerusalem and, because he did not

[1] The comparison of the spiritual life to a pilgrimage is at least suggested in Scripture (Heb. xi. 13, and 1 Peter ii. 11), and it is found in St Augustine (*De Doctrina Christiana*, 1, 4, 10 (P.L., xxxiv, col. 20, 21, 23) though not developed at all in the way that it is here. We are perhaps apt to forget how relevant it was to the life of Hilton's day. For us the Canterbury Pilgrimage may appear little more than a literary device, but pilgrimage played a prominent part among the activities of fourteenth-century England. Remarkable evidence of the feats which the apparently most unlikely people could perform in this respect came to light with the publication of *The Book of Margery Kempe* (London, 1936). Fr Baker incorporated this parable of the pilgrim in his *Sancta Sophia*, Tr. I, Sect. 1, chap. 6. Hilton stresses two points to which it is perhaps worth drawing attention: the necessity for (1) a strong determination to reach the goal; (2) humility and charity. The first is the whole point of the parable, the second is summed up in the saying that the pilgrim is recommended to repeat to himself: "Humility says, I am nothing, I have nothing. Charity says, I desire only one thing, and that is Jesus" (p. 194). With this should be compared what he says about the desire for Jesus in chap. 47 of Book I and about the necessity for humility and charity in chap. 51 of the same Book.

know the way there, he asked another man who, he hoped, would be able to tell him. This man replied that he would not be able to get there without great difficulty and labour, for the way, he said, is long and dangerous because of thieves and robbers, and there are many obstacles in the way of a man going there. Furthermore there are several roads that seem to lead to it, but every day men are slain and robbed and cannot reach their destination. There was however, he said, one road by which he would guarantee that a man should reach the city, Jerusalem, and never lose his life on the way. He would be robbed and beaten and suffer great distress, but his life would be saved. Then the pilgrim said, "As long as my life is spared and I come to the place I desire, I do not mind how much I have to suffer on the way. Whatever advice you give to me I will promise to carry it out." The other man replied, "Well, I will set you on the way. This is it, and you must carry out the instructions that I give you. Do not stop over anything that you hear, or see, or feel that would hinder you on your way. Make no pause for it, do not look at it, do not take pleasure in it, do not fear it. Keep on your way and have no aim but to be at Jerusalem, for that is what you desire and nothing but that. And if you are robbed, or beaten, or treated with contempt, do not resist, if you wish to keep your life. Put up with the harm you suffer and continue as though nothing had happened, lest you should suffer greater harm. And if men wish to keep you by telling you false tales to amuse you and turn you from your pilgrimage, do not listen and do not reply to them, but only say that you wish to be at Jerusalem. And if men offer you gifts and to make you rich with this world's goods, pay no heed to them, keep your mind always on Jerusalem. If you will keep to this way and do as I have said, I will answer for it that you will not be slain but that you will come to the place that you desire."

In the spiritual sense Jerusalem is the vision of peace[2] and represents contemplation in the perfect love of God. For contemplation is nothing else than the vision of Jesus, who is true peace. And if you desire to come to this blessed vision of true peace and to be a pilgrim to Jerusalem, I will put you on the way as far as I am able, even though I have never been there myself. The beginning of the way is reform in faith, and this, as I have said, is based on humility and faith and the laws of the Church. You can be assured that whatever sins you may have committed before, if you have been reformed by the sacrament of Penance according to the law of the Church, you are in the right way. Now if you wish to make good progress, there are two things that you must often have in mind, humility and charity. That is, I am nothing, I have nothing, I desire only one thing. The sense of these words must be your constant guide, even though the words themselves are not formulated in your mind, for that is not necessary. Humility says, I am nothing, I have nothing. Charity says, I desire only one thing, and that is Jesus. These two strings united by the thought of Jesus will produce harmony in the harp of your soul, when they are skilfully touched with the finger of reason. The lower you strike on one, the higher the other will sound. The less you feel that you are, or that you possess, through humility, the more you will desire to possess Jesus in love. I am not referring to the humility that a soul feels at the sight of its own sin or weakness and at the misery of this life, nor yet that which it feels at the sight of the virtues of other men, for though such humility is genuine and helpful, still it is harsh and worldly, not pure, and gentle, and charming. But I am referring to the humility that the soul feels through grace in the contempla-

---

[2] *Sicut Jerusalem interpretatur visio pacis, ita Sion speculatio, id est visio et contemplatio.* St Augustine, *Enarr. in Ps.*, Ps. lxiv, n. 3 (P.L., xxxvi, col. 774).

tion of the infinite being and the great goodness of Jesus. [3] If you cannot yet see this with the eyes of your spirit, believe that it is so. For the knowledge of His being that comes through perfect faith or through contemplation will make you consider yourself not only the most miserable creature in existence, but as absolutely nothing, even though you had never committed a sin. And such humility is beautiful. For in comparison with Jesus, who is in truth all, you are nothing. And in the same way you ought to judge that you possess nothing, but are like an empty vessel that has no power to fill itself. For however many exterior and interior good works you perform, till you are conscious of the love of Jesus, you have nothing. For with that precious liquor only may your soul be filled and with no other. For since that alone is so precious, consider anything that you have and do as unable to satisfy you without the contemplation and the love of Jesus. Put everything else behind you and forget it that you may have that which is best.

A real pilgrim going to Jerusalem leaves house and lands, wife and children, and strips himself of all his possessions that he may go easily on his way without hindrance. In the same way, if you wish to be a spiritual pilgrim, you must strip yourself of all your possessions; good works as well as bad, you must put them all behind you, and make yourself so poor in spirit that you rest in no work of your own, but are always desiring the grace of greater love and are always seeking the spiritual presence of Jesus. If you do this then you are setting your heart wholly on being at Jerusalem and nowhere else but there. Your heart is wholly intent on having nothing but the love of Jesus and what spiritual vision

[3] Hilton will develop the distinction he makes here between humility which is the product of reason and that which is the result of contemplation in Bk. II, chap. 37. *The Cloud of Unknowing*, chap. 13, has substantially the same teaching.

of Himself He will give you. It is for that alone that you were
created and redeemed; that is your beginning and your end,
your joy and your happiness. And therefore, whatever you
possess, that is, however rich you may be in good works,
hold it as nothing as long as you have not experienced this
love of which I am speaking. If you keep this purpose before
you and cling to it earnestly, it will bring you safe through
the perils of your journey. Thieves and robbers may despoil
and beat you, that is the evil spirits may attack you with
various temptations, but your life will always be spared. In
a word, if you will follow my instructions, you will escape
all dangers and quickly come to the City of Jerusalem.

Now you are on the road and you know the name of the
place to which you are going, so you may proceed with your
journey. The setting-forth is nothing else than spiritual
effort, and bodily too, as far as there is need. You may act,
with discretion, in this way. Any bodily or spiritual occupation which is in accordance with your state of life, I consider suitable for you[4] provided that it furthers this desire to
love Jesus that grace inspires in you, that it makes it more
complete, more agreeable, and more effective in producing
virtue. It may be praying[5] or meditating, reading or working, but as long as it strengthens your will to love Jesus and
withdraws your mind and your affections from love of the
world, it is good for you. And if it happens that through custom its virtue grows less, and you think another occupation
will help you more, and that grace inspires you to it, then

[4] "What work that it be that thou should do, after the degree and the
state that thou standest in bodily and ghostly." I have taken *bodily* and
ghostly to refer to the work and not the state. The fifteenth-century Latin
translation interprets the passage in the same way.

[5] The printed texts have *preaching*, which is evidently not a suitable
occupation for an anchoress. There is, however, manuscript support for
praying (Bodleian MS., Rawlinson C 285, and very likely others), and the
Latin translation has *oratione*.

take it up and leave your former one. For though the desire of your heart for Jesus should be always unchanged, the spiritual exercises that you use in prayer or meditation to feed this desire may be various, and may well be changed according to the dispositions you find in yourself through grace.

The more sticks are laid on a fire the larger it is, and so the more different spiritual exercises that a man makes use of to enkindle his desire for God, the stronger and more burning it will be. If then you are free and are not bound by any particular rule, consider carefully the occupation that is best fitted to you and that furthers most this desire for Jesus, and give yourself to that. Do not tie yourself unchangeably to bodily practices that might hinder your freedom of heart in loving Jesus, if grace visits you in a special way. Anything that leads to the acquirement of virtue and hindering of sin is always good and must not be given up, for you must always practise humility and patience, temperance and chastity, and the other virtues. But any practice that gets in the way of a better is to be left when time and opportunity offers. For example, if a man is accustomed to say so many rosaries, or to meditate in a certain way for a certain time, or to watch or kneel for so long, or to perform any other bodily action, these practices are to be omitted sometimes for a reasonable cause, or if a different and greater grace is given.

THE TWENTY-SECOND CHAPTER

How a man who is on this road will have enemies to fight against, and how he must overcome them by the knowledge of our Lord Jesus, by confession, and contrition, and satisfaction

NOW that you are on the way and know how you ought to go beware of enemies who will do their best to hinder you if they can. What they seek is to put out of your heart this desire and longing that you have for the love of Jesus, for there is nothing that pains them more. And they will endeavour to drive you back to the love of temporal pleasures. These enemies are principally the desires of the flesh and vain fears which arise in your heart because of the corruption of human nature. These things will hinder your desire for the love of God and engross your heart, and they are your greatest enemies. There are others too; evil spirits that are full of tricks to deceive you. But there is one remedy, as I said before; whatever they say, do not believe them, but keep steadily on and desire nothing but the love of Jesus. Always answer: I am nothing, I have nothing, I desire only one thing, and that is the love of Jesus.

Do not believe these enemies of yours, if to begin with they disturb you by suggesting that your confessions have not been good, that there is some former sin unconfessed that you are unaware of, and therefore that leaving your desire you must turn back on the road and go and make a better confession. They are not speaking the truth, and there is nothing wrong with your confessions. Believe firmly that you are on the right road and that there is no need for you to examine your past confessions. Hold on your way and fix your mind on Jerusalem. And again, if they say that you are not worthy to have the love of God, and why should you desire that which you cannot obtain and do not deserve to obtain, do not pay any attention to them. Continue on your way and say, "Not because I am worthy but because I am unworthy, I desire the love of God; for if I had it, it would make me worthy. And since I was created for this end, I will seek it even though I never attain it, and will pray for it and believe that in the end I may come to it." If your enemies see that you are growing bold and confident in your effort, they will begin to be afraid of you.

But as long as you are on the road they will not cease to trouble you—threatening and menacing you on the one hand, and flattering you and offering false pleasures on the other, to make you give up your purpose and turn back. They will say, "If you continue to strive after this desire for Jesus with as much effort as you began, you will become ill, or fall into delusions or madness, as you see happens to some; or you will be reduced to poverty, or suffer some physical mishap, and no one will be willing to come to your aid; or you will be assailed by secret temptations which you cannot surmount. It is a dangerous thing for a man to leave the world and give himself wholly to the love of God, and to seek nothing else. Many unknown dangers may overwhelm him. Return therefore and give up this desire, which you will never be able to achieve, and act like other men in the world."

This is what your enemies will say, but do not believe them. Continue in your desire and repeat always that it is Jesus that you would have and Jerusalem where you would be. They will see then that you are determined, that you will not give up because of sin or illness, delusions or madness, fear of spiritual temptations, misfortune or poverty, not for life or for death. They will see that you seek only one thing and are deaf to all they have to say, that you keep firmly to your prayers and other spiritual exercises without any relaxation, but with discretion according to the advice of your superior or of your spiritual director, and they will be angered and begin to attack you more vigorously. They will rob you and beat you and put you to all the shame they can. You will begin to experience this when all your actions, however good they may be, are judged to be bad by other men, and taken amiss. Anything that you wish to do, whether for the good of your body or of your soul, will be thwarted, and you will fail in all your most reasonable aims.[1] And their hope in all this is that you will be moved to anger or melancholy or ill-will against your neighbour.

But against all these troubles, or any others that may come on you, use this remedy. Think of Jesus, do not get angry over your trials, do not dwell on them, but recall your teaching that you are nothing, you have nothing, anything that you lose of temporal goods is in fact no loss, and you desire nothing but the love of Jesus. Keep on your way to Jerusalem without making any change in your way of acting. And if at times you are troubled by your own weakness and the inconveniences that arise through the ill-will of men or the malice of the devil, as soon as you can, recollect yourself, cease thinking about your difficulties and continue with your work. Do not dwell too long on your troubles lest your enemies profit by them.

[1] The general difficulties described in this and the following chapter are to be connected with the suffering described in chap. 28 which will occur in what Hilton calls the period of justification (see n. 4 to that chapter). In particular it may be noted that the experience of failure and misrepresentation described in this passage is frequently met with in the lives of the saints.

THE TWENTY-THIRD CHAPTER

A general remedy against evil movements that arise in the heart from the flesh, the world, and the devil

AND then, when your enemies perceive that in spite of all they can say and do you do not become angry or depressed or irritated about anything, that you are determined to accept whatever may happen to you, comfort or discomfort, praise or the lack of it, and that you will give your attention to nothing but keeping your mind and your will on the love of God, they will be greatly disconcerted. But then they will tempt you with flattery, and false pleasure. They will put before you all your acts and virtues, and impress upon you that all men praise you and speak of your holiness, and that they love and honour you for your holy life. They will do this in the hope that you will believe them, and that you will take delight in this false pleasure and rest in it. But if you are wise, you will hold all such nonsense falsehood and flattery, that your enemy offers to you like a poisoned drink mixed with honey. Therefore refuse, and say that you will have none of it, but that you wish to be at Jerusalem.

Such are the difficulties you will encounter, or others like them, whether from the flesh, the world, or the devil; more than I can tell you now. For as long as a man allows his thoughts to range about the world considering all sorts of things he feels few difficulties. But as soon as he concentrates all his thought and all his desire on one object, to possess it, to see and know and love it, and that object is Jesus, then he will encounter many painful hindrances. Whatever he feels that is not the object of his desire is a hindrance to him. I have given you some examples, and beyond this I say in general that whatever movement you feel, whether of the flesh or the devil, pleasant or painful, bitter or sweet, attractive or terrifying, joyous or sad, if it draws your mind and your will from the love of Jesus to the vanity of the world, and puts an end to your desire of Him, so that it comes to occupy you fully, despise it, do not accept it, do not dwell on it.

But if it is a question of some external work that you have to do for your neighbour or for yourself, do it as quickly as you can so that it does not weigh on you. If it is something that is not necessary or is no affair of yours, do not undertake it or concern yourself with it. Do not get angry about it, do not fear it, do not take pleasure in it, but put it away altogether. Repeat, "I am nothing, I have nothing, I neither seek nor desire anything but the love of Jesus." Concentrate your mind on this desire, strengthen and foster it with prayer and other spiritual exercises so that you do not lose sight of it, and it will lead you on the right way and save you from all dangers. You may be very conscious of them, but they will not overcome you, and I am confident that this desire will bring you to the perfect love of our Lord Jesus.

On the other hand, any practice that furthers your desire, strengthens and nourishes it, and turns your mind from the desire of the world to seek the love of God with more fervour—whether it is praying or meditating, keeping silence or speaking, reading or listening, solitude or the company of others, moving about or keeping still—make use of it for as long as it helps you. And for your eating and drinking and sleeping, do these things as a pilgrim does, and with discretion, according to the advice and directions of your superior. For however much haste a pilgrim makes he must at times eat and drink and sleep. Do the same, for although it hinders you at one time, it will help you at others.

THE TWENTY-FOURTH CHAPTER

Of an evil day and a good night, and what they signify; and how the love of the world is compared to an evil day and the love of God to a good night

IF you want to know what this desire consists of, it is in truth Jesus. For He creates this desire in you, and it is He who desires in you, and who is also the object of your desire. He is everything and He does everything, if you could but realize. You do nothing but allow Him to act on your soul and consent with great joy of heart to what He deigns to do in you. You are nothing but His instrument, though you are endowed with reason. And therefore, when at the touch of His grace you feel your mind caught up by a strong desire to please Him and love Him, believe that you possess Jesus. For He is indeed the object of your desire. Consider Him earnestly, for He does not appear in bodily form, but invisibly by the inward presence of His power. See Him with the eyes of your spirit if you are able, or else with the eyes of faith, and follow Him wherever He leads, for He will lead you in the right way to Jerusalem, which is the vision of peace in contemplation. This was how the prophet prayed to the Heavenly Father: *Emitte lucem tuam et veritatem tuam; ipsa me deduxerunt in montem sanctum tuum, et in tabernacula tua* (Ps. xlii. 3). Father of heaven, send out your light and your truth, that is your Son Jesus; and He will lead me by desire to your holy hill and to your tabernacles, that is to the experience of perfect love and to the height of contemplation.

Of this desire the prophet says: *Memoriale tuum Domine in desiderio animae. Anima mea desideravit te in nocte, sed et spiritus meus in praecordiis meis* (Isa. xxvi. 8, 9). Lord Jesus, the memory of you is imprinted in the desire of my soul, for my soul has desired you in the night and my spirit has sought you in

all my meditations. And why the prophet said he desired
God in the night, and what he meant by it, I will tell you.
You know well that the night is a space of time between two
days. For when one day is ended another does not come at
once, but first there comes the night and separates the days;
sometimes it is long and sometimes short, and then there
comes another day. The prophet was referring not only to
this sort of night, but to a spiritual night. You must know
that there are two days or two periods of light; the first is a
false light, the second a true one. The false light is the love
of this world that a man has because of the corruption of his
human nature; the true light is the perfect love of Jesus felt
in the soul through grace. The love of the world is a false
light, for it passes away and does not last, and so it does not
perform what it promised. The devil promised this light
when he persuaded Adam to sin and said: *Aperientur oculi
vestri; et eritis sicut dii* (Gen. iii. 5). Your eyes shall be opened
and you shall be as gods. And he spoke the truth, for when
Adam had sinned his inward eye was closed and spiritual
light withdrawn, and his outward eyes were opened, and he
felt and saw a new light of bodily pleasure and love of the
world that he did not see before. And so he saw a new day,
but it was an evil day. It was the day that Job cursed when he
said: *Pereat dies in qua natus sum* (Job iii. 3). May the day
perish in which I was born. It was not the day in the course
of the year created by God that he cursed, but the day made
by man, that is the concupiscence and love of the world into
which he was born without knowing it. It was of this day
that he asked of God that it should perish and no longer endure.

But the everlasting love of Jesus is a true day and a blessed
light. For God is both love and light and He is everlasting,
and therefore he who loves Him is in everlasting light, as St
John says: *Qui diligit Deum manet in lumine* (1 John ii. 10).

He who loves God dwells in light. The man who perceives that the love of this world is false and does not last, and for this reason wishes to forsake it and seek the love of God, cannot immediately experience His love, but must stay for a time in the night. For he cannot come suddenly from one light to the other, that is from the love of the world to the perfect love of God. This night consists in nothing else than a withdrawal of the soul from the things of earth by a great desire and longing to love and see and experience Jesus and spiritual things. This is the night; for just as the night is dark and material objects are hidden in it and exterior occupations cannot be carried on, so a man who determines to fix his mind on Jesus and to desire only his love, must give neither his thoughts nor his love to bodily creatures. In this way his thoughts will be made free and his affections will not be entangled in anything beneath him. If he can do this, he is in the night, for he is in darkness.

But this night is good and the darkness luminous, for it keeps out the false love of the world and brings nearer the true day. And indeed the darker the night, the nearer is the true day of the love of Jesus. The more the soul is withdrawn from the tumult of the desires of the flesh and impure thoughts through its longing for God, the nearer it is to experiencing the light of His love; and it is in fact very near. It seems that this was what the prophet meant when he said: *Cum in tenebris sedero, Dominus lux mea est* (Mic. vii. 8). When I sit in darkness our Lord is my light. That is, when my soul is free from all movements of sin, as though it were asleep, then our Lord is my light, for then by His grace He draws near to show me His light. But this night is sometimes distressing, and sometimes easy and comforting. It is distressing at first, when a man is much stained by sin, for grace has not accustomed him to the darkness, and yet he wishes to be in it, and he directs his thoughts and his will to God as far as he is able, and endeavours not to feel or think of anything but Him. And because He cannot easily achieve this, he is distressed. Habits of sin, his previous familiarity with it and with the desires of the flesh and the things of earth, his external activities, all press upon him with powerful influence and draw down his soul to them, so that he cannot escape from them as quickly as he would like. And so this darkness is distressing to him, and especially when the effects of grace are slight. Nevertheless, if you find it so, do not be too depressed, and do not struggle too much, as though you would put these things out of your mind by force, for you cannot do that. Wait till grace comes, be patient and do not let your efforts be too violent; if you can, quietly turn your will and your thought to Jesus as though you attached no importance to these feelings.

For be sure of this; when you would desire and think of nothing but Jesus and find this impossible, because worldly thoughts press in on you, you have already got out of the false day and are entering into the darkness. But this darkness is not peaceful, because you are not accustomed to it, and because of the lack of understanding and the impurity in you. And so give yourself to it often, and it will by custom and by the grace of God become easier and more peaceful. That is, your soul by grace will become so unimpeded and strong, and so recollected, that it will find no attraction in earthly thoughts, and no material thing will prevent it from thinking of nothing. [1] Then it is in a fruitful darkness.

[1] "Lust not to think on right nought." A double negative which I take to have merely an intensifying effect, as often in Middle English. It does not care to think of anything [worldly]. This interpretation is borne out by the Latin translation, *quod non delectatur de aliquo cogitare*. In the next phrase Hilton uses the expression "to think of right nought" in a curious technical sense reminiscent of *The Cloud of Unknowing* (e.g. chap. 3) but different, I believe, to its sense (see Bk. I, chap. 52, n.). Hilton goes on to explain what he means by it in the next paragraph.

When I say that the soul thinks of nothing, I mean that by
grace it is recollected, free and self-sufficient, and not driven
against its will to think of, or feel an attachment for, any sin
or anything of the earth. When this is so the soul thinks of
nothing, for it does not think with attachment of any earthly
thing. This is a fruitful nothing, and this nothing and this
night are a great comfort to the soul that desires the love of
Jesus. It is no longer troubled by the thought of earthly
things, but all its thought is for Jesus. Though it is not distracted by earthly thoughts, it is fully occupied with thinking of Him.

What does this darkness consist of then? Truly nothing
else than a desire through grace to have the love of Jesus.[2]
For its desire and its longing for the love of God, for the
vision and the possession of Him, drives out of the heart all
worldly interests and all desires of the flesh, and makes the
soul recollected and occupied only with how it may come to
His love, and so it brings it into this fruitful nothing. And all
is not darkness and nothingness when it is so occupied. For
though it is darkness in relation to the false light, it is not all
darkness in relation to the true light. For Jesus, who is both
love and light, is in this darkness, whether it is distressing or
peaceful. He is in the soul making it labour with desire, and

[2] It should be noted that here as in Book I (chaps. 46–54) the basis
of all the soul's activity is simply what he calls the desire for Jesus (cf. also
Book II, chap. 21, n. 1, and this same chapter, p. 205). To desire Jesus
means of course necessarily to turn the mind and the will to Him, it is
essentially prayer, and the process he is describing here is essentially that
which he described in chaps. 46 and 47 of Book I. He went on there
to point out (especially chap. 48) that the first result of this desire
for God was to bring a man to a realization of his own sins, and the whole
of the second part of the Book (from chap. 55) was devoted to a consideration of the sins so revealed. Here the sins and the difficulties are not
ignored (e.g. chaps. 22, 23, and 25) but the emphasis is on the positive
attainment of contemplation that is going to ensue from this seeking
Jesus.

long for the light, but He is not yet in it making it rest in love, and He does not yet show His light.[3] And therefore it is called night and darkness, in as much as the soul is hidden from the false light of the world and does not yet fully experience the true light, but it is waiting for that blessed love of God which it desires.

If, then, you want to find out when you are in this safe darkness and when not, you may test yourself in this way, and do not try to do so in any other way. When you feel that your will is fully concentrated on seeking God and thinking only of Him, ask yourself whether you desire to have anything on earth for its own sake, or whether you wish the satisfaction of your bodily senses through any creature. And if your eye answers that it wishes to see nothing, and your ear that it would hear nothing, your mouth that it wishes to taste nothing, and not to speak of earthly matters; your nose that it would smell nothing, and your body that it would feel nothing; if your heart says that it does not wish to think about creatures or to love them, but only to be occupied with the thought and love of God, and if all your faculties answer thus, as they easily may under the effect of grace, then you have entered into this darkness. For though you

---

[3] This sentence usefully summarizes the state of the contemplative soul. We may note three things about this state : (1) It is essentially supernatural, the outcome of divine action and in some way of divine indwelling (cf. Book II, chap. 34, n. 2); (2) Jesus may be in the soul making it labour with desire; or (3) He may be in it making it rest in love, and illuminating it.

(2) I take to be the time of justification and (3) that of exaltation of which he speaks in chap. 28. As pointed out in n. 4 to that chapter these states are not rigidly divided one from another but alternate, (2) predominating at first and later (3). So in this chapter he says the night is sometimes distressing and sometimes easy and comforting, and later on, "give yourself to it often, and it will by custom and the grace of God become easier and more peaceful" (p. 206). Cf. also chap. 25, p. 210.

may perceive gleams and suggestions of idle thoughts and carnal desires pressing in on you, nevertheless you are in this fruitful darkness as long as your mind is not fixed on them. Idle imaginings that crop up unexpectedly trouble this darkness and distress the soul, because it would be quit of them and cannot be so, but they do not take away the value of the darkness, for through it the soul will come to peace. And the darkness is peaceful, when for the time being the soul is free from all these idle thoughts and rests peacefully in the desire and longing it has for the spiritual vision of Jesus, as will be said later. That does not last long, but though it is only for a short time it is a most valuable experience.

THE TWENTY-FIFTH CHAPTER

How the desire of Jesus felt in this luminous darkness destroys all movements of sin, and enables the soul to perceive the spiritual light of the heavenly Jerusalem, that is of Jesus

THEN, since this darkness, or night, which is nothing else than the desire of Jesus accompanied by a blind movement of the intellect towards Him, is so fruitful and brings so much peace, even though it does not last long, how much better it must be to experience His love and to be illumined by His holy, invisible light to see the truth. This is the light that a soul receives when the night passes and the day comes, and it was to this night, I think, that the prophet referred when he said: *Anima mea desideravit te in nocte* (Isa. xxvi. 9). My soul desired Thee in the night. It is much better to be cut off from the view of the world in this dark night, however painful this may be, than to dwell outside occupied with the world's false pleasures, though these appear so attractive and agreeable to those whose eyes are closed to the light of

the spirit. For when you are in this darkness you are much
nearer to Jerusalem than when you are in the false light.
Open your heart then to the movement of grace and accus-
tom yourself to dwell in this darkness, strive to become
familiar with it, and you will quickly find peace, and the true
light of spiritual understanding will flood your soul—not all
at once, but gradually. As the prophet says: *Habitantibus in
regione umbrae mortis, lux orta est eis* (Isa. ix. 2). To those who
dwell in the land of the shadow of death light has sprung up.
That is, the light of grace has arisen, and it will shine on
those who can dwell in the shadow of death, that is in the
darkness which is like death. For as death slays a living body
and all its sense perception, so the desire to love Jesus which
is felt in this darkness slays all sins, all the desires of the flesh,
and all impure thoughts, and when this occurs, you have
come very near to Jerusalem. You have not yet reached it,
but by the gleams of light that escape from it you will be able
to see it in the distance before you come to it. For be certain
of this, that though your soul is in this peaceful darkness and
untroubled by the vain joys of the world, it has not yet
reached its goal, it is not yet clothed in light or transformed
into the fire of love. It is aware of something above it that it
does not know and does not yet possess, but which it wants
and yearns after eagerly. And what it longs for is nothing but
the sight of Jerusalem, which is like the city that the prophet Ezechiel saw in his vision (Ezech. xl).

He says that he saw a city standing on a hill which sloped
to the south, and when it was measured before his eyes it
was no more in length and breadth than a rod, that is six
cubits and a palm. But when he was brought into it, it seemed strangely large; he saw many halls and rooms, both public and private, he saw gates and portals outside and in, and
many other buildings many hundred cubits in length and
breadth. And he was amazed that this city was so large in-

side, that appeared so small when he was outside it. This
city signifies the perfect love of God, and it is set on the hill
of contemplation. To the soul that has had no experience of
it but that strives for it with desire it seems only small, six
cubits and a palm in length. The six cubits represent the perfection of human effort, the palm a little touch of contemplation.[1] He sees that there is something which surpasses the
attainment of all human effort, as the palm goes beyond the
six cubits, but he does not see what this is. But if he is able to
get inside the city of contemplation, he sees much more
than he saw at first.

THE TWENTY-SIXTH CHAPTER

*How a man may distinguish the false light, which is an illusion
of the devil, from the true light which comes from Jesus*

You should beware the noon-day devil who makes light to
appear as though it came from Jerusalem when in truth it
does not do so. For the devil perceives that our Lord Jesus
shows the light of truth to those who love Him, and so to
deceive the foolish he shows a false light under colour of a
true one. I will explain how the light of truth coming from
God may be distinguished from the feigned representation
of the devil by an example taken from the sky.

Sometimes one sees in the sky a shaft of sunlight which
one takes to be the sun, but in reality it is not so, and sometimes the sun truly appears. The two appearances may be
distinguished in this way. The false sun only appears between
two black rain clouds. The sun is behind them, and a shaft of
light shines out between the clouds that looks as though it

[1] This interpretation is to be found in St Gregory (*Hom. in Ezech.*,
Bk. II, hom. v, n. 1, P.L., LXXVI, col. 984–5).

were the sun. But the true sun appears when the sky is clear, or at least when there are not many black clouds. Applying this to our subject. Some men appear to forsake the love of the world and to wish to come to the love of God and to the light of His knowledge, but they are not willing to pass through the darkness that I have been speaking about. They will not learn to know themselves truly and humbly—what they previously were, and what they still are through sin, nor how they are nothing in their own nature in comparison with God. They will not trouble to enter into themselves, leaving aside all exterior things ; they will not put down all evil movements of pride, envy, anger, and other sins that arise in their hearts, by cultivating a constant desire of Jesus in prayer and meditation, in silence and tears, and in other corporal and spiritual exercises, as holy and devout men have done before them. As soon as they have forsaken the world exteriorly, or very soon after, they think that they have achieved holiness and the spiritual understanding of the Gospels and Holy Scripture. And especially if they are able to keep the Commandments of God literally and refrain from bodily sins, they think that they love God perfectly. And so they want immediately to preach and instruct all other men, as if they had received the gift of understanding and perfect charity through a special gift of the Holy Ghost. And they are all the more incited to this, because they are sometimes conscious of great lights suddenly given to them without much effort on their part, and they have an ardent love, it seems, urging them to preach truth and righteousness to their fellow-men. They take this as a grace from God which is given to them in preference to others. But if they will consider carefully, they will see that the intellectual light and the ardent love that they experience do not come from the true sun, that is our Lord Jesus, but from the devil, who produces a false light which looks like the sun. And so they may be known by the example that I have given.

The false intellectual light that is given by the devil to a soul in darkness always appears between two black rain clouds. The higher cloud is presumption and self-exaltation, the lower one is contempt and under-estimation of one's neighbour. Whatever knowledge or fervour appears in a soul along with presumption, and exaltation of self, and disdain of one's neighbour, is not the light of grace given by the Holy Ghost. The knowledge may be true in itself, but it comes from the devil if it is acquired suddenly, or else from a man's natural powers if it comes as the result of consideration. And in this way it can clearly be recognized that this false intellectual light is not the light of the true sun.

Those that have knowledge of this sort are full of spiritual pride, but they are unaware of the fact. They are so blinded by this false light that they consider their pride and disobedience to the laws of Holy Church as perfect submission to the Gospel and to the laws of God. They think that the following of their own will is freedom of spirit, and errors and heresies come from them like rain from black clouds. All their preaching leads to damnation, strife, discord, and the condemnation of other walks of life and of other persons. And yet they claim that all is charity and zeal; but it is not so, for St James the Apostle says: *Ubi enim zelus et contentio, ibi inconstantia et omne opus pravum. Non est sapientia haec desursum descendens a Patri luminum, sed terrena, animalis et diabolica* (James iii. 16, 15). Wherever there is envy and contention there is instability and every evil work. And therefore the wisdom which produces such sins does not come from God, the Father of Light, but it is of the earth, brutish and devilish. And so it is by these signs, pride, presumption, disobedience, indignation, defamation, and the like—the things which come from it—that the false light may be distinguished from the true. For the true sun does not impart intellectual light and the fullness of charity unless the sky is first clear of clouds, that is, unless the conscience is first purified in this darkness by the fire of a burning desire for Jesus, which destroys and burns up all evil movements of pride, vainglory, anger, envy, and other sins; as the prophet says: *Ignis ante ipsum praecedet, et inflammabit in circuitu inimicos ejus* (Ps. xcvi. 3). Fire will go before him; that is, the desire of love will go before Jesus in a man's soul, and it will burn up all his enemies, that is, it will destroy all sins.

For if a soul is not first made humble by fear, and then well tried in this fire of desire and purified from its spiritual uncleanness by a long time spent in devout prayers and other spiritual exercises, it cannot bear the shafts of spiritual light nor receive the precious liquor of the perfect love of Jesus. But when it has been purified and refined by this fire, then it can receive the grace of spiritual knowledge and perfect love. Holy Scripture says: *Vobis qui timetis Dominum orietur sol justitiae* (Mal. iv. 2). The true sun of justice, that is our Lord Jesus, will shine on you who fear Him; that is, on humble souls who rank themselves beneath their neighbours through the knowledge of their own misery, and cast themselves at the feet of God by the consideration that they are nothing in themselves. It is a reverent fear and the steady spiritual contemplation of God that produces this perfect humility.

For such souls, the true sun will rise and illumine their reason to know truth and will enkindle their affections with burning love, and then they will both burn and shine. By the power of this heavenly sun they will burn with perfect love and shine with the knowledge of God and spiritual things, for then they are reformed in feeling. And so whoever does not wish to be deceived should humble himself and hide in this darkness. He should avoid all dealings with other men, as I said, and forget the whole world, if he can, and follow Jesus with steady desire in prayer and meditation. For I am

sure that the light that follows this darkness is safe and true
and shines from the city of Jerusalem. It comes from the true
sun to a soul that labours in darkness and cries out for light
to show it the way and comfort it in its struggle. For I think
that a false light never follows true darkness. That is, if a
man really and truly sets himself to forsake the love of the
world and by the grace of God comes to knowledge of himself, he will be deceived by no errors or heresies or illusions.
For all of these come in by the gate of pride, and if pride is
kept out, they will find no place in the soul. Even if they
knock at the gate, they will not get in. For the grace that the
soul feels in this lowly darkness will teach it the truth, and
show all such advances to be tricks of the devil.

THE TWENTY-SEVENTH CHAPTER

*How it is very profitable for a soul to be brought by grace into
this luminous darkness, and how a man should dispose himself
to come to it*

THERE are many devout souls who by grace come into this
darkness and learn to know themselves, and yet do not fully
understand their state. And that ignorance is to some extent
a hindrance to them. They often feel their mind and their
will withdrawn from the things of earth and brought into a
profound and very sweet peace, undisturbed by vain thoughts
or the bodily senses. Their spirit is free to think peacefully
of Jesus, and they can offer prayers and psalms to Him with
great relish and sweetness as long as the weakness of human
nature will allow it. They know that this feeling is good, but
they do not know what it is. To such I would say that it
seems to me that this sort of experience, even if it only lasts
a short time and comes but seldom, is indeed this darkness

that I have been speaking about. It is first of all a consciousness of themselves and a rising above themselves through a
burning desire to see Jesus, or to speak more truly, it is already a spiritual sight of Jesus. And if they can remain in
that peace, or by grace make it habitual, so that they can
easily and freely have it when they desire, and keep themselves in it, then they will no more be overcome by temptations of the devil or the flesh, nor fall into errors or heresies.
They have reached the gate of contemplation and are able
and ready to receive the perfect love of Jesus. So he that has
it should humbly recognize it, guard it carefully, and cultivate it assiduously. No creature should hinder him from attaining it when it offers. He should forget and ignore everything that might interfere with his practice of it, provided
he has no obligations and may do what he likes without scan-
dalizing or offending his neighbour. For I do not think that
he can come to this peace easily unless he has great grace and
is very faithful in obeying its inspirations. And he ought to
be careful to be so. For grace needs to be free from the obstacles of sin and worldly affairs and everything that hinders
its effects, even though they are not sin.

But he who has not yet received this fullness of grace and
who desires to come to the spiritual knowledge of Jesus
must prepare himself for it as well as he can, and so far as possible remove all hindrances to it. He must learn to die to the
world and truly to forsake the love of it. First he must renounce pride, bodily and spiritual. He must seek neither the
respect nor the praise of the world, neither celebrity nor
position, power nor skill, neither riches nor fine clothes.
In a word, he must not seek anything that would lead to his
being honoured above other men. He must desire none of
these things; and if they come to him, he should receive
them with fear, so that, if he cannot be both inwardly and
outwardly poor, he should be so at least inwardly. He should

desire to be forgotten by the world, so that men regard him no more—however rich or able he may be—than the poorest man alive.

Also, he must not take pleasure at the sight of his own good works or virtues, thinking that he does better than others, because he has left the world and others have not done so. He must suppress all rising of ill-will, anger, and envy towards his neighbour, offending or angering no man unreasonably by word or act. He should be free; no man dependent on him, nor he on any man. He must renounce covetousness; only asking what is necessary for his bodily sustenance, and considering himself well recompensed when God moves other men to give him anything at all. He must not trust in his worldly possessions nor in the help or favour of friends, but only in God, for if he does otherwise, he puts himself under an obligation to the world, and this may interfere with his freedom to think of God.

And in the same way he must renounce gluttony and lust and all other bodily impurity, and especially the carnal love of women. The sort of blind love which exists sometimes between a man and a woman can seem good and honest, in as much as they would not sin in act; but none the less in the sight of God it is impure and culpable. For it is a great sin for a man to allow his heart, which ought to be given to Jesus and to virtue and purity of spirit, to be given deliberately in carnal love to any creature. And especially is this so, when the love is so strong that it takes possession of the mind and disturbs it, so that it can no longer savour the things of God. I take it to be deliberate, when a man does it, even though he says it is no sin, [1] or else, when he is so blinded that he re-

---

[1] This sentence presents some difficulty. Hilton says simply, "Thus I hold it wilfully that a man doth it and saith it is no sin." Earlier editors (e.g. Dalgairns) and the translators of the French edition have taken it in the sense that it is deliberate when a man does it even though he ac-

fuses to see that it is sin. He must not seek the mere pleasure of his senses in food and drink, but be satisfied with such food as is offered to him; that is, provided his health is good, such food as will take away his hunger and keep the body in normal strength for the service of God. He must not grumble nor be contentious about his food, though it is sometimes not as good as he would like.

These and all other sins must be renounced in will, and, when the occasion offers, in act, and so must anything else that hinders a man from occupying his mind with Jesus. As long as these things stand in the way a man cannot die to the world nor attain this obscure knowledge of himself, and he cannot attain it unless he does all this, as St Paul did, who said: *Mihi mundus crucifixus est, et ego mundo* (Gal. vi. 14). The world is slain and crucified to me, and I to the world. He who, for the love of God, renounces the love of the world and honour and riches, and does not seek these things, but is well satisfied to be without them, and would not have them if he could, is truly dead to the world, for he takes no delight in it. If the world sets him at nought, does not consider him, pays him no honour or respect, but forgets him as though he were dead, then he is dead to the world. This was absolutely St Paul's state, and it must to some degree be the state of any man who would follow him and come to the perfect love of God. He cannot live fully to God unless he first dies to the world.

This dying to the world is this darkness and it is the door[2]

---

knowledges it to be a sin. This makes better sense, but the texts do not seem to warrant it.

[2] The word *gate* is used frequently in this paragraph. It could in Middle English mean either *door* or *way*. The Latin translation made in the fifteenth century translates it always by *via*, but this seems to lose the point of the contrast between *many ways* and only one *door*. It is the idea of many roads converging at one point, which is the true entrance to contemplation.

of contemplation and of reform in feeling, and there is no other. There may be a variety of ways leading souls to contemplation, for there are various exercises adapted to the various dispositions of men and to different states of life, as for example, the religious and the secular. But there is only the one door. It does not matter what exercise a man makes use of, he has not reached reform in feeling nor come truly to contemplation, unless he has attained this humble self-knowledge and is dead to the world as far as his affections are concerned. From time to time he must feel himself in this peaceful darkness in which he is hidden from the world and sees himself for what he is. And if he will enter by any other door, he is a thief and housebreaker, and will be cast out as unworthy. But the man who can reduce himself to nothing and die in this way stands at the door, for he is dead to the world and lives to God. It was of these that St Paul said: *Mortui enim estis, et vita vestra abscondita est cum Christo in Deo* (Col. iii. 3). You are dead, that is, you, who for the love of God renounce the love of the world, are dead to the world, but your life is hidden from men, as the life of Christ is hidden in the Godhead from the sight of those who love the flesh.

Our Lord Himself pointed out this door in the Gospel when He said: *Omnis qui reliquerit patrem aut matrem, fratrem aut sororem propter me, centuplum accipiet, et vitam aeternam possidebit* (Matt. xix. 29). Everyone who for love of Me leaves father or mother, sister or brother, or any earthly possession, shall have a hundredfold in this life, and afterwards the happiness of heaven. The hundredfold that a soul will have if it leaves the world is nothing else than the enjoyment of this luminous darkness, which I called the door of contemplation. For he who is in this darkness and is hidden by grace from the vanity of the world has no desire for the things of the world; he is not troubled by them, does not seek them or care for them, and so he possesses a hundred times more than a king or a man most greedy of earthly possessions. He who seeks nothing but Jesus has a hundredfold, for he has more rest, more peace of heart, more true love and delight in his soul in one day, than the most covetous man in the world, who has all its wealth at his command, possesses in his whole life.

This is, then, a fruitful darkness and a profitable nothingness that brings a soul to such spiritual ease and sweetness. I think David was referring to this night or this nothingness when he said: *Ad nihilum redactus sum, et nescivi* (Ps. lxxii. 22). I was brought to nothing and I knew it not. That is, the grace of our Lord Jesus sent into my heart has slain and brought to nothing in me all the love of the world, and I know not how. For it is through no effort of my own and not by my own will, but by the grace of our Lord Jesus. And so he who wishes to have the light of grace and to feel the love of Jesus abundantly in his soul, must leave the false light of worldly love and remain in this darkness. And if at first he is afraid to dwell in it, let him not turn again to the love of the world, but suffer for a time and put all his hope and trust in Jesus, and he will not be long without some spiritual light. The prophet says: *Qui ambulavit in tenebris, et non est lumen ei, speret in Domino, et innitatur super Deum suum* (Isa. l. 10). He who walks in darkness and has no light, that is, he who wishes to hide himself from the love of the world and may not readily feel the light of spiritual love, let him not despair or turn again to the world, but let him hope in our Lord and lean upon Him, that is, trust in God, cling to Him by desire, and wait patiently, and he shall have light. It is as if a man has been a long time in the sun and then comes suddenly into a dark house. He will be as if blind at first, and see nothing, but if he will wait a bit, he will soon be able to see about him; at first large objects, and then small, and then everything

that is in the house. It is the same spiritually; he who renounces self-love and acquires knowledge of himself is in the
dark to begin with. But if he perseveres and continues with
assiduous prayer, and often repeats his determination to love
Jesus, he will come to see many things, great and small, of
which he was at first unaware. The prophet seems to have
promised this when he said: *Orietur in tenebris lux tua, et tenebrae tuae erunt sicut meridies. Et requiem dabit tibi Dominus Deus
tuus, et implebit animam tuam splendoribus* (Isa. lviii. 10, 11).
Light will spring up for you in darkness. That is, the light of
blessed love and the spiritual knowledge of God will arise
for you who truly forsake the light of worldly love and bury
your mind in this darkness. *And your darkness shall be as mid-
day*. The darkness of your desire and your blind trust in God
will turn into clear knowledge and certainty of love. *And
God will give you rest*. That is, your carnal desires and your
painful fears and doubts, and the evil spirits that have ceas-
lessly troubled you, will all grow weak and lose their power.
You will be made so strong that they will not hurt you, for
you will be hidden from them in peace. *And then our Lord
Jesus will fill your soul with light*. That is, when you have been
brought into this peace, you will more easily tend to God
and be occupied with nothing but the love of Him. He will
fill all the powers of your soul with beams of spiritual light.
Do not be surprised that I call the leaving of worldly love
darkness, for the prophet called it so, saying: *Intra in tenebras tuas, filia Chaldaeorum* (Isa. xlvii. 5). Enter into your
darkness, daughter of Chaldee. That is, Soul, who is a
daughter of Chaldee through your love of the world, leave
it and enter into your darkness.

THE TWENTY-EIGHTH CHAPTER

The work of our Lord Jesus in the reform of the soul has four stages: the call, justification, exaltation, and glorification

I HAVE told you something of the disposition necessary if you wish to be reformed in feeling, but I do not say that you can bring this about by yourself, for I know very well that it is our Lord Jesus who perfects this work as He pleases. For it is His grace alone that moves a soul and brings it first into this darkness and then into light; as the prophet says: *Sicut tenebrae ejus, ita et lumen ejus* (Ps. cxxxviii. 12). Just as the light which consists in the knowledge and experience of spiritual love is from God, so the darkness, that is, forsaking of worldly love, is from Him. It is He who does everything; He forms [creates] and reforms. He forms by Himself alone, but He reforms with our co-operation.[1] For it is His grace with the co-operation of our will that brings it about. And of the way he does this St Paul says: *Quos Deus praescivit fieri conformes imaginis Filii ejus, hos vocavit; et quos vocavit, hos justificavit; et quos justificavit, hos magnificavit; et quos magnificavit, hos et glorificavit* (Rom. viii. 29, 30).[2] Those whom God foreknew should be conformed to the image of His Son, those He called and justified, those He exalted and glorified.

Though these words may be said of all the elect who are in the lowest degree of charity and are reformed only in faith, they may more particularly be understood of those souls who are reformed in feeling, to whom our Lord God

[1] *Qui ergo fecit te sine te, non te justificat sine te.* St Augustine, Serm. CLXIX, cap. xi, n. 13 (P.L., XXXVIII, col. 923).

[2] Hilton uses this text as the basis of his four stages in the reform of the soul. It may be noted that he does so by making use of the phrase *hos magnificavit*, which does not appear in the Clementine Vulgate. It has, however, authority in some Vulgate manuscripts.

has given great grace and for whom He has been especially solicitous. For they are His special sons, who are fully conformed to the likeness of His Son Jesus. In these words St Paul divides the work of God into four phases. The first is the period of calling a soul from the vanity of the world, and that period is often easy and comfortable. For in the beginning of his conversion a man who is called to great grace receives so vivid an impression and in so sensible a manner, feels often such sweetness of devotion, and has so many tears of compunction, that he thinks sometimes that he is already half in heaven. But these consolations pass away after a time, and then is the second period, that of justification. [3] It is laborious; for when he begins to advance on the road of righteousness, to set his will firmly against all sin, and to reach out with desire to virtues and the love of Jesus, a man feels many difficulties both within, from the waywardness and hardness of his own will, and without, from temptations of the devil, and he is often greatly tormented. And that is not surprising, for he has so long been bent to the false love of the world, that he cannot be made straight without great effort; just as a bent bar cannot be straightened without being forged in the fire. So our Lord Jesus, seeing what is necessary for a wayward soul, allows it to be tested by spiritual trials till the rust of impurity is burnt out of it. Interiorly such fears and doubts and perplexities will arise that the soul will almost fall into despair. It will seem to be forsaken by God and delivered into the hands of the devil, except that it will always have a little secret trust in the goodness and mercy of God. For our Lord Jesus leaves that secret trust in such a soul, however much He departs from

[3] Hilton is here using justification in a non-technical sense. As a technical theological term it is used to describe the result of the infusion of sanctifying grace. Here he is using it to describe the second stage in the rise of the soul to contemplation.

it, and it saves the soul from despair and spiritual harm. It will be mortified exteriorly too, and suffer much pain in its bodily senses, either through illness, or physical suffering caused by the devil. Or again by the secret operation of God the unfortunate soul will suffer so mysteriously through its union with this wretched body that it would not be able to remain united to the body, if our Lord Jesus did not enable it. [4] And yet the soul would rather suffer all this pain than be blinded by the false love of the world. For such a soul that would be hell, while the suffering of all this pain is no more than purgatory. And for this reason it suffers gladly and would not escape from its pains if it could, because they are of such profit to it. Our Lord brings all this about to the great benefit of the soul in order to prevent it resting in its bodily life and in order to wean it from the love of the senses, so that it can receive spiritual light.

After this, when the soul has been mortified in this way and brought from the love of the world into this darkness, so that it no longer takes pleasure in the world, but finds it

[4] This second stage that Hilton calls justification corresponds in general with what came in later mystical literature to be called by the rather dramatic title of the Great Desolation. The ingredients are all there, the interior doubts and perplexities and the rather mysterious physical sufferings, yet through it all the soul is sustained, as Hilton puts it, by "a little secret trust in the goodness and mercy of God". A schematic exposition of the contemplative life such as Hilton gives here, though useful and true in the main, is necessarily rather misleading, because it suggests that the soul is uninterruptedly immersed in these periods one after the other. But there seems no doubt that the period of suffering is not uninterrupted any more than the period of contemplation and that these two experiences alternate, though no doubt after the first fervour there is a period—it is St John of the Cross's *dark night of the soul*—in which suffering will predominate. It seems, further, that only those souls called to a high degree of contemplation feel this suffering in an intense form. In these periods of suffering the soul is experiencing contemplation even though it is unaware of the fact. It is indeed the divine action on the soul which is the cause of the suffering. See Bk. II, chap. 40, n. 5.

bitter as wormwood, there comes the third period, that of exaltation. That is when the soul is partly reformed in feeling, and it is a time of great peace. And then comes the fourth period, that of glorification, and that is when the soul is fully reformed in the happiness of heaven. For these souls that are called from sin and justified by being made to pass in one way or another through the fire and water of trials are then exalted and will finally be glorified. Our Lord will give them all that they desired while they were here, and more. He will raise them above all the elect and make them equal to the cherubim and seraphim, since they excelled all others in knowledge and love in this life.

So let him that would come to this exaltation not fear the justification, for it is the way he must go. By the prophet our Lord spoke words of great comfort to all souls that are tried in the fire of suffering: *Puer meus noli timere; si transieris per ignem, flamma non nocebit te* (Isa. xliii. 2). My child, if you pass through fire, do not fear, for the flame shall not hurt you. It will cleanse you from all the defilement of the flesh and make you able to receive the spiritual fire of the love of God. And that cleansing must be accomplished first, for, as I said before, the soul cannot else be reformed in feeling.

THE TWENTY-NINTH CHAPTER

How it sometimes happens that beginners and those still making progress in the spiritual life show more outward signs of love than the perfect, and yet their love is not really greater

BUT you may say, how can this be so? For there are many souls still at the beginning of their conversion who receive great spiritual favours. Some have great sorrow for their sins, and some great devotion and fervour in prayer, and

spiritual light in their understanding; some again feel a consoling heat and great sweetness, and yet these souls never
really enter this peaceful darkness that I have been speaking
of; they never arrive at this ardent desire and continual
thought of God. You ask whether these souls are reformed
in feeling or not? It seems that they are, inasmuch as they
have these exceptional spiritual experiences which other
men, who are reformed only in faith, do not have.

To this I say, that it seems to me that these spiritual experiences, whether they consist of feelings of compunction,
or devotion, or imaginary visions, are not the experiences
which will come to a soul by the grace of contemplation. I
do not deny that they are genuine and the result of God's
grace. But the souls which experience them are not yet reformed in feeling, and have not yet come to perfection nor
to the burning spiritual love of Jesus that they may come to.
And yet it often seems otherwise; that such souls feel more
of the love of God than those who have attained perfection,
inasmuch as their experience manifests itself much more
exteriorly, in tears, prayers, prostrations, locutions, and
other bodily phenomena. So much so, that they seem to an
onlooker to be continually in an ecstasy of love. And though
I do not think that it is so, I am aware that these experiences,
the fervours of devotion and compunction that they feel, are
gifts of God's grace granted to chosen souls to draw them
from the love of the world and the lusts of the flesh that have
for long had possession of their hearts. And they cannot be
withdrawn from such things except by these sensible experiences.

And yet the fervour which manifests itself so strongly in
exterior signs is not the result only of the greatness of their
love; it is on account of the weakness of their souls, which
are not able to bear the lightest touch of God. They are still,
as it were, carnal, entangled in the flesh, and not yet freed

from it by the mortification of the spirit. And therefore the least touch of love or the smallest spark of spiritual light sent from heaven into such a soul is so great and consoling, so sweet and delectable, so superior to any pleasure it ever felt before in the senses or in the things of earth, that the soul is overwhelmed by it. It is something so new, so sudden, and so unfamiliar, that the soul has not the strength to bear it, but breaks out in tears, sobs, and other exterior manifestations. Just as, when new wine in all its vigour is put into an old barrel, the barrel swells and almost bursts, until the wine has fermented and got rid of all impurity. But when the wine has purified itself and cleared, it does not work any more, and the barrel remains intact. So with one who has grown old in sin; when he receives a touch of the love of God, so vital and so powerful is it, that the body would be in danger of breaking down if God did not keep it intact. Even as it is, the eyes break out in tears and the mouth in words, but that is more because of the weakness of the soul than the greatness of its love. Afterwards, when the fermentation caused by this fervour has removed all the impurity from the soul, its love becomes pure and tranquil. Both body and soul are in greater peace, and yet the soul has much more love than previously, though this manifests itself less exteriorly. For the soul is now at rest within, and its fervour scarcely shows itself. And so I say that these souls that feel such great bodily fervour, though they have great grace, are not yet reformed in feeling, though they have gone a long way towards it. For I think that a man who has been much defiled by sin will not be reformed in feeling unless he is first purified by strong feelings of compunction. On the other hand a soul that has not been much defiled by the love of the world, but has remained innocent of serious sin may come to this reform more easily and more quietly, without great outward manifestations of fervour.

The truth is, I think, that consolation and the fervour that a soul feels when it is in the state of a beginner or while it is still advancing, are, as it were, spiritual food sent from heaven to strengthen it on the way. Just as a pilgrim who journeys all day without food or drink and is nearly overcome with fatigue reaches at last a good inn, where he eats and drinks and is refreshed for the time being, so in the spiritual sphere, it sometimes happens that a devout soul wishing to renounce the love of the world and to love God, and directing all its efforts to this end, spends the whole day in prayer and spiritual or bodily exercises without feeling either consolation or delight. Then our Lord, who has pity on all His creatures, sends it His spiritual food and consoles it with such devotion as seems good to Him, lest it should fall by the way or yield to depression or complaint. And when the soul feels any spiritual consolation, when it fares well at the end of the day through the experiencing of grace, it considers itself well recompensed for all the labour and difficulty that it has undergone.

Souls that have already advanced far in grace have the same experience. They feel the effect of the grace of the Holy Ghost, both in the understanding of spiritual matters, and in love of them. But they are not yet reformed in feeling; they are not yet perfect. And why? because all these experiences come to them, as it were, unexpectedly; they come and go before they are aware of them, and they cannot attain them again. They do not know where to seek them or where to find them. They are not yet at home with these experiences, and are not yet masters of themselves by stability of thought and a continual desire for Jesus, and their eyes are not yet opened to the sight of spiritual things, although they are fast approaching that state. And so they are not yet reformed in feeling and have not yet the full gift of contemplation.

THE THIRTIETH CHAPTER

How a man shall come to a knowledge of his own soul and how he should direct his love to Jesus, God and man in one Person

A SOUL that wishes to come to the knowledge of spiritual things must first know itself, for it cannot know a higher nature unless it first knows its own. It does this when it is so recollected and detached from the consideration of earthly things and from the use of the senses that it knows itself as it is in its own nature, apart from the body. So if you wish to know your soul as it is, do not look for it as though it was contained in your heart in the way that your heart is contained in your body.[1] If you look for it in that way you will never find it. The more you seek it as though it were something material, the further you will be from it. For your soul is not material but an invisible and living substance.[2] It is not hidden and contained in your body as a lesser object

[1] It is certainly tempting to think that there may be here an allusion to *The Revelations of Dame Julian of Norwich*. In chap. 67 of her *Revelations* she says, "And then Our Lord opened my spiritual eye and showed me my soul in midst of my heart." Hilton appears to have taken occasion in *The Scale* to refute views of which he disapproved (see notes to chaps. 26 and 44 of Bk. I), and if he did know Julian's writings, he may have thought it well to point out that her experience, whatever it was, only provided an imaginative representation which was not strictly in accordance with the facts. But it is open to question whether any relation can really be shown to exist between *The Scale* and *The Revelations*, though the French editors think that Julian was influenced by *The Scale*. Her revelations took place in 1373, and she says that she received further enlightenment on them twenty years later. In that case her book could not have been finished before 1393. If Hilton wrote *The Scale* at the very end of his life, he might have referred to Julian's expression here, but that he did so is only surmise.

[2] Hilton here and in the next paragraph says a *life* (cf. Bk. I, chap. 43, n. 1).

229

may be hidden and contained in a greater one, but it contains and animates your body, and is of much greater power.

If, then, you wish to find your soul, you must withdraw your mind from everything material, including your own body, and as far as possible from all your five senses, and reflect on the nature of a rational soul in a purely intellectual manner, using the same process that you would to know a virtue, truth, or humility, or any other.[3] In the same way consider that your soul is a living substance, immortal and invisible, and that it has power to know the Supreme Truth and to love the Supreme Goodness which is God. When you appreciate this, then you understand something of yourself; and do not seek to do so in any other way. And the more fully and clearly that you can reflect on the nature and the excellence of a rational soul, what it is, and what is its natural manner of operation, the better you will see yourself. It is very difficult for a soul that is unrefined and weighed down by the flesh to know itself, or an angel, or God. It imagines a material form, and thinks in that way to have an idea of itself, and so of God and other spiritual Beings. But that cannot be, for spiritual things are known by the intellect and not by the imagination. The soul comes to know itself by the intellect, just as it sees by its intellect that the virtue of justice consists in giving to every man his due.

[3] Hilton's remarks here naturally recall what he said in Book I about considering the nature of the soul and getting to know its powers (chaps. 40 and 42). He says nothing in Book II to contradict anything that he said in Book I, and the essential process of "seeking Jesus" by desire forms the basis of all the soul's activity in both Books (cf. Bk. II, chap. 24, n. 2). Taking all he had said in Book I about considering the nature of the soul for granted, and referring to the same process, he is here refining on it. The point which he will develop in this chapter is that in the higher kinds of mystical experience the imagination must be transcended, and he is introducing that idea by giving a warning against considering the soul in a crude, imaginative way.

But I do not say that your soul should remain satisfied with
this knowledge, but through this it should seek a higher
knowledge of something above itself, that is of the nature of
God. For your soul is a spiritual mirror in which you may
see God. [4] So in the first place you must discover your mirror
and keep it bright and clean from the defilement of the flesh
and the vanity of the world, and then hold it well up from
the earth, so that you may be able to see it, and also our Lord
reflected in it. All the elect are striving for this in intention
all their lives, even though they are not aware of it. And so,
as I have said before, many souls at the beginning and in the
early stages of their spiritual lives experience great fervour
and sweetness of devotion and seem all on fire with love, and
yet they have not got perfect love or the intellectual knowledge of God. For be sure of this, that however much fervour a soul feels, even if it feels so much that it thinks the
body cannot bear it, or that it dissolves in tears, as long as its
conception of God is principally, or altogether, in the
imagination and not in the intellect, it has not yet attained
perfect love or contemplation.

Our love of God has three stages. [5] All are good but they

[4] cf. Richard of St Victor in the *Benjamin Minor*, chap. 72 (P.L.,
cxcvi, col. 51). The chapter is entitled *Quomodo per plenam cognitionem
sui sublevetur animus ad contemplationem Dei*. Richard also uses the figure of
the mirror, but we cannot say whether Hilton got his idea from this place.

[5] It is to be noted that Hilton marks three progressive stages in love
and not in knowledge, but progress in love will follow progress in knowledge, and in fact Hilton distinguishes his three stages by the degrees of
knowledge appropriate to them. Of these three stages the first is simply
the state of the ordinary Christian; Hilton says so explicitly. In the second
stage the imagination is enabled by special grace to picture Christ in His
humanity. It is clear that Hilton means no less than this; what came later
to be called an imaginative vision. In the third stage there is some sort of
intellectual perception (*ghostly sight* is his expression) of the divinity.
He goes on to make it clear that this knowledge is purely in the intellect
and is free from sense images and the use of the imagination. But it is with

become progressively better. The *first* is by faith alone without any knowledge of God given in the imagination or the intellect by grace. This love exists in every soul that is reformed in faith, even if it only has the lowest degree of charity. It is good, for it is sufficient for salvation. In the *second* stage of love the soul knows God through faith, but also knows Him in the humanity of Jesus through the imagination. This love, in which the imagination is moved by grace, is of a much higher kind, because there is a certain contemplation of our Lord's humanity. In the *third* kind of love the soul's contemplation extends to the divinity that is united to the humanity, in so far as this is possible here. It is the best and highest of the three and is perfect love, and a soul does not experience it until it is reformed in feeling. Beginners, and those who are still advancing in their spiritual course, do not possess love of this kind, for they cannot think of Jesus or love Him in His divinity, but only in a human and carnal fashion in His human nature, and all their thoughts and affections are exercised on Him in that state. They reverence Him as man, and adore Him and love Him principally through their imaginations, and they cannot go beyond this. For example, if they have sinned and wronged God, they think that He is angry with them as a man would be whom they had wronged, and so they cast themselves with great contrition,

---

love that he is primarily concerned, and his teaching in this chapter may be summarized by saying that in the second stage, which is the first that is truly contemplative, love will spring principally from the imaginative perception of Christ's humanity, but the soul should endeavour to go beyond this to a love which springs from the perception of His divinity. This perception is necessarily in the intellect and not in the imagination or the senses, and is the result of a special divine illumination. Our love for God as it becomes more intense becomes more spiritualized, more independent of the body and its powers, and in saying this Hilton is, of course, only in line with the common teaching.

as it were at the feet of our Lord and ask His mercy. This way of acting is excellent, but it is not as spiritual as it might be. In the same way, when they wish to adore God, they imagine our Lord in bodily form surrounded by a bright light, and they adore Him with reverent fear, and throw themselves on His mercy, begging Him to do with them what He wills. So, when it is a question of loving God, they consider Him, adore Him, and reverence Him in the passion, or some other act of [Christ's] life, but as man, and not yet as God in man. However, these considerations move them greatly to the love of God.

All this is good and inspired by grace, but it is much less elevated than is the use of the intellect in which the soul by grace contemplates the divinity in the humanity. For there are two natures in our Lord Jesus, the human and the divine. And just as the divine is superior to the human and more excellent, so the contemplation of the divinity in the humanity is more excellent, more intellectual, and more meritorious, than the contemplation of the humanity alone, whether it is seen in its mortal state or glorified. In the same way, the love that a soul experiences in contemplating the divinity in the human nature, when this is revealed by grace, is more excellent, more spiritual, and more meritorious, than the fervour of devotion that is excited by the imagination of the humanity alone, however much this may be accompanied by outward manifestations. The love of the humanity is only a human thing in comparison with the love of the divinity. For our Lord does not show Himself to the imagination as He is, nor does the imagination grasp the fact of His divinity,[6] for on account of the frailty of the flesh the soul could not support such an experience.

But in order that souls who are unable to have this intel-

[6] I have thus translated, "Our Lord does not show Him in imagination as He is, nor that He is."

lectual contemplation of the divinity should not be led astray
in their devotion, but that they should be consoled and
strengthened through some sort of inward contemplation of
Jesus to forsake sin and the love of the world, God tempers
the incomprehensible light of His Godhead and encloses it
in the bodily form of the humanity [of Christ]. He shows
this to the eyes of the soul, and gives it spiritual nourishment
through the love of His precious body. And this love is of
such power that it puts to death all evil love in the soul, and
gives it strength to endure bodily penance and other bodily
suffering, as need may arise, for the love of Jesus. And this
is the way our Lord protects a chosen soul from the fire of
worldly love under His shadow. For as in order that there
may be a shadow there must be light and a material object, so
it might be said that this spiritual shadow cast on a devout
soul comes from the blessed incomprehensible light of the
divinity and the human nature which is joined to it. It is of
this shadow that the prophet says: *Spiritus ante faciem nostram
Christus Dominus; sub umbra ejus vivemus inter gentes* (Lam. iv.
20). Our Lord Christ is a spirit before our face; under His
shadow we shall live among the nations. That is, our Lord
Jesus in His divinity is a spirit that cannot be seen as He is in
His blessed light by us who live in the flesh. Therefore we
must live under the shadow of His humanity as long as we
are here. But although it is true that this love, which works
through the imagination, is good, [7] nevertheless a soul should
desire to have spiritual love of the divinity, for that is the end
and the perfect happiness of the soul, and all other bodily
contemplations are but means leading to it. I do not say that

[7] The value of this love of the humanity of Christ with its sense appeal
is brought out by St Bernard, *Serm. in Cant.*, Serm., xx, n.6–9 (P.L.,
CLXXXIII, col. 870–2). He does not, however, as Hilton does, bring out
the desirability of passing to a higher form of love, which is yet not
separated from the humanity of Christ.

we ought to separate the divinity from the humanity, but we should love Jesus as both God and man, God existing in man and man in God, but our love should be of a spiritual and not a carnal nature. [8]

Our Lord taught this to Mary Magdalen, whose vocation it was to be a contemplative, when He said: *Noli me tangere, nondum enim ascendi ad Patrem meum* (John xx. 17). Do not touch Me, I have not yet ascended to My Father. That is to say, Mary Magdalen loved our Lord Jesus ardently before His passion, but her love was largely carnal and only spiritual to a small extent. She believed firmly that He was God, but she did not love Him greatly as God, for she could not at that time, and so she allowed all her affection and all her thought to dwell on Him in His human state. And our Lord did not blame her, but gave her great praise. When He had arisen from the dead and appeared to her, she would have adored Him with the same sort of love that she did before, and then our Lord forbade her and said, "Do not touch Me." That is; Do not let your heart and your love rest in the human nature that you see with your bodily eyes. For in that state I have not ascended to My Father, that is, I am not equal to the Father; for in My humanity I am less than He. Touch Me not in this state, but fix your mind and your love on that state in which I am equal to the Father; that is in My divinity. Love, know, and adore Me as God and man, and not as man only. So you shall touch Me, for being both God and man I am to be loved and adored as God who took the nature of man. And therefore treat Me as God in your heart and in your

[8] This sentence is very note-worthy and illustrates to what an extent Hilton's teaching is indeed Christo-centric. His highest form of spiritual experience is love springing from an immediate apprehension of the divinity united to the human nature of Christ, a coming to the divinity through the humanity—"the soul by grace contemplates the divinity in the humanity" (p. 233). When he says this he can only mean that the soul is divinely illumined to *realize* in some way the fact of Christ's divinity.

love, and adore Me in your intellect as Jesus, God Incarnate, Supreme Truth, Supreme Goodness and Blessed Life, for that is what I am. This is what our Lord taught her as I understand it, and so He teaches all other souls to act that are fit for contemplation.

Nevertheless, it is good for souls that are not disposed by nature, or are not yet raised by grace, to persevere by their own efforts in the imagination with human love, until greater grace is given to them. It is not prudent for a man to leave something good until he knows and has tried something better. And the same may be said of other sorts of phenomena that are physical in their nature, such as hearing sweet song, and the feeling of comforting heat, or perceiving certain lights, or the taste of sweet flavours. These are not spiritual experiences, for spiritual experiences occur in the powers of the soul, principally in the intellect and the will, and little in the imagination. But these experiences are in the imagination, and therefore they are not spiritual. At their best they are only outward signs of the inner grace that is experienced in the powers of the soul. This can be proved clearly from Holy Scripture: *Apparuerunt apostolis dispertitae linguae tamquam ignis, seditque supra singulos eorum Spiritus Sanctus* (Acts ii. 3). The Holy Ghost appeared to the apostles in the day of Pentecost in the form of tongues of fire, and inflamed their hearts, and rested upon each of them. Now it is certain that the Holy Ghost, that is the invisible God Himself, was not that fire that was seen, nor the burning that was felt; but He was invisibly felt in the powers of their souls, for He enlightened their reason and kindled their affections through His blessed presence so clearly and ardently that they suddenly possessed the intellectual knowledge of truth and the perfection of love, as our Lord promised when He said, *Spiritus Sanctus docebit vos omnem veritatem* (John xvi. 13). The Holy Ghost will teach you all truth. So the fire and the burning was nothing else than a bodily sign showed exteriorly in witness of the grace that was experienced interiorly. And as it was with them, so it is with other souls that are visited and interiorly enlightened by the Holy Ghost, and have along with that experience sensible feelings and consolations in witness of the interior grace. And yet that experience does not come, I think, to all perfect souls, but only to those to whom God wills to send it. It is not good for imperfect souls that have the sensible feelings, and have not yet received the interior grace, to rely too much on such feelings, but let them make use of them in so far as they help the soul to fix its thought more steadily on God and to feel greater love. For some of these experiences may be genuine and some false, as I said before.

THE THIRTY-FIRST CHAPTER

The meaning of the expression reform in feeling as applied to the soul; the way in which it is brought about, and how the doctrine is found in the writings of St Paul

I HAVE said something about reform in faith and have also touched a little on the further reform in feeling to which the soul may advance. Not that it is my intention to confine God's operations to limits laid down by me, to say that God must act in a soul in this way and in no other. I do not mean to do that, but I merely say that I think God acts in this way with some of his creatures. No doubt He also acts in other ways that exceed my knowledge and my experience. But in whatever way He acts, and by whatever means, in a long time or a short, with great labour for the soul or with little, if the same end is attained, namely the perfect love of Him, then all is well. For if He chooses to give the full grace of contemplation to a soul in one day without any labour on its part, as He very well can, then such grace is as fruitful for the soul as twenty years of trials and sufferings, mortifications and purifications. Take my words then in the sense that I have said and that I intend to give them. For now with God's help I will speak more fully of reform in feeling, of what it consists, how it is brought about, and of the nature of the spiritual experiences that it brings to a soul.

But first, in order that you should not think that this expression of reforming a soul in feeling is mere fiction or fantasy, I will base myself on St Paul's words: *Nolite conformari huic saeculo, sed reformamini in novitate sensus vestri* (Rom. xii. 2). That is: You are reformed in faith by grace, do not now conform to the way of the world in pride, covetousness, and other sins, but be reformed in newness of feeling.[1] You see here that St Paul speaks of reform in feeling, and what that new feeling is he relates in another place. *Ut impleamini in agnitione voluntatis ejus, in omni intellectu et sapientia spirituali* (Col. i. 9). That is, we pray that you may be filled with the knowledge of God's will, with understanding, and every

[1] *Reformamini in novitate sensus vestri.* This text of St Paul is the origin of Hilton's phrase "reform in feeling" (cf. Bk. II, chap. 5, n. 1). It is evident that by *feeling* Hilton meant much more than we mean when we talk of having a feeling that something is going to happen, or than the expression, "I have a feeling that God loves me", would ordinarily mean. It is clear from all he says about this state (see for example the beginning of the next chapter) that he meant by it the quasi-direct knowledge of God that comes from infused contemplation as distinct from the knowledge of faith.

His translation is a legitimate interpretation of the Latin as it stands, though it is to be noted that it does not in fact appear to be the correct interpretation of the Greek, where the word used is νους. "Be transformed by the renovation of your mind" would be a literal translation, and the sense would seem to be that given to it by Mgr Knox, "there must be an inward change, a remaking of your minds", which hardly implies all that Hilton meant by the phrase.

sort of spiritual wisdom. This is to be reformed in feeling. For you must know that the soul feels or knows in two ways; externally by the five bodily senses, and internally by the spiritual senses, which are properly the powers of the soul, memory, understanding, and will. When grace perfects these powers to understand God's will and His wisdom, then the soul has this new and supernatural knowledge. The truth of this is shown in another place: *Renovamini spiritu mentis vestrae, et induite novum hominem, qui secundum Deum creatus est in justitia, sanctitate, et veritate* (Eph. iv. 23, 24). Be spiritually renewed; that is, be reformed, not in your external senses, nor in your imagination, but in the higher part of your intellect. And put on the new man that is conformed to God in justice. That is: your reason, where the image of God is properly found, must through the grace of the Holy Ghost be clothed in the new light of truth, holiness, and justice, and then it is reformed in feeling. For the soul is reformed when it has a perfect knowledge of God. St Paul says: *Exspoliantes veterem hominem cum actibus suis; induite novum, qui renovatur in agnitione Dei, secundum imaginem ejus, qui creavit eum* (Col. iii. 9, 10). Put off the old man with all his acts; that is, put away the love of the world and all worldly behaviour, and put on the new man; that is, be renewed in the likeness of God by knowing Him.

You can see by these words that St Paul would have men's souls reformed by the perfect knowledge of God, for that is the new knowledge that he is speaking about. And so basing myself on him, I shall with the grace of God speak more fully of this reform. There are two ways of knowing God. One is principally in the imagination, with the intellect playing little part; chosen souls at the beginning of their spiritual course, and while they are advancing in it, possess this sort of knowledge. They know God and love Him in a human and not in a spiritual way, with human affection, and using, as I have already said, corporeal images. This sort of knowledge is good; it is, as it were, the milk by which they are nourished in their spiritual childhood, till they are able to come to their Father's table and receive solid bread from His hand. The other sort of knowledge is principally in the intellect, strengthened and illumined by the Holy Ghost, and in it the imagination plays little part. For the intellect is the mistress and the imagination is her maid, serving her when occasion arises. This knowledge is solid bread, food for perfect souls, and it is reform in feeling.

THE THIRTY-SECOND CHAPTER

How God opens the eyes of the soul to reveal Himself to it, not all at once, but by degrees; and of an example illustrating the three kinds of reform

WHEN a soul has been withdrawn from the love of the world and has been justified and tested, mortified and purified, in the way that I have explained, God in His goodness and in His own time reforms it in feeling. He opens the eyes of the soul, illuminating the intellect so that it can know Him. He does not do it all at once, but gradually, a little at a time, as the soul is able to bear it. The soul does not comprehend God's Nature, for no creature in heaven or earth may do that, nor does it see Him as He is, for that is reserved for the happiness of heaven. But it sees that He is immutable Being, supreme Power, Truth, and Goodness, blessed Life, and everlasting Happiness. The soul sees all this and much more, not in an obscure, abstract fashion, lacking all sweetness, as does a theologian who knows Him only in a scientific way by the mere use of his reason. But its intellect is strengthened and illumined by the gift of the Holy Ghost, and it sees Him with great reverence and ardent love, with spiritual sweetness and heavenly joy, more clearly and more fully than can be described.[1]

This experience, though it only lasts a short time, is so elevated and of such effect that it takes away from the soul all thought and remembrance of earthly things, so that it would enjoy nothing else if it could. This experience is the source of all the soul's activity, for in it it reverences God in man as Truth, admires Him as Power, loves Him as Goodness. This knowledge of God, and the love that springs from it, may be called the reforming in faith and feeling that I have spoken of. It is with faith, for it is still obscure in comparison to the full knowledge that we shall have in heaven. For then we shall see not only that God is, but we shall see Him as He is. In St John's words: *Tunc videbimus eum sicuti est* (1 John iii. 2). Then we shall see Him as He is. Nevertheless it is in *feeling* also in comparison with the blind knowledge that a soul has only by faith. For the soul that has had this experience knows something of the divine nature of Jesus through this supernatural knowledge, but a soul that has not had it has only belief in the fact of His divinity.

That you may better understand what I mean, I will explain these three degrees of reform in the soul by the example of three men standing in the sun. One is blind, the second can see but his eyes are closed, the third has his eyes open.

The blind man has no way of knowing that he is in the sun except by believing, if an honest man tells him so. He represents a soul that is only reformed in faith, that believes in God according to the teaching of the Church, but has no direct knowledge of what it believes. This state is sufficient for salvation.

The second man sees the light of the sun, but he does not

---

[1] This is the true contemplative experience that Hilton is referring to, when the soul begins to have some direct awareness of the Being of God.

see it clearly, for his eyelids prevent him. But, nevertheless, he sees a glimmer of light through them, and he represents a soul that is reformed in faith and feeling, and so one who is a contemplative. By grace he sees something of the divinity of Jesus, but he does not see it clearly or fully, for his eyelids, that is his bodily nature, are still a barrier between him and the divine nature of Jesus, and prevent him from having a clear view of it. But according as he has more or less grace, he sees through the barrier that Jesus is God, and that He is supreme Goodness, supreme Being, divine Life, and the source of all other goodness. The soul sees this through grace in spite of its union with the body. But the purer and more refined the soul becomes, and the more it is independent of the body, the clearer is its view and the stronger its love of the divinity in Jesus. This experience is so powerful that, even if no other man alive would believe in Jesus, or love Him, he would do so none the less. His knowledge is so real that he is unable not to believe.

The third man, who sees the sun openly, does not believe, because he has unimpeded vision. He represents a blessed soul that sees the face of God openly in the happiness of heaven without any barrier of the body or of sin intervening. Faith does not enter in, and therefore he is fully reformed in feeling.

In this life a soul cannot get beyond the second of these reforms, for this is the state of perfection and the high-road to heaven. But all souls that are in this state are not equally far advanced. Some have this experience only to a slight degree; it lasts a short time and comes at rare intervals; some have a higher degree, lasting a longer time and coming more frequently, and some have it in a very intense form over long periods of time as the result of abundant grace. And yet they all have the gift of contemplation.[2] For the soul does not

[2] Hilton gives here a valuable exposition of the various degrees to

have perfect knowledge of God all at once. At first it sees only a little, and then it advances and attains a greater experience, and as long as it is in this life it may increase in knowledge and love of God. And indeed I do not know what remains for a soul that has enjoyed a little of this experience but, leaving everything, to strive for a clearer knowledge and deeper love of Jesus, and in Him of all the Holy Trinity.

The knowledge of God is, as I see it, the opening of heaven to the eyes of a pure soul of which the saints speak in their writings. Not as if, as some think, the opening of heaven means that a soul can see in imagination how our Lord Jesus sits above the firmament in His majesty in light as bright as that of a hundred suns. It is not so. However high a man sees in that way, he does not see the heaven of the spirit. The higher above the sun he rises by his imagination, the lower he falls on earth. However, this way of considering our Lord may suit simple souls who do not know better how to seek Him who is invisible.

THE THIRTY-THIRD CHAPTER

How Jesus is heaven to the soul, and why He is called fire[1]

WHAT does heaven mean for a rational soul? Nothing else than Jesus, God. For if that is heaven which is above every-

which contemplation may be present in the soul.

[1] In the general plan I have called the section beginning with this chapter *the nature of contemplation*. The distinction between this and the previous section which was *the contemplative life* is admittedly not very pronounced, but it must be remembered that these titles are only convenient labels and the divisions I have assigned to them more or less arbitrary. It remains true, nevertheless, that in the previous section (chaps. 21–32) Hilton does, as it were, stand back and view the career of the contemplative as a whole without attempting much analysis of the actual ex-

thing else, then only God is heaven to the human soul, for
He alone is above the nature of the soul. And if a soul is able
through grace to know the divine nature of Jesus, then indeed it sees heaven, for it sees God.

Many fail to understand statements made about God, because they do not understand them in a spiritual sense. Scripture says that a soul that wishes to find God must lift up
its eyes and seek God above itself. Some wishing to carry
this out understand this expression, "above itself", as referring to a higher and more honourable position in the
physical sense, as one element or planet is set in a higher or
more honourable position. But this is not the meaning when
the expression is applied to spiritual things. A soul is above
all material things not by its physical position, but because
of the spirituality and dignity of its nature. In the same way
God is above all bodily and spiritual creatures not by physical position, but through the spirituality and dignity of His
immutable divine nature. And so the man who wishes to
seek God wisely and with hope of success must not reach out
in his thought as though he would climb above the sun and
range across the firmament, and imagine God's glory as
though it were the light of a hundred suns. He ought rather
to put the sun and all the firmament beneath his feet, forgetting them and counting them with all material things as
nothing, and consider both God and himself in a spiritual
way. The soul that can do this sees above itself, and it sees
heaven.

And the word "within" must be understood in the same
way.[2] It is commonly said that a soul should see God within

perience of contemplation. In this section, and particularly in chaps. 34
and 40, he is more concerned with the special relationship of the soul
with God in contemplation.

[2] The same sort of warnings that Hilton gives in this chapter are to be
found in *The Cloud of Unknowing*, see particularly chaps. 51, 52, and 57.

all things and within itself. Certainly God is within all creatures, but not in the way that the kernel is within the shell
of a nut, or as a small object is contained in a large. He is
within all creatures maintaining and conserving them in being. He is there in a spiritual way through the power of His
own divine nature and invisible purity. For just as something
which is very precious and clean is put away most carefully,
so, it may be said, the nature of God, which is very precious,
very pure, very far removed from all corporeal substance, is
hidden within all things. And so he who will seek God within must first forget all material things, for they are not within, and he must forget his own body and even his own soul,
and think of that uncreated nature that is God, who made
him, gave him life, and maintains it, and endowed him with
understanding, memory, and love. For he has these things
through the power of God. This is how the soul must act
when grace touches it, or else it will be of little use to seek
God in itself or in creatures.

In the same way it is said in Holy Scripture that God is
light. St John says: *Deus lux est* (1 John i. 5). God is light.
That must not be taken in a physical sense, but in this way.
God is light; that is God is truth, for truth is spiritual light.
So he who by grace has the clearest knowledge of truth has
the clearest knowledge of God. But there is a resemblance
to the light of the physical world in this way. As the sun reveals itself and all material objects by its light, so God, who
is truth, reveals Himself to man's intellect, and in so doing
imparts all the knowledge of spiritual matters that man needs
to have. The prophet says: *Domine, in lumine tuo videbimus
lumen* (Ps. xxxv. 10). We shall see Thee that art truth by
Thyself. In the same way it is said that God is fire: *Deus noster
ignis consumens est* (Heb. xii. 29). God is a consuming fire.
That is to say, God is not the element fire that heats objects
and burns them, but God is love and charity. For as fire con-

sumes all material objects that are inflammable, so the love of God burns and consumes all sin out of the soul, and makes it pure, as fire purifies metal. These expressions, and all others that Holy Scripture applies to God in comparing Him with material objects, must be understood in a spiritual sense, or else they have no meaning. The reason why such expressions are applied to God in Scripture is this. We are so materially minded that we cannot speak of God or think of Him unless we use such expressions to begin with. But when the eye of the spirit is opened by grace to have some sight of God, then the soul can easily enough understand these material expressions in a spiritual way.

This opening of the eyes of the spirit to the knowledge of the Godhead I call *reform in faith and feeling*. For then the soul understands something of what it knew before only by faith, and that is the beginning of contemplation, of which St Paul said: *Non contemplantibus nobis quae videntur, sed quae non videntur; quae enim videntur, temporalia sunt, quae autem non videntur, aeterna sunt* (2 Cor. iv. 18). Our contemplation is not of things visible, but invisible. For the visible things pass away, but the invisible things are eternal. It is these that every soul should desire to obtain, partially while it is still on earth, and fully in the happiness of heaven. For it is in that sight and knowledge of God that the full happiness and eternal life of a rational soul consists. *Haec est autem vita aeterna: ut cognoscant te unum Deum, et quem misisti Jesum Christum* (John xvii. 3). This is eternal life, that thy chosen souls know Thee, Father, and Thy Son whom Thou has sent, as the one true God.

THE THIRTY-FOURTH CHAPTER

How it is not through created love that a soul comes to the spiritual vision of God, but it is through uncreated Love, that is God Himself

BUT since the soul's happiness and its end lies in this knowledge of God, perhaps you are surprised that I said before that a soul should desire nothing but the love of God, and said nothing about its desiring this knowledge.

In answer, I say that the knowledge of God constitutes the complete happiness of a soul, but this happiness comes not from the knowledge only but from the love which follows it. But, because love follows knowledge and not the other way about, the soul's happiness is said to consist principally in the knowledge of God, but with love accompanying it, and the greater the knowledge, the greater the love. But it was because the soul cannot attain this knowledge or the love that comes from it without Love, that I said you ought to desire Love.[1] For it is Love that brings a soul to this knowledge, and that Love is not the soul's love for God, but God's love for the sinful soul that is itself unable to love Him. It is this which brings the soul to this knowledge and the love that follows it. And how that is so I will tell you more clearly.

[1] There is an apparent difficulty. He has just said that love follows knowledge, for we cannot love what we do not know. Now he says that the soul must desire love first, for it is this which brings knowledge. He resolves the difficulty by the distinction which he introduces into the meaning of the word love. The love which brings a soul to the knowledge of God is God Himself. It is the uncreated Love, the Holy Ghost, which gives knowledge, and so leads to the soul's love for God, which is created love.

I have used capitals to distinguish love when it refers to the uncreated Love, the Holy Ghost.

The saints say, and rightly, that there are two sorts of spiritual love. One is called uncreated and the other created. Uncreated Love is God Himself, the Third Person of the Trinity, that is the Holy Ghost. He is uncreated Love; as St John says: *Deus dilectio est* (1 John iv. 8). God is love, that is the Holy Ghost. Created love is the love that the Holy Ghost arouses in a soul at the sight of truth, that is of God. This love is called created because it is brought about by the Holy Ghost. Being created it is not God Himself, but it is the love which the soul feels at the contemplation of God, when it is drawn to Him alone. Now you can see how created love is not the cause of a soul coming to the contemplation of God. For there are some who think that they can love God so ardently, as it were by their own powers, that they can merit the contemplation of Him, but it is not so. It is uncreated Love, that is God Himself, who is the cause of all this knowledge.[2] For owing to sin and the weakness of its human nature the poor, blind soul is so far from the clear knowledge of God and the enjoyment of His love that it would never be able to attain them, if it were not for the infinite greatness of God's love. But because He loves us so much, He gives us His love, that is the Holy Ghost. He is both the giver and the gift, and by that gift makes us know and love Him. This is the love that I said you should desire, this uncreated Love that is the Holy Ghost. And indeed a lesser gift than He will not avail to bring us to the blessed knowledge of God. Therefore we should desire and ask of God only this gift of Love; that in the greatness of His blessed love He would illumine our hearts with His incompre-

---

[2] This is an important passage for it brings out the essentially supernatural character of contemplation. He says explicitly that it is uncreated Love, God Himself, who brings about this experience, and this is in keeping with what he will say later about contemplation as an awareness of grace (see chap. 40, n. 4).

hensible light that we may know Him, and that He may impart His blessed love to us, that as He loves us, so we may love Him in return. St John says : *Nos diligamus Deum, quoniam ipse prior dilexit nos* (1 John iv. 19). Let us love God now, for He has first loved us. He loved us much when He made us in His likeness, but He loved us more when He redeemed us from the power of the devil and from the pains of hell through His precious blood by voluntarily undergoing death in His human nature. But He loves us most when He gives us the gift of the Holy Ghost, that is Love, by which we know Him and love Him and are assured that we are His sons chosen for salvation.[3] We are more bound to Him for this love than

[3] Hilton is here touching on very difficult matter. There are really two questions, the gratuity of grace, and the predestination of certain men in the decrees of God to receive grace.

Since the end of man, the vision of God in heaven, is strictly supernatural, it follows that man can in no way acquire it by his own efforts, he cannot unaided make the jump from the natural to the supernatural plane. He must have the help of God. Nothing that he can do on the purely natural plane, which is the only one he can act on by himself, can merit a supernatural reward. He cannot even take the first step, and this is what Hilton means when he says that, "It is the gift of this uncreated Love that brings about all good in our souls, and it is given to us before we love Him," and "The most that we do is to give voluntary assent to the action of His grace in us. And yet that very act of our will is not our own but is His work" (p. 251).

The more difficult question is the distribution of this grace. We have seen that man by himself can do nothing to merit it, hence it follows that God gives grace to whom He wills, and that those to whom He will give it, and those who will persevere in it, are known to Him from all eternity. These are the elect. It is in this sense that Hilton says in Bk. II, chap, 4, that God has predestined a certain number of souls to salvation, or in Bk. I, chap 21, "Believe you are chosen by the mercy of God to be saved as one of His elect". The Church has always rejected the view put forward by Calvin and Jansenius that God has predestined certain souls to eternal punishment. He wills all men to be saved, and if they are not, it must be through their own responsibility. So Hilton says in this chapter, "The redemption is common to us and to all rational souls, to Jews, and

for any other that He has shown to us, either in creating or
redeeming us. For though He had created us and redeemed
us, if He had not saved us as well, what profit would it have
been for us? None indeed.

The greatest sign of love that has been given to us, it seems
to me, is this, that He gives Himself to our souls in His
divinity. He gave Himself first in His humanity to redeem
us when He offered Himself to the Heavenly Father on the
altar of the Cross. This was a glorious gift and a great token
of love. But when He gives Himself to us in His divinity for
our salvation, and makes us know and love Him, then He
loves us fully, for then He gives Himself to us; He could not
give us more, and less would not suffice us. And for this
reason it is said that the justification of a sinful soul through
the forgiveness of its sins is ascribed and appropriated principally to the power of the Holy Ghost. For the Holy Ghost
is love, and in the justification of a soul God most shows His
love, for He takes away all sin and unites the soul to Himself.
That is the greatest thing that He can do for a soul, and therefore it is appropriated to the Holy Ghost.

The creation of a soul is appropriated to the Father on
account of the supreme power that He shows in creating it.
The redemption is appropriated to the Son, for the supreme
wisdom that He manifested in His humanity, for He over-
came the devil principally through His wisdom and not
through strength. But the justification and salvation of a soul

Saracens, and unworthy Christians. For He died for all souls and redeemed them, if they are willing to profit by His act, and His death sufficed for the redemption of all, though all do not benefit by it." The re-
conciliation of these two clearly revealed facts, namely that grace is an
absolutely free gift which God gives to whom He wills, and yet does not
withhold unjustly from any man, has been a fruitful source of debate, and
perhaps Hilton is right in saying (Bk. II, chap. 45) that it is only through
a very special revelation that God shows "how justly He abandons sinners
and leaves them in their sin without doing them any wrong".

by the forgiveness of sins is appropriated to the Third Person, that is, to the Holy Ghost. For it is in our justification that God most shows His love for us, and it is that which most demands our love in return. Creation we have in common with irrational creatures. He made them out of nothing as He made us, and so this is the work of greatest power but not of greatest love. So, too, the redemption is common to us and to all rational souls, to Jews, and Saracens, and unworthy Christians. For He died for all souls and redeemed them, if they are willing to profit by His act, and His death sufficed for the redemption of all, though all do not benefit by it. And this was the work of wisdom rather than of love. But the justification and sanctification of our souls through the gift of the Holy Ghost is the work only of love, and that is not common to all, but is a special gift to the elect, and is the special work of love for us who are His chosen children.

This is the love of God that I said you should desire, for this love is God Himself, the Holy Ghost. It is the gift of this uncreated Love that brings about all good in our souls, and it is given to us before we love Him. It cleanses us from our sins in the first place, and makes us love Him, strengthens our wills against sin, and moves us to prove ourselves in all virtues by various bodily and spiritual exercises. It moves us also to forsake the love of the world; it slays in us the risings of sin, the desires of the flesh, and worldly anxieties. It shields us from the malicious temptations of the devil and separates us from worldly occupations and from intercourse with the worldly-minded. The uncreated Love of God performs all this when He gives Himself to us. We do no more than allow Him to act and consent to His action. The most that we do is to give voluntary assent to the action of His grace in us. And yet that very act of our will is not our own but is His work, so that it seems He brings about in us whatever is good; and yet we do not realize this. And not only does He act in this way, but He goes further. He opens the eyes of the soul and shows it in a wonderful way the vision of God and the knowledge of Him; as the soul is able to bear it, a little at a time. And by that knowledge all the love of the soul is caught up to Him.

And then the soul begins to know Him in a spiritual way and to love Him ardently; then it sees something of the divine nature of God, how He is all and does everything, and how all good acts and good thoughts are only from Him. For He is supreme Power, and Truth, and Goodness; and therefore every good act is done through Him and by Him, and the honour and the thanks are due to Him alone. For though evil men steal His honour here for a while, neverthe-less at the Last Day truth will show that God did all and man did nothing by himself. Then those who have stolen the honour which is due to God alone, who have not been re-conciled to Him here in this life for the evil they did, will be condemned to death, and God will receive the adoration and the thanks of all the blessed for the work of His grace.

This love is nothing else than God Himself, who does all this in a man's soul by love, and reforms it in feeling to His likeness, as I said before and as I shall further explain. This love brings the fullness of virtues into the soul, virtues which are pure and true, gentle and easy, and it makes their per-formance a matter of love and pleasure; and how this hap-pens I shall go on to tell you. This love elevates the soul from a carnal to a spiritual state, from being immersed in the things of earth to enjoying those of heaven, from the vain consideration of earthly things to the contemplation of the spiritual world and the secrets of God.

THE THIRTY-FIFTH CHAPTER

How some souls love God with sensible fervour and their own
human affections, which are moved both by grace and reason.
And how some love Him more peacefully with a purely spiritual
love by the special inspiration of the Holy Ghost

IT may be said that he who possesses the highest degree of
love in this life is most pleasing to God, and he will have the
clearest vision of Him in heaven precisely because he had the
highest love on earth.

Love of this nature cannot be obtained by a man's own
efforts, as some think. It comes by the gift of God's grace,
after much effort of body and soul. For there are some lovers
of God who force themselves to love Him, as it were by
their own efforts. They strain themselves with great vio-
lence, and aspire so urgently that they break out into sensible fervour. They act as though they would pull God down
to them from heaven, saying in their hearts and with their
mouth, "Ah, Lord, I love Thee, and I will love Thee. I would
for Thy love, suffer death." And acting in this way they feel
great fervour and great grace. And indeed I think such action
is good and meritorious, if it is tempered with humility and
discretion. Nevertheless, these people have not the gift of
Love that I spoke of, and they do not seek it. For a man who
has the gift of Love, that is who contemplates God through
grace in the way that I mean, or who desires to do this, is
careful not to strain beyond his powers after sensible fervour and the experience of God's Love, as though he could
obtain these by bodily strength. He considers himself nothing and able to do nothing by himself. He is as it were dead
and only held up by the mercy of God. He sees that God is
everything and does everything, and therefore he asks nothing but the gift of His Love. Since he sees that his own love

is nothing, he would have God's Love, for that is all he needs. What he prays for and what he desires is that God would illumine Him with His blessed light, that he might have some awareness of His gracious presence, for then he could not but love Him. And this is the way that the gift of Love, that is God, comes to a soul.

The more the soul annihilates itself by grace at the sight of God's truth, sometimes without any external manifestations of fervour, and the less it is conscious of loving and seeing God, the nearer it is to recognizing the gift of divine Love. For Love is in charge then and acts on the soul, making it forget itself and be aware only of the divine action. And then the soul is more passive than active, and that is the state of pure love. St Paul was referring to this when he said: *Quicumque Spiritu Dei aguntur, ii filii Dei sunt* (Rom. viii. 14). All those who are fashioned by the Spirit of God are God's sons. That is what he calls those souls that are so humble and so obedient to God that they do not rely on themselves, but allow the Holy Ghost to move them and produce in them the feelings of love, while they themselves are completely submissive to His action. These are in a special way the sons of God and are most conformable to His likeness.

Souls that cannot love in this way, but that strive through their own affections and meditations, and by performing external exercises, to bring about in themselves the experience of love with fervour and bodily manifestations do not love in a supernatural way. Their affections are good and meritorious as long as they are humble and know that they are not manifestations of love brought about by grace, but that they are purely human affections, which are the product of reason. Nevertheless, because the soul does what it can, the goodness of God transforms these affections produced by human effort into divinely inspired aspirations, and makes them correspondingly meritorious. It is God's great kind-

ness shown to humble souls to transform all these affections of natural love into the aspirations of His own love.
Affections so transformed may be called aspirations of divine
Love, but ones which are acquired, and not infused directly
by the Holy Ghost.[1] I do not say that a soul can produce even
these human affections by itself without grace, for I know
well that St Paul says that we can neither do nor think
anything good by ourselves. *Non enim quod sufficientes simus
cogitare aliquid ex nobis, quasi ex nobis; sed sufficientia nostra ex
Deo est* (2 Cor. iii. 5). That is, we who love God do not think
that we are sufficient to love or to think anything good by
ourselves, but our sufficiency is from God. For God works
in us both to will and to accomplish, as St Paul says: *Deus est
qui operatur in nobis et velle et perficere pro bona voluntate* (Phil.
ii. 13). It is God who produces in us both good will and its
accomplishment. But certainly aspirations made by the soul
itself according to the general grace that He gives to all the
elect are good. But, as I have explained, they are not the
fruit of special grace and of the touch of God present in the

---

[1] The distinction between affections, or acts, which are produced by
human effort with the ordinary grace of God and those which are directly
infused is well known. Father Baker called them respectively "forced
acts" and "aspirations", and I have adopted his terminology. Hilton talks
about one being transformed into the other, which would naturally imply
simply that one is succeeded by the other. This, however, does not appear
to be quite what he means. So transformed they are affections of divine
love, or aspirations, but with a difference; they are aspirations "by
purchas," he says, which I have translated *acquired*. On the face of it it
is not at all clear what he means. Lower down he talks of ordinary forced
acts being produced indirectly by the Holy Ghost, as distinct from aspirations, which are produced directly. Perhaps he means here that the
acts are still the indirect work of the Holy Ghost, inasmuch as they are
produced through the agency of the powers of the soul, but that they are
the work of a special assisting grace and not of just the ordinary concomi-
tant grace of God. It is a curiously fine distinction which seems peculiar
to Hilton.

soul, as is the case with those who love Him perfectly. For in those who love God imperfectly, Love acts indirectly, through human affections, but in those who love with a perfect love It acts directly by means of Its own aspirations, and for the time being destroys all other affections, whether they are sensible or are simply natural and human,[2] and that is the proper action of divine Love. A pure soul may have this Love partially here through the contemplation of God, but in the happiness of heaven it is perfected by a clear vision of the Godhead, for then all the aspirations of the soul will be divine, and purely in the spirit.

THE THIRTY-SIXTH CHAPTER

How, among all the gifts of God, the gift of Love is the most excellent and the most useful, and how God is the author of all good in those who love Him, and is so only out of love. And how Love makes the exercise of all virtues light and easy

Ask nothing from God, then, but this gift of Love, that is, the Holy Ghost. For among all His gifts there is none so good and useful, so noble or so excellent as this. For this is the only gift of God in which the giver is identified with the gift, and for this reason it is the best and most noble. Prophesying, working miracles, knowledge and counsel, performing great feats of fasting and penance, are all great gifts of the Holy Ghost, but they are not the Holy Ghost, for they can exist in a reprobate soul. And so gifts of this nature are not greatly to be desired and they should not have much store set by them. But the gift of Love is the Holy Ghost, God

[2] Natural and human presumably in the sense that they are produced by the human soul, but uninfluenced by the bodily passions, or emotions. What Fr Baker would call spiritual as distinct from sensible acts.

Himself, and no soul can have this gift and suffer damnation, for it is He who saves it from damnation, and He makes it His son, heir of the heritage of heaven. And this Love, as I said before, is not the love that is created in a soul, but it is the Holy Ghost Himself, uncreated Love, who is the soul's salvation. For He gives Himself to a soul in the first place, before the soul loves Him; and He creates love in a soul and makes it love Him for Himself alone. And further, by this gift the soul loves itself and its fellow-Christians equally for God alone. It is this gift of Love that separates the elect from the reprobate, that makes peace between God and the soul, and unites all the blessed in God. By it God loves us and we love Him and love one another in Him.

Desire, then, this gift of Love before all else, as I have said. For if He will of His grace give it in this way, it will illumine your mind to see truth, that is God and all spiritual things. It will move you to love Him perfectly. He will act as He pleases in your soul, and you will contemplate God with adoration and with sweetness of love, and you will understand His action. He tells us by His prophet that we should do this, saying: *Vacate, et videte quoniam ego sum Deus* (Ps. xlv. 11). Be at rest, and see that I am God. That is, you who are reformed in feeling and have the eyes of your soul opened to see the things of the spirit, be at rest from external activity and see that I am God. That is, "See only what I, Jesus, God and man, do. Behold Me for I do everything. I am Love, and love is the motive of all that I do, and you do nothing. And I will show you the truth of this, for there is no good work or thought in you, except it is through Me, that is through Power, and Wisdom, and Love; otherwise it is of no value. But it is the truth that I, Jesus, am Power and Wisdom and blessed Love, and you are nothing and I am God. It is I that produce all good effects in you, whether of action, or thought, or love, and you contribute nothing.

And yet these good deeds are attributed to you, not because you are their principal author, but because I make them yours out of the love that I have for you. And therefore, since I am God and do all this out of love, cease to consider yourself, attach no importance to yourself, and look at Me and see that I am God who does all this." This is something of what that verse of David means.

See, then, what Love does to a chosen soul reformed in Its likeness, when the intellect is illumined a little to know Jesus and to be aware of His love. Love brings all virtues into the soul and makes them agreeable and pleasant, as it were without effort on the soul's part; for the soul does not struggle to attain them as it did before, but it possesses them easily and rests in them through the gift of Love, that is the Holy Ghost. It is a great comfort and unspeakable joy, when without knowing how, it suddenly finds that humility and patience, temperance and constancy, chastity and purity, and all the other virtues, which were previously laborious, painful, and difficult to practise, have become agreeable and pleasant and strangely easy. There seems to be no great achievement or difficulty about practising them, but only pleasure.[1]

[1] The effect described here is that which theology attributes to the Gifts of the Holy Ghost, which modern writers in particular make to play so large a part in contemplation (e.g. Garrigou-Lagrange, *Perfection chrétienne et contemplation*). St Thomas describes them as *quaedam habituales perfectiones potentiarum animae, quibus redduntur bene mobiles a Spiritu Sancto*. "Certain habitual perfections of the soul's powers whereby these are made readily responsive to the Holy Ghost" (*Summa*, IIa IIae, q, XIX, art. 9). They impart a certain docility and receptiveness to the soul, an aptness to respond to actual graces. We receive the Gifts of the Holy Ghost with sanctifying grace and it is particularly when a higher stage of grace has been attained that their operation becomes manifest. It is, then, quite in accordance with Hilton's view of contemplation as brought about by an intensification of sanctifying grace that the particular effects of the Gifts should become apparent in the contemplative soul.

Others, who possess an ordinary degree of charity and are not so advanced in grace but act according to their own reason, strive against their sins all day in order to acquire virtues, and sometimes they are on top and sometimes underneath, as wrestlers are. Such men do well. They possess virtues through their reason and their will, but there is no pleasure or love in their practice of them, for they have to contend with their own evil inclinations as it were by brute force in order to acquire them. And for that reason they are never really at peace and are never wholly successful. They will have a high reward, but they are not yet sufficiently humble. They have not put themselves fully at God's disposal, for they do not yet see Him.

But a soul that has attained to this intellectual vision of God does not greatly concern itself with striving for virtues; it does not particularly occupy itself with them. All its efforts are directed to fostering its vision of God. It seeks only to fix its mind, to concentrate its love, and as far as possible it is oblivious of everything else. When it does this, then God does indeed override all sins in the soul, and His presence overshadows it and obtains all virtues for it. The soul is so comforted and upheld with the delightful feeling of love that comes from this vision of God that it feels no external trials. And in this manner Love puts to death sin in the soul and reforms it with a new consciousness of virtues.

THE THIRTY-SEVENTH CHAPTER

How in the contemplation of God, which is the fruit of grace,
Love stifles all movements of pride and takes away pleasure and
delight in worldly honour

I WILL treat now more in particular of how Love destroys
sin and infuses virtues into the soul[1]; and first of pride and
its contrary, humility. You must know that there are two
sorts of humility, one is the product of the reason, but the
other is the special gift of Love. Both in fact are gifts of Love,
but the first is the result of Love acting through the reason,
the second is produced by Love directly. The first is imperfect, but the second perfect.[2]

The first sort of humility arises in a man from the consideration of his own sins and misery. Seeing these he thinks
himself unworthy of any grace or of any recompense from
God. It seems to him enough that God should in His mercy
forgive his sins, and he considers himself worse than the
greatest sinner alive, and that everyone is better than he is.
These considerations lead him to put himself in thought below all men, and to fight against the movements of pride as

[1] The idea put forward in these chapters (37–9) that the divine action
in contemplation is in itself purifying to the soul is of course common
teaching and is to be found in *The Cloud of Unknowing* (chap. 12), though
in a notable passage the latter work goes beyond anything that Hilton
says. See *The Cloud*, chap. 25, and Dom Justin McCann in the Introduction to his edition (London, 1952), p. xix.

[2] Hilton goes on to explain that the humility into which a man can
argue himself by considering his sins and frailty is good and necessary,
but it is of an altogether different quality from that which comes to the
soul when the Holy Ghost Himself shows it "how Jesus is all". *The Cloud*
(chap. 13) makes exactly the same distinction between humility which is
the result of considering our own weakness and that which is the result
of realizing "the overabundant love and the worthiness of God in himself".

far as he can, both the pride of the flesh, and spiritual pride. He despises himself and does not give his assent. And if sometimes he falls into pride and sins by taking pleasure in honour, or praise, or his ability, or in anything else, as soon as he perceives it, he is displeased with himself. He feels contrition and asks forgiveness from God, accuses himself humbly to his confessor and receives a penance. This humility is good but it is not yet perfect. It is characteristic of beginners and those still advancing spiritually, and is caused by the consideration of their sins. Love produces it through the reason.

But perfect humility comes when the intellect is illumined to see God. For when the Holy Ghost illumines the reason to see the truth, how God is all and does all, the soul is so carried away by love and joy that it becomes oblivious of itself, and gives itself to the contemplation of God with all the love of which it is capable. It gives no thought to its own unworthiness nor to the sins it has committed. It ignores itself with all its sins and all its good works, as if nothing existed outside God. David was humble in this way, when he said : *Et substantia mea tamquam nihilum ante te* (Ps. xxxviii. 6). O God, the sight of Thy blessed uncreated substance and Thine infinite being shows to me that my substance and the being of my soul is nothing in comparison to Thee. So, too, such a man never judges his neighbour, or considers whether he is better or worse than he is. He thinks of himself and all other men as equal, all alike nothing compared to God. And that is no more than the truth, for all the good in himself or in them is from God. He sees Him as everything, and therefore considers all creatures, himself included, as nothing. The prophet was humble in this way when he said : *Omnes gentes quasi non sint, sic sunt coram eo, et quasi nihilum et inane reputatae sunt ei* (Isa. xl. 17). All men are as nothing and as empty before our Lord, and they are accounted as nothing to Him. That is, compared to the infinite being and immutable nature of God, mankind is nothing. For it was created out of nothing and to nothing it would return unless He kept it in being who created it. This is the truth, and if through grace the soul can realize it, then it has reason to be humble. So when Love opens the inward eyes of the soul to see the truth and all that it entails, the soul begins to be truly humble. For then as a result of this vision of God it sees itself as it is, and it no longer looks at, and relies on, itself, but gives itself entirely to the contemplation of Him. When this experience comes to a man, he considers all worldly joy and honour as nothing. For the pleasures and honour of the world are so slight in comparison with the joy and the love that he feels at the contemplation of God and the knowledge of the truth, that even if he could have them without sin he would not do so. If the world honoured and praised him, showed him all sorts of favours, or gave him great position, it would give him no pleasure. Just as it would give him no pleasure to be skilled in all the seven liberal arts, in theology, and in every conceivable craft, or to have the power of working miracles. He would have no more taste for these things than for gnawing on a dry stick. He would rather forget all these and be alone out of sight of the world, than to think of them and be honoured by all men. For the heart of a true lover of God is so enlarged through a little sight of Him and a little experience of His love that all the pleasures on earth would not suffice to fill a corner of it. And he understands that the miserable lovers of the world, who are as if in an ecstasy of love at the honour paid to them, and who pursue it with all their energies, have no taste for this humility. They are indeed far from it. But the lover of God has this humility continually, without difficulty and without effort, but rather with pleasure and joy. And it gives him joy, not because he has forsaken the honour of the world, for that would be a proud humility such as a hypocrite might possess, but because his mind is illumined to know the truth and the excellence of God through the gift of the Holy Ghost.

This contemplative adoration and love of God brings the soul such comfort and elevates it so powerfully and so sweetly that it can take pleasure and rest in no earthly joy, and it has no wish to do so. The man who experiences it is indifferent to praise or blame, honour or contempt. He does not trouble to be pleased if men's contempt makes him humble, nor to be sorry for their honour and praise. He had rather forget both the one and the other, and to think only of God and get humility in that way. And that is much the safest way for whoever can attain it. David did so when he said: *Oculi mei semper ad Dominum, quia ipse evellet de laqueo pedes meos* (Ps. xxiv. 15). My eyes are always turned to God, for He will preserve my feet from the snares of sin. When a man acts in this way he forsakes himself entirely and casts himself wholly at the feet of God. Then he is in safe keeping, for the shield of truth which he holds protects him so well that no movement of pride will hurt him as long as he keeps behind it. As the prophet says, *Scuto circumdabit te veritas ejus; non timebis a timore nocturno* (Ps. xc. 5). Truth shall encompass you as a shield, if, leaving all other things, you regard it alone. For then you will not fear the terror of the night, that is, you will not be afraid of the spirit of pride, whether it comes in the night or in the day, as the next verse says: *A sagitta volante in die* (Ps. xc. 6). When a man is despised and reproved by men so that he is in danger of falling into depression and sorrow, it may be said that pride comes by night to attack him, but when he is honoured and praised, whether for worldly works or spiritual ones, so that he is tempted to rest with vain pleasure in passing things, pride may be said to be an arrow flying in the day. This arrow is piercing and dangerous; it flies swiftly, strikes unperceived, but wounds mortally. But the lover of God, who turns to Him steadily with devout prayers and assiduous meditation, is so surrounded by the safe shield of truth that he has no fear, for the arrow cannot enter into his soul; even though it reaches him, it glances off and passes harmlessly on. And this, as I understand it, is the way a soul is made humble by the action of the Holy Ghost, that is, the gift of Love. He opens the eyes of the soul to see and love God in peace and security, and quietly and gently He destroys all the movements of pride, the soul knows not how, and so with truth and love He brings in the virtue of humility. Love does all this, but not for all His lovers alike. Some have this grace but for a short time and in a slight degree. They have, as it were, the beginnings of it, and a little trial of it, for their conscience is not yet fully cleansed by grace. And some have it more fully, for they have a clearer sight of God, and they feel more of His love. And some have the highest degree, for they have the full gift of contemplation. But he who has the least degree of it has perfect humility, for he has the gift of perfect love.

THE THIRTY-EIGHTH CHAPTER

How Love gently destroys movements of anger and envy in the soul and re-establishes in it the virtues of peace and patience and perfect charity to other men, as It did especially for the apostles

LOVE acts in a soul at Its own good pleasure, wisely and gently; It has great power to destroy anger, envy, melancholy, and all the passions that come in their train, and it brings into the soul the virtues of patience, gentleness,

peace, and love of one's neighbour. A man who is guided
only by his own reason finds it very hard to be patient, tranquil, sweet-tempered, and charitable to his fellow-men
when they trouble him unreasonably and do him wrong. He
will be greatly tempted to show anger or depression, either
in word or act, or in both. Nevertheless, he is patient, if, in
spite of his emotion, his trouble, and his agitation, he does
not go beyond the bounds of reason, and if he restrains his
hands and his tongue, and is ready to forgive a wrong done
when pardon is asked. His patience is still weak and unde-
veloped, but it is real in so far as he desires to possess it and
struggles to restrain his unruly passions in order that he may
have it, and is sorry that he has not got it to the degree that
he should. But to one who truly loves God there is no great
difficulty in putting up with all this, because Love fights for
him and destroys these movements of anger and melancholy
with surprising facility. The sight of God and the consciousness of His love makes the soul of such a man so much at ease
and peaceful, so ready to bear all, and so conformed to God,
that neither contempt nor rebukes, injustice nor injury,
shame nor ill treatment, make any difference to him. He is
not greatly moved by these things and he will not allow himself to be, for if he were he would lose the interior comfort
that he feels, and that he is unwilling to do. It is easier for
him to forget all the wrong done to him, than it is for another
man to forgive it when pardon is asked of him. He had rather
forget than forgive, for that seems to him easier.

And it is Love that brings all this about, for Love opens
the eyes of the soul to the vision of God, and confirms it in
the joyous love that springs from that vision. It comforts a
man so much that he has no anxieties and is quite indifferent
to what men say or do against him. The greatest harm that
could come to him would be to forgo the vision of God,
and he would suffer any injury rather than that. A man can

do all this without much difficulty and without much interference to his contemplation when it is a question of external evils which do not touch the body, such as defamation,
contempt, or loss of material goods. All this is nothing. But
it is another matter when the flesh is touched. He feels the
pain and it is harder to bear. But although it is difficult, and
indeed impossible, for weak human nature to endure bodily
pain gladly and patiently without anger and feelings of depression, it is not impossible for Love, that is the Holy
Ghost, to effect this in a soul when He gives Himself to it.
Even in the midst of pain He makes the soul experience His
love and unites it to Himself, taking away all feeling in the
senses through His secret power. He brings it such sweet
comfort through His holy presence that the soul is conscious
of little or no pain. This is a special grace which is given to
the holy martyrs, and which was given to the apostles, as the
Scripture says: *Ibant apostoli gaudentes a conspectu concilii,
quoniam digni habiti sunt pro nomine Christi contumeliam pati*
(Acts v. 41). The apostles came joyfully from the council of
the Jews when they were beaten with scourges, and they
rejoiced that they were worthy to suffer bodily pain for the
love of Jesus. They were not moved to anger or bitterness
or to take vengeance on the Jews who beat them, as a worldly-minded man would be who suffered ever so small an injury from his neighbour. Nor were they moved by pride to
think well of themselves and to despise and condemn the
Jews, as is the case with hypocrites and heretics, who will
suffer great physical pain, and sometimes even death, with
great joy and constancy, as though in the name of Jesus and
for love of Him. But indeed the love and the joy that they
feel in physical suffering are not from the Holy Ghost, not
from the fire that burns on the high altar of heaven, but they
are feigned by the devil burning in the fire of hell. Their feelings are entirely composed of pride and presumption, scorn

and condemnation, and contempt of those who punish them. They think that they are all the work of charity and that they suffer for the love of God, but they are deceived by the noon-day devil. When a true lover of God suffers at the hands of his fellow-men, he is strengthened through the grace of the Holy Ghost and is made so truly humble and patient and peaceable that, whatever wrong or injury he suffers, he always retains his humility. He does not despise his persecutors or speak ill of them, but prays for them with pity and compassion more tenderly than for those who never harmed him. And he does indeed love them more, and more fervently desires their salvation, because he sees that he will have such great spiritual gain from their evil deed, even though they never intended that he should. But this kind of love and humility, which are beyond human nature, are only brought about by the Holy Ghost in those whom He makes true lovers of God.

THE THIRTY-NINTH CHAPTER

How Love destroys covetousness, lust, and gluttony, and pleasure in all the senses, with sweetness and facility through the contemplation of God by grace

THE action of Love also frees the soul from covetousness, for it makes it desire spiritual good and heavenly riches so ardently that it puts no value on earthly riches. Under its influence the soul takes no more pleasure in a precious stone than in a piece of chalk, and feels no more drawn to a hundred pounds of gold than to a pound of lead. All perishable things appear of the same value, and it cares no more for one than another, for it knows without doubt that all the things of earth to which men of the world attach such great importance, and which they love so much, will pass away and come to nothing, both the thing in itself and the love of it. And so in thought the soul possessed by Love makes them already what they will become and considers them as nothing. And while the lovers of this world strive and beg for the possession of earthly goods, the lover of God strives with nobody, but remains at peace and is content with what he has, and seeks nothing more. He wants no more of the riches of the earth than will barely suffice for his bodily sustenance to keep him alive for as long as it is God's will. And since he can easily obtain so much, he has no further desires. He is very well satisfied when he has only what he needs for the time being, so that he is not troubled about the guarding and administration of his possessions, and can give his whole attention to seeking God and finding Him in purity of spirit. That is what he desires, because only the clean of heart shall see God. So, too, the love of father and mother and friends does not weigh upon him. The sword of the love of God cuts this love off from his heart, so that he has no more affection for his parents than for anyone else unless he recognizes more grace or virtue in them. Except, that he would rather see in his father and mother the same degree of grace that he sees in some others; but if they have not so much, then he prefers those who have more, and that is charity.[1] In this way the Love of God destroys worldly covetousness and brings the soul poverty of spirit.

[1] Hilton seems to teach a hard doctrine here, but it is incontestable that charity, which is the love of God and the love of our fellow-men in and for God, must take precedence over natural affection. It is important to remember though, that our love of our neighbour, like our love of God, is a matter of will not of feeling. We are bound to esteem more highly those who are closer to God, but natural affection can have scope in desiring the spiritual good of those who are bound to us by natural ties, and these do indeed impose an obligation on us to further the good, both spiritual and also temporal, of those related to us.

And Love brings this about, not only in those who have no worldly property, but also in some who have great position and great riches. Love so far removes covetousness from some of these that they do not value their possessions at a straw. If their goods are lost through the negligence of those who have charge of them, they are not upset. The reason is that the heart of him who loves God is by the gift of the Holy Ghost so fully occupied with that which is most precious and most excellent that it can find room for no other love which is opposed to this.

And furthermore Love destroys the pleasures of lust and bodily impurity and brings true chastity into the soul, and causes it to take pleasure in it. The soul feels such joy at the sight of God that it rejoices in being chaste and finds no great difficulty in it, for in that state it is most at ease and most at rest.

And in the same way Love destroys gluttony and makes a man sober and temperate, and so uplifts him that he can find no satisfaction in the pleasures of food and drink, but takes what best suits his bodily constitution and can most easily be obtained. He does this not from love of self but from love of God. One who loves God understands that he must preserve the life of his body with food and drink for as long as God wishes him to live. And so for one who experiences this love of God, discretion, as I see it, will consist in taking such bodily sustenance as will most conduce to the preservation of the grace that he has and enable him to make the best use of it. The food which least oppresses him and is sufficient to maintain the strength of the body, whether it is meat or fish, or only bread and ale, will be that which he chooses when he can obtain it. For his whole concern is to keep his mind constantly on God with devout love and to prevent, if possible, anything from interfering with this. And so, since other things must interfere to some extent, the less food and drink

T   269

do so the better he is pleased. He would rather make use of
the best and most expensive food if it interfered less with
the custody of his heart, than live on bread and water if that
interfered more. He has no desire to get a great reward for
the pain of fasting if he loses sweetness of temper through it.
All he is concerned with is to keep his heart as steadily as he
can in the sight of God and in the experience of His love.
And indeed I think he might well take less pleasure in the
richest food than a man who regulates his life by his reason
alone, without this special gift of Love, might take in the
worst. But I would make exception for rare foods very delicately prepared, for these are never suitable for a spiritual
man. On the other hand, if poor food, only bread and ale
for example, brings him greater peace of heart, then he
would prefer to have nothing more; and especially if the
gift of Love itself maintains his bodily strength.[2]

And Love does more, for it destroys *accidia* and bodily
idleness, and makes a man active and prompt in the service of
God. It makes him want always to be well occupied, that is in
the contemplation of Him, for through this he finds pleasure
in prayer and meditation, and in the performance without
depression or bitterness of whatever may be his duty according to his state of life, whether he be a religious or a layman.

So, too, Love puts an end to all useless indulgence of the
five bodily senses. First with regard to sight: It brings it
about that a man takes no pleasure in seeing the things of the
world. He is, rather, distressed at the sight of them, however beautiful or precious or admirable they may be. As

[2] The only concern of the true lover of Jesus is to keep his heart stead-
fastly on God, and whether or not he practises particular mortification in
food and drink is in itself indifferent to him. Hilton advocates a wise discretion in this matter and his advice coincides with that of the author of
The Cloud of Unknowing (chap. 42) and is the theme of "An Epistle of Discretion" (*The Cell of Self-Knowledge*, ed. E. G. Gardner (London, 1925),
p. 95).

lovers of the world run after new things, to admire them and feed their hearts with the empty sight of them, so the lover of God is at pains to avoid the sight of such things, so that his inward vision may not be interfered with. For in the spirit he sees something much more beautiful and admirable, and he has no wish to lose that vision.

It is just the same with regard to speech and hearing. It is painful to such a man to speak about or to hear anything that might distract him from the thought of God. Song or music that distracts his mind so that he cannot freely and peacefully pray or meditate is displeasing to him; the more delightful it is to other men, the more distasteful it is to him. And to hear others speaking, unless it concerns the advancement of his soul in the love of God, gives him no pleasure. He is soon bored by it. He would rather be at peace and neither listen nor speak, than listen to the most learned man on earth using all the resources of human intelligence, if he could not speak from experience and movingly of the love of God. For that is the craft that interests him, and therefore he has no desire to speak or hear or see anything that will not lead him to a better knowledge and a deeper experience of God. It is clear that he has no taste for speaking of worldly things or for hearing about them, and neither secular stories, nor news, nor anything that does not concern him has any interest for him.

So of smell and taste and touch; the more his mind is distracted from spiritual peace by the use of his sense of smell or taste, or any other sense, the more he flees from them. The less he experiences them the better he is pleased, and if he could live in the body without experiencing any of them, he would rather it was so. For they often trouble the heart and disturb its peace, and yet they cannot be altogether avoided. But the love of God is sometimes so strong in a soul that it overcomes everything that is opposed to it.

THE FORTIETH CHAPTER

Of the virtues and graces that a soul receives through the open-
ing of the spiritual eyes and the contemplation of God, and
how these may not be obtained through man's efforts alone, but
only when these are helped by special grace

THE action of Love in a soul, when it opens the eyes of the
spirit to contemplate God by the inspiration of a special
grace, is of this nature. It makes a soul act in an entirely
spiritual way and enables it to rise to contemplation. What
this opening of the eyes of the spirit involves the greatest
theologian could not conceive or express. For this experience cannot be obtained by study or human effort; it comes
principally through the grace of the Holy Ghost, but with
man's effort co-operating. I am afraid to say anything about
it, for I do not think I am able; it is beyond my powers and
my lips are unclean. Nevertheless, because I think Love asks
it of me, and indeed commands, I shall say a little more as,
I hope, Love may inspire me. This opening of the eyes of the
spirit is that luminous darkness and rich nothing that I spoke
about before. All these terms are used of it: *Purity and rest of*
spirit, inward silence and peace of conscience, elevation of thought
and integrity of soul, an awareness of the life of grace and seclusion
of heart, the wakeful sleep of the spouse and tasting of heavenly
savour, ardent love and shining light, the entry of contemplation
and reform in feeling. All these expressions are found in the
writings of the saints,[1] for each of them spoke of it according
to the grace which he had received, and though they differ
verbally, they all mean the same truth.

[1] The French editors give references to the works of a number of
authors in which these or similar phrases occur, but they are probably
right in thinking that Hilton had no particular passages in mind, but
quoted these expressions because they were current in the spiritual literature of his time.

For if one of these expressions applies to a soul, then they all do. A soul that is yearning to see the face of God, on being touched by the special grace of the Holy Ghost, suddenly feels itself transformed. In the first place it is admirably detached from the love of earthly things and recollected in itself; to such an extent that it has lost all taste for its life in the body and for everything save God alone. And then it is *clean from all the defilement of sin*—so much, that the remembrance of sin and all inordinate affection for creatures is suddenly swept away. Nothing keeps the soul from God but its union with the body. *And then it is in spiritual rest*, because all painful doubts and anxieties and all the temptations of its spiritual enemies are driven out of the heart; they do not trouble it or make any impression on it while this experience lasts. It is at rest from the distractions of worldly affairs and the distressing movements of evil inclinations, but it is well occupied in the free exercise of love; and the more it is occupied with this the more repose it feels.[2]

This restful action is something very different from phy-

---

[2] This witness to the activity of the soul in contemplation is well in accord with later teaching (cf. A. Tanquery, *The Spiritual Life* (Tournai 1930), p. 654; and is why Father Baker, for example, calls ordinary infused contemplation "active contemplation" (*Sancta Sophia*, Treatise III, Sect. ii, chap. 1, p. 85, and Treatise III, Sect. i, chap. 7, pp. 74 ff, edit. 1657). Contemplation is infused inasmuch as it is produced by the action of God and not by the soul's own efforts, but the soul co-operates. We may compare what Hilton says here about the activity of the soul in contemplation with what he says in the earlier chapters of this section. In chap. 34 he says, "We do no more than allow Him to act and consent to His action. The most that we do is to give voluntary assent to His action in us" (p. 251). And in chap. 35, after stressing that contemplation is a free gift of God, he says that souls "allow the Holy Ghost to move them and produce in them the feelings of love, while they themselves are completely submissive to His action" (p. 254). In these cases the emphasis is certainly on the passivity of the soul, but in each case he makes definite allowance for its co-operation.

sical idleness and from blind security. There is great spiritual activity, but it is called a state of rest, because grace lifts the heavy yoke of carnal love from the soul and makes it strong and free through the gift of the Holy Spirit of Love to act with joy and peace and delight. And therefore it is called a holy idleness and a most active rest, and it is in this way that the soul is *in silence* from the clamour and tumult of the desires of the flesh and of impure thoughts.

The inspiration of the Holy Ghost produces this silence in the contemplation of God, because His voice is so sweet and so strong that it reduces the noise of all other voices in the soul to silence. It is the voice of power which sounds gently in the pure soul of which the prophet says : *Vox Domini in virtute* (Ps. xxviii. 4). The voice of God is in power. This voice is a living and effectual word as the Apostle says : *Vivus est sermo Domini et efficax, et penetrabilior omni gladio* (Hebr. iv. 12). The word of God is living and effectual, more piercing than any sword. Carnal love is extinguished through the utterance of His word and the soul is preserved in silence from all evil suggestions. The Apocalypse says of this silence : *Factum est silentium in caelo, quasi media hora* (Apoc. viii. 1). There was silence in heaven as it were for half an hour. Heaven represents a pure soul raised by grace from earthly love to heavenly conversation, and so such a soul is in silence. But because that silence cannot last uninterruptedly by reason of the corruption of human nature, it is said to be for half an hour.[3] However long it is it seems short to the soul, and so it is called half an hour. And then again the soul has *peace of conscience*. And why? Because grace puts an end to the trouble and annoyance, the tumult and contention, that are the accompaniments of sin, and brings peace and harmony, and unites the soul to the will of

[3] There is a fairly close parallel to the thought here in St Gregory's *Morals on Job* (Bk. xxx, chap. 16, n. 53, P.L., LXXVI, col. 553).

God. The soul receives no reproach for its sins or reproof for its faults, for God has given it the kiss of His love. They are friends and all the soul's wrong-doing is forgiven. So it feels a profound but humble security and great interior joy. And this union brings with it a great assurance of salvation, for the Holy Ghost witnesses inwardly to the conscience that the soul is one of the elect predestined to the heritage of heaven. So St Paul says: *Ipse Spiritus testimonium perhibet spiritui nostro, quod filii Dei sumus* (Rom. viii. 16). The Holy Ghost bears witness to our spirit that we are the sons of God. This witness which grace brings to the conscience is the true joy of the soul as the apostle says: *Gloria mea est testimonium conscientiae meae* (2 Cor. i. 12). My joy is the witness to my conscience; that is, the joy felt bears witness to the peace and union, the true love and friendship, between God and the soul. And when the soul enjoys this peace it is *elevated in thought*.

When the soul is held in bondage by the love of the world, it is beneath all creatures, for they all dominate it and hold it down by their tyranny so that it can neither see God nor love Him. For as the love of the world is a worthless and carnal thing, so the consideration and use of creatures is a carnal thing, and it is servitude for the soul. But when the eyes of the soul are opened to contemplate God, it acquires a new love and it is raised above all material things in accordance with its real nature. And then it considers them and makes use of them in a spiritual way, for its love is spiritual. It will not condescend to subject itself to the love of material things, for grace puts it high above them. It sets no store by the world which will perish and pass away. While the soul enjoys this elevation of heart no error or deceit of the devil can reach it, for its view is fixed on God, and all things are beneath it. The prophet speaks of this when he says: *Accedat homo ad cor altum; et exaltabitur Deus* (Ps. lxiii. 7, 8). Let man come to elevation of heart and God shall be exalted. That is, a man who by grace comes to be raised in thought shall see that God alone is exalted above all creatures and that he himself is exalted in Him.

And when this happens the soul is alone, completely alienated from the fellowship of worldly men, though the body is still among them. It is completely despoiled of all base affection for creatures, and does not care if it never sees a man or speaks with one or receives any consolation from one, so long as it can always enjoy its internal experiences. It is so intimately aware of the presence of God that for love of Him it can easily dispense with the love of creatures and even the very remembrance of them. I do not say that it will in fact cease to love or think of creatures, but it will only think of them at suitable times, and it will consider them and love them in a spiritual way, keeping its liberty, and not in a carnal way and with pain as it did before. The prophet speaks of this solitude thus : *Ducam eam in solitudinem, et loquar ad cor ejus* (Osee ii. 14). I shall lead her into solitude and speak to her heart. That is, the grace of God leads a soul from the troublesome throng of carnal desires into solitude of thought and makes it forget the pleasures of the world and inspires it with words of love. A soul is in solitude when it loves God and attends solely to Him, and no longer has a taste for the world and its consolations. In order that it may enjoy this sort of solitude it flees the company of men and seeks external solitude, because that conduces to this solitude of soul and to the unimpeded action of Love. The less it is hindered by useless talk without, or useless thought within, the more free it is for contemplation, and in this way it is in *solitude of heart*.

While a soul is overlaid and blinded by the love of the world it is entirely extraverted. It lies open to everything like a highway, for every impulse of the flesh or the devil makes itself felt. But then by grace the soul is withdrawn into a secret chamber where it sees God and hears His secret counsels, and it is wonderfully consoled. Of this the prophet says: *Secretum meum mihi; secretum meum mihi* (Isa. xxiv. 16). My secret to myself, my secret to myself. That is, the lover of God, free from the sensible feeling of worldly love, and ravished into the secrets of spiritual love by the inspiration of His grace, gives thanks to Him saying: *My secret to myself.* That is, my God, Thy secret is shown to me and hidden from all lovers of the world, for it is called hidden manna. It is easier to ask what this is, than to give the answer (cf. Exod. xvi. 15). God makes this promise to His lover: *Dabo sibi manna absconditum quod nemo novit, nisi, qui accipit* (Apoc. ii. 17). I shall give a hidden manna that no man knows but he who takes it. This manna is the food of angels as Holy Scripture calls it. For angels are nourished with the clear view and ardent love of God, and that is this manna. For we can ask what it is, but we can never understand. He who loves God is not filled with this food on earth, but as long as he is in this bodily life he only enjoys a little taste of it.

This tasting of manna is an awareness of the life of grace, [4]

[4] *An awareness of the life of grace.* This definition of contemplation, which is what the opening of the eyes of the spirit means (cf. p. 246), is very noteworthy. The natural deduction would seem to be that contemplative union is an intensification of sanctifying grace. A union is effected by grace, but when it reaches a certain intensity there is "an awareness of the life of grace", an awareness of the union. It should be remembered that grace is being used strictly here in the sense of sanctifying or habitual grace, that is, a quality in the essence of the soul by which it is supernaturalized, brought into a totally different relation to God from that which it was in before. St Thomas says it is none other than *quaedam participatio divinae naturae* (*Summa*, Ia IIae, q. CII, art. 1). The mystery of grace is how man can share in this divine life without becoming merged in God in a pantheistic sense, but it is only in virtue of this co-naturality that man has with God that he can see Him in the Beatific Vision. The

which comes from the opening of the soul's eyes. And this grace does not differ from the grace that an elect soul feels at the beginning of its conversion; it is the same grace but experienced in another way, because the progress of the soul and grace are interdependent. The purer and more detached from the love of the world the soul is, the stronger is the grace, the more interior and spiritual the experience of the presence of God. So the same grace that first turns men from sin and then makes them set out and advance on the spiritual road by the practice of virtues and good works makes them perfect, and it is called an *awareness of the life of grace*, for he who has it is conscious of the grace within him. He recognizes it as a principle of life in the soul, which is wonderfully invigorated by it, so that it is unconscious of the suffering caused by bodily weakness and sickness, because under its influence the body and the soul are at their strongest, are most healthy and restful.

Once it has experienced it the soul cannot live happily without this grace. It thinks that it will be able to keep it always and that nothing will take it away, and yet it is not so, and it passes away only too easily. Nevertheless, though the overwhelming consciousness of it passes, the effect still remains and keeps the soul calm and makes it desire its return. And this is also what is called the wakeful sleep of the spouse,[5] of which Holy Scripture says: *Ego dormio, et cor*

---

soul in a state of grace is already in a truly supernatural state, which admits of degrees and culminates in this Vision. The act of contemplation is an experience more or less intense of the Being of God, falling indeed far short of the Beatific Vision, but of the same nature in so far as it is direct and not through creatures.

[5] Talking of the awareness of the life of grace he has just said that it "passes away only too easily. Nevertheless, though the overwhelming consciousness of it passes, the effect still remains." This state he goes on to describe as *the wakeful sleep of the spouse*, one of the phrases that he used earlier in this chapter (p. 272) to describe contemplation. This chapter

meum vigilat (Cant. v. 2). I sleep and my heart watches. That is: I sleep spiritually, when the love of the world is extinguished in me by grace, and the evil impulses of the desires of the flesh are so much deadened that I hardly feel them, and they are no trouble to me. My heart is made free, and then it watches, for it is alert and ready to love God and see Him. The more I sleep to external things, the more I am awake to the knowledge of God and inward things. I cannot wake to God unless I sleep to the world. And therefore the grace of the Holy Ghost shutting the bodily eyes, the soul sleeps to the worthlessness of the world, and the spiritual eyes being opened, it wakes to the sight of God's majesty hidden under the cloud of his precious humanity.

The Gospel says of the apostles when they were with our Lord at the Transfiguration that first they slept and then, *vigilantes viderunt majestatem* (Luke ix. 32). Wakening they saw His majesty. The sleep of the apostles represents death to worldly love through the inspiration of the Holy Ghost, their awakening represents contemplation of God. Through this sleep the soul is brought into peace from the clamour of the lusts of the flesh, and through the wakening it is raised up to the sight of God and spiritual things. The more that the eyes are shut to the things of earth in this sort of sleep, the clearer is the inward vision which loving contemplation brings of the beauty of heaven. Love brings about this sleep and this waking in the soul of the lover of God through the light of grace.

---

therefore clearly recognizes a contemplation that is real though unfelt, and it is in accordance with this that he says in chap. 24 (p. 207) that Jesus is in the darkness whether it is distressing or peaceful. The experience would seem to be what came later to be called by St John of the Cross dim or secret contemplation (see *The Dark Night of the Soul*, Bk. I, chaps. 9 and 10), and it means that the divine action on the soul may be present whether it is felt or not.

THE FORTY-FIRST CHAPTER

How the special grace of contemplation of God is sometimes withdrawn from a soul, and how a soul should behave both in the absence and the presence of God, and how it should always desire His presence

SHOW me a soul whose eyes are opened by grace to the contemplation of God, a soul detached and withdrawn from the love of the world so that it has obtained purity and poverty of spirit, rest, interior silence and peace of conscience, elevation of thought, solitude and seclusion of heart, and the wakeful sleep of the spouse; a soul that has ceased to find pleasure and joy in the world, which is captivated by heavenly delights, and which is always thirsting and sighing gently for the presence of God, and I do not hesitate to say that such a soul is consumed with love and enveloped in spiritual light, worthy to be called and to be the spouse of Christ. It is reformed in feeling and ready for contemplation. These are the signs of the inspiration which accompanies the opening of the soul's eyes; for when its eyes are opened the soul enjoys all these gifts.

Nevertheless, it often happens that grace is partially withdrawn,[1] because of the corruption and frailty of human na-

---

[1] *Grace is partially withdrawn.* It is clear from what immediately follows that what is withdrawn is not in fact grace, but the "awareness" of it, and indeed at the beginning of the next paragraph he says so explicitly, "Do not be surprised that this awareness of grace is sometimes withdrawn" (p. 281). In other words, the substantial union effected by sanctifying grace remains, but the awareness of it comes and goes (see below, p. 285 and n. 5). If this be true, then it would seem that the contemplative soul acquires a certain degree of sanctifying grace more intense than a less advanced soul possesses, and this remains, unless it is increased by correspondence or diminished by lack of correspondence with God's work. But it may remain at a given intensity quite independently of whether the

ture, and the soul is allowed to fall back into its dependence
on the body, and this is a matter of sorrow and anguish to it,
for it is blind, without any taste for the things of the spirit,
and incapable of all good. It is weak and feeble, encumbered
with the body and the bodily senses. It desires and seeks for
the grace of God and is unable to find it. For Holy Scripture
says of God: *Postquam vultum suum absconderit, non est qui con-
templetur eum* (Job xxxiv. 29). When God has hidden His
face there is none who may behold Him. When He shows
Himself, the soul cannot fail to see Him, for He is light;
and when He hides Himself, it is unable to see Him, for
it is in darkness. His hiding of Himself is only a delicate
trial of the soul, His revelation of Himself is to console it by
a striking effect of His merciful goodness.

Do not be surprised that the awareness of grace is sometimes withdrawn from the lover of God, for Holy Scripture
says of the spouse: *Quaesivi et non inveni illum: vocavi et non
respondit mihi* (Cant. iii. 1).[2] I sought Him and did not find
Him; I called Him and He did not answer. That is, when I
sink back into my natural weakness, grace is withdrawn; and
if it is withdrawn, my failure is the cause, and not because
He has departed from me. But His absence makes me feel
my misery. I seek Him with great desire of heart, and He
gives me no answer that I can recognize. And then I cry with
all my soul: *Revertere dilecte mi!* (Cant. ii. 17). Return again,
my Beloved. And yet it seems as though He did not hear me.
The painful consciousness of self, the assaults of sensible love
and fear, and my lack of spiritual strength, form as it were

---

soul is conscious of experiencing contemplation or not. For contemplation as an awareness of grace see Bk. II, chap. 40, n. 4. It is of course in
accordance with all teaching on the subject that the state of contemplation is not continuous, and Hilton has many references to the fact, see
for example chap. 24, p. 209, and later in this chapter p. 286.

[2] The last part of this quotation is not in the Vulgate.

a continual cry from my soul to God. And yet He estranges Himself for a time and does not come, however much I cry to Him. And the reason is that He is sure of His lover; He knows he will not turn again fully to the love of the world, because he has no taste for it, and so He holds Himself aloof.

But at last, in His own good time, He returns, full of grace and truth, and visits the soul which is languishing with desire and sighing lovingly after His presence. He touches it and anoints it with the oil of gladness and takes away all its suffering. And then the soul cries out joyously with the voice of the spirit: *Oleum effusum nomen tuum* (Cant. i. 2). Thy name, O God, is oil poured out. Thy name is Jesus, that is Saviour. As long as my soul is sick through sin, oppressed with the heavy burden of the body, anxious and disturbed by the dangers and miseries of this life, so long, O Lord, Thy name is for me oil, not poured out, but withheld. But when my soul is suddenly illumined with the light of grace, cleansed from all the defilement of sin, and feels itself filled with consolation, with spiritual strength and unspeakable joy, then I can say to Thee with delighted praise and in joy of spirit, "Thy name O Lord, is for me oil poured out. For the grace of Thy visitation makes me fully understand the true meaning of Thy name, which is Jesus, Saviour.[3] For it is Thy gracious presence that saves me from sorrow and from sin."

Happy is the soul that is ever nourished by the experience of love when He is present, and is upheld by desire of Him when He is absent. He is wise and well instructed in the love of God who keeps himself temperately and reverently in

[3] It is perhaps going too far to say, as the French editors do, that this passage is inspired by Richard Rolle's *Encomium Nominis Iesu* (Horstman, vol. I, p. 186), but Rolle has the same interpretation of the Holy Name, Saviour.

His presence, who contemplates Him lovingly without care-
less levity, and is patient and at ease in His absence without
harmful despair and sore bitterness.

These alternations of the absence and presence of God
that a soul feels do not constitute perfection, but on the
other hand they are not incompatible with the grace of perfection or of contemplation, but they mean that the degree
of perfection is less. For the more a soul is interrupted from
the continual awareness of grace, the less degree of grace it
possesses. But the grace which it has is nevertheless the
grace of contemplation. [4] This alternation of the absence and
presence of God occurs both in the perfect and in beginners,
but in a different way. For just as the presence of grace is felt
differently in these two states, so is its absence. And so he
who cannot recognize the absence of grace is liable to be
deceived, and he who cannot recognize the presence of grace
will be ungrateful when it comes, whether he is among the
beginners or the perfect. Nevertheless, the more stable grace
is, the less interrupted, the more beautiful is the soul and the
more like to Him in whom, as the apostle says, there is no
change (James i. 17). And it is fitting that the soul should be
like its divine spouse in behaviour and in virtue, fully re-
sembling Him in the stability of perfect love. But that occurs
rarely, and only in the chosen spouses of Christ.

For the man who perceives none of these fluctuations of
grace, but who thinks that he always possesses it completely
and stably without interruption, is either very perfect or
very blind. He is perfect who is cut off from all carnal affections, from all intercourse with creatures, who has broken
down all the obstacles that corruption and sin raise between

---

[4] This seems to imply the secret contemplation previously referred to
(chap. 40, n. 5). What he means presumably is that the grace which the
soul has is a sufficiently intense degree of sanctifying grace to constitute
contemplation, whether felt or not.

his soul and God, who is completely united to Him in calm love. But this is a grace that surpasses the state of human nature. That man, on the contrary, is very blind who thinks that he has received grace without feeling God's inspiration, and who considers himself confirmed in the experience of special grace; who thinks that whatever he feels, interiorly or exteriorly, is a grace, and who sees the effect of grace in all his words or actions. If there is such a man, and I hope there is not, he knows very little about the manner in which grace makes itself felt.

But you may say that we should love only by faith and not desire spiritual experiences or pay any attention to them if they come, for the apostle says *Justus ex fide vivit* (Heb. x. 38). The righteous man lives by faith. Certainly I say we ought not to desire bodily experiences, however enjoyable they may be, nor pay much attention to them if they come. But we should always desire the sort of spiritual experiences that I am referring to now, if they come in the way that I described. Such experiences are the extinguishing of all love of the world, the opening of the eyes of the spirit, purity of spirit, peace of conscience, and the rest. We should desire to feel always, if we can, the effects that the presence of God produces in the soul. We should desire to contemplate Him always with reverence, and to feel the sweetness of His love in the admirable intimacy of His presence. This should be our life; this is the experience that we should strive to have according to the measure of His grace in whom all grace resides, and who gives to some more to others less. For He makes His presence felt in various ways, as He chooses. And to the possession of this gift we ought to consecrate all our lives and all our activities; without it we do not truly live, for as the soul is the life of the body, God is the life of the soul by His gracious presence. And yet however vivid the experience of grace may be, it is only in faith, and it is not that which we shall have of God Himself in the happiness of heaven.

How we ought to desire this feeling! Every rational soul ought with all its strength to desire to approach God and to be united to Him through the perception of His invisible presence. What that presence means may be known better by experience than by books. To the chosen soul that has once enjoyed it, it is life and love, strength and light, joy and peace, and therefore the soul cannot suffer its loss without pain; it is unable not to desire it, since it is so good in itself and so consoling. For what is more consoling to a soul on earth than to be withdrawn by grace from the trouble of worldly affairs, from the defilement of desiring and the vanity of loving creatures, into the peace and sweetness of spiritual love, where it inwardly perceives God's presence and is satisfied with the light of His countenance? Truly, nothing, as it seems to me. Nothing can make the soul of one who loves God truly happy but the presence of God as it can be made known to a pure soul through grace. The man whose soul experiences this is never depressed or sad except when the consciousness of his body presses on him, he is never completely joyous and happy but when he escapes from himself to be with God. And yet even then his joy is not perfect, for he is weighed down by the corruption of the body, which greatly interferes with his spiritual joy, and it must always be so as long as he is in this life.

However, lest you should fall into error on this point, when I speak of the variations of grace, how it comes and goes, I am not referring to the ordinary grace that manifests itself in faith and charity to God. For unless a man possesses and preserves this he cannot be saved, and it is in the least of the elect. But I am referring to a special grace that comes from the inspiration of the Holy Ghost, as I explained above.[5] The ordinary grace, that is charity, remains whatever a man does, as long as his will is truly fixed on God so that he does not consent to mortal sin by doing anything deliberately which is forbidden under pain of mortal sin. And in order that a sin should be mortal it is necessary that a man should act against the witness of his conscience, or else that his conscience is so blinded that he does not hold it a mortal sin to act deliberately in a way which God and the Church condemn as such.

The special grace that accompanies the invisible presence of God and makes the soul perfect does not always remain at its most intense, but comes and goes, as I said. *Spiritus ubi vult spirat; et vocem eius audis, et nescis unde veniat, aut quo vadat* (John iii. 8). The Holy Spirit breathes where He wills and you hear His voice, but you do not know whence He comes or whither He goes. Sometimes He comes secretly when you are least aware of Him, but you cannot fail to recognize Him before He goes, for He moves your heart marvellously and excites it strongly to the contemplation of His goodness, so that it melts with joy in the sweetness of His love like wax before the fire, and this is the sounding of His voice. But then, before you are aware, He has gone. He withdraws partially, not entirely. The soul no longer experiences His

[5] It is evident that this *special grace* that comes from the inspiration of the Holy Ghost is in reality the awareness of grace of which he spoke earlier (chap. 40, p. 277, n. 4). "The *ordinary grace* that manifests itself in faith and charity" that he has just spoken of is evidently sanctifying grace, for it is necessary to salvation. This grace remains, for it is, as he says, "in the least of the elect", that is, in all those who are in a state of grace. The *special grace* (which is the awareness of grace) comes and goes. There is a certain confusion owing to the fact that the word grace is unfortunately used in two senses and the proper theological qualification is not always applied, nor has Hilton applied it here. Sanctifying grace has been explained above (chap. 40, n. 4). Actual grace is a supernatural transient aid or favour which God grants to the soul. The *special grace* that he talks about here is an actual grace, the *ordinary grace* is sanctifying grace.

presence in a superabundant manner, but only in moderation. The intensity of the experience passes away but grace
remains substantially and in all its effects as long as the soul
keeps pure and does not fall deliberately or recklessly into
indulgence of the flesh, or occupy itself unnecessarily with
outward things. It will do this sometimes, not because of the
pleasure it takes in them, but because of its natural frailty.
This is the fluctuation of grace that I have been speaking of.

THE FORTY-SECOND CHAPTER

*A commendation of the prayer which a contemplative soul offers
to God; how there is security in persevering in prayer; how
every experience of grace in a favoured soul may be called an
experience of God; how this grace is more elevated as the soul
is purer*

MAN's soul is dull and inept in performing spiritual exercises, incapable of making any headway in them, when it is
not touched by a special grace. Its natural weakness brings
this about, for it is by nature cold and dry, lacking in devotion and in a taste for the things of the spirit.[1] But when the
light of grace shines on it it becomes a responsive and delicate instrument, ready and able to engage in spiritual activity. It has great liberty and is prompt to obey the movements of grace, and at times it will happen that grace moves
it to pray. Of the manner of its prayer then I will now tell
you something.

The prayers that are most made use of and are most consoling to men are, if I am not mistaken, the Our Father and

[1] The soul is a spiritual being but it informs a body, and only with difficulty does it transcend the things of sense. This is no doubt what Hilton
means by its natural weakness.

287

the Psalter; the Our Father for the uneducated, and psalms
and hymns and the services of the Church for the educated.
Now a man under the special influence of grace will not
make use of these prayers in the way that he did before, nor
in the way that men ordinarily do, speaking in full or moderate tones, but his prayer will be in a very low voice and with
fervour of heart, because his mind is not distracted by exterior things but is entirely recollected, and his soul is, as
it were, in the presence of God. And therefore every word
and every syllable is pronounced with appreciation, sweetly,
and with delight, the lips and the heart in full accord. For the
soul is then on fire with love, and every word of its prayer
is like a spark springing up from a blazing log, so that all its
powers are enkindled and glow with love, and this brings
such consolation that it wishes to pray always in this manner
and never to be occupied in any other way. The more the
soul practises this prayer, the better it is able to do it, the
stronger it is. For grace helps it greatly and makes its task
light and easy, so that it delights with a spiritual and heavenly
joy in singing the psalms and the praises of God.

This kind of prayer is the food of the soul and is of great
effect. It puts to flight all the temptations of the devil, both
secret and open, it takes away all remembrance of the world
and of sins of the flesh, and all pleasure in them. It preserves
both body and soul from feeling the miseries of life. It makes
the soul conscious of grace and the action of Love, and it
keeps it glowing with love as sticks do a fire, taking away all
depression, and creating joy and gladness of spirit. Of this
prayer David says: *Dirigatur oratio mea sicut incensum in conspectu tuo* (Ps. cxl. 2). May my prayer be directed, O Lord, as
incense in Thy sight. For as incense thrown on the fire makes
a sweet smell from the smoke rising into the air, so a psalm
sung or said devoutly from an ardent heart sends up a sweet
odour before the Lord and all the court of heaven.

No fly dares to rest on the edge of a pot that is boiling on the fire. So no sensual pleasure touches a pure soul which is embraced and warmed with the fire of love, and which this fire makes, as it were, to boil over with psalms and praises to God.[2] This prayer is always heard by God, it gives homage to Him, and is recompensed again by grace, making the soul intimate with God and with all the angels of heaven. Let him use it who can; it is good and the result of grace.

Although it is not full contemplation in itself, nor the effect of Love alone, this sort of prayer is nevertheless a degree of contemplation. For it cannot be achieved except through a large measure of grace and the opening of the eyes of the spirit. And so the soul that can give itself to prayer of this kind, and taste its sweetness and delight, has in a certain manner the grace of contemplation.[3]

It is an offering rich in devotion, which is taken up by the angels and presented before the face of God. The prayer of men who are occupied with active works has, as it were, a twofold expression, one is formed in the heart through

[2] The French editors point out that this comparison occurs three times in the writings of St Catherine of Sienna, once in the dialogue and twice in the letters (edit. Gigli, t. IV, p. 138, t. II, pp. 486, 514). St Catherine died in 1380 and I do not know that there is any evidence of the Dialogue being known in England during Hilton's lifetime. It is, however, of some interest that Harleian MS. 2409 attributes to Hilton a translation of part of the De Remediis contra Tentationes of William Flete, the English Augustinian Hermit, who was a close friend and disciple of St Catherine. See Life of the Spirit, July 1950, p. 20.

The French editors also state that this comparison occurs in writings anterior to Hilton, but without giving references, and I have not come across it.

[3] The explanation of this otherwise rather baffling chapter seems to be that the soul, apart from the experience of full contemplation in the accepted sense, may expect to have, at least at intervals, this special grace which will make the recitation of vocal prayers a more or less contemplative experience.

thinking of worldly affairs, while the words of the psalm form another. And yet, if these men have a right intention, their prayer is good and acceptable to God, although it is lacking in devotion and sweetness. But the prayer of a contemplative has only a single expression. It is all one in the heart and on the lips. And indeed the soul is so strengthened through grace, so liberated from the senses, that the body is completely subject to it. The body is no more than an instrument, a trumpet, on which it sounds the praises of God. This is the trumpet that David speaks of: *Buccinate in neomenia tuba, in insigne die solemnitatis vestrae* (Ps. lxxx. 4). Sound with a trumpet in the time of the new moon. That is; O souls, reformed in the spiritual life through the opening of the inward eyes, sound psalms devoutly with the trumpet of your bodily tongues. This prayer is so pleasing to God and so valuable to the soul that anyone who is newly turned to God, and who wants to please Him and experience His special grace, does well to desire it. He should seek by grace to attain the ability to offer his prayers constantly, stably, and devoutly, with an undistracted mind and ardent love to God, so that this habit may prepare him to receive the movement of grace when it presents itself.

There is nothing deceptive about this prayer, and it gives security. If you can achieve it and maintain it, you have no need to go about here and there asking every spiritual man what you should do, how you should love God, and how you should serve Him, and speaking of spiritual matters that surpass your understanding, as perhaps some do. It is not profitable to do that unless there is real necessity. Hold firmly to your prayer, with effort at first, till you can pray peacefully in this spiritual way, and then it will teach you all you need to know without danger of deceit or illusion. Persevere in it, if you have reached it, and do not give it up. But if grace comes and takes it from you for a time, manifesting itself in another way, then leave it and return again to it later. He who has the grace of this sort of prayer does not ask, as some do, on what he shall fix his thought while he is praying, whether on the words or on God or on the name of Jesus. He knows well enough from the experience of the grace, for the eyes of the soul are turned inwards and contemplate God clearly, and the soul is assured that it experiences and sees Him. I do not mean that it sees the fullness of the divinity, but it sees Him in the measure in which He is willing to show Himself to a pure soul that is still in the body, and according to the degree of its purity. For be sure of this, that every experience of grace is an experience of God, and may be said to be God; and according as the grace is greater or lesser the soul experiences God to a greater or lesser degree. Indeed, the first experience of special grace that comes to a beginner, the grace of compunction and contrition for sins, is an experience of God Himself, because it is He who produces contrition in the soul by His presence. But at that stage the soul experiences God in an imperfect manner, and is far from any fine appreciation of the divinity, because of its impurity. But if it later increases in virtue and purity, then with the aid of grace it will come to experience God, but in a more spiritual way, one more in accordance with the divine nature. And indeed what God loves above all in a soul is to see it by spiritual contemplation and love of Him become by grace what He is by nature. For that is the goal of all who truly love God. You may be sure that whenever you feel your soul moved by grace in the way I have described, by the opening of the spiritual eyes, that it is God whom you see and experience. Hold fast to Him while you can, preserve His gift of Himself, and do not easily let Him depart. Seek God alone by receiving His grace in a manner ever more in accordance with His nature, so that you may always be attaining a higher degree of it. And because you have not the full awareness of God as He is in His divinity, do not be afraid that you are deceived in giving yourself to what you do feel. If you love God, have confidence that your experience is genuine, that you truly see and experience Him by grace in the way that is possible to you on earth. And so give yourself up to this experience when grace brings it to you. Cherish it so that you may come to a more perfect knowledge of God. For grace will always guide you, if you will follow it, till you reach your goal.

Perhaps you wonder why I say at one time that grace performs all this, at another time Love, or Jesus, or God. I reply that when I say that grace does it I mean Love, Jesus, God; they are all the same. Jesus is Love, Jesus is grace, Jesus is God; for He does everything in us by grace, as God, and for Love. For this reason I can use which word of the four I please in this book.

THE FORTY-THIRD CHAPTER

How a soul, when its spiritual eyes are opened, receives a gift which enables it to understand Holy Scripture, and how God, concealed in the Scriptures, reveals Himself to those who love Him

WHEN a soul has this experience of God in prayer it is persuaded that it can never lose it. Nevertheless, it sometimes happens that grace causes a soul to leave vocal prayer and moves it to see God in another way. It sees Him first in the Scriptures, for God, who is truth, is hidden there under the beauty of the words as under a soft silk. He can only be recognized by the pure of heart, because truth will not reveal itself to those who are hostile, but only to those who love it and seek it with humility. For truth and humility are sisters joined together by love, and there is no divergence in their counsels. Humility relies on truth and not at all on itself, and truth trusts in humility, and so they agree well together. The soul of one who loves and desires God sees Him in proportion to the degree in which it is made humble by the infusion of grace and the opening of the spiritual eyes, and in so far as it understands that it is nothing of itself but is entirely dependent on the mercy and goodness of God, and that it is upheld only by His favour. It sees the truth of the Scriptures wonderfully revealed to it in a way that it could not do by study and its own natural intelligence, and this is a kind of experience or perception of God, for God is the source of wisdom, and by imparting a little of His wisdom to a pure soul He can enable it to understand the whole of Scripture. He does not impart this knowledge all at once in a single act of enlightenment, but through His grace the soul receives a new habitual ability to understand the texts which come to its mind.

This light and clearness in the intelligence is produced by the presence of God. The Gospel tells us that as two of the disciples were going to Emmaus, speaking of Jesus and on fire with love, He appeared to them in the likeness of a pilgrim and instructed them in the prophecies concerning Himself: *Aperuit illis sensum, ut intelligerent Scripturas* (Luke xxiv. 45). He gave them intelligence to understand Holy Scripture. In the same way the indwelling of God illumines the intelligence of those who love and ardently desire Him, and brings to their minds by the ministry of angels the words and the texts of Scripture without their searching for them or thinking about them, and it makes their meaning clear however difficult or obscure they may be in themselves.[1] The

---

[1] This kind of enlightenment is that which theologians attribute to that Gift of the Holy Ghost which is known as the Gift of Understanding, the gift of insight into revealed truths. Cf. also p. 295 for the same effect.

more difficult they are and the less able to be understood by
the ordinary light of reason, the more delightful is their exposition when it comes from God. The interpretation is
literal, moral, mystical, and heavenly, if the matter allows
of it.² By the literal interpretation, which is the easiest and
most obvious, the natural intelligence of man is fortified; by
the moral sense of Scripture the soul is instructed about
vices and virtues, how to distinguish one from the other. By
the mystical sense it is illumined to see the operation of God
in the Church, to apply the words of Scripture to Christ our
head, and to the Church, His mystical body. The fourth, the
heavenly sense, is concerned only with the operation of love,
and it consists in applying to love all the truth of Scripture.
Since that comes nearest to the experience of heaven, I call
it heavenly.

The lover of God is His friend, not because he has deserved to be, but because God in His merciful goodness has
made him so by a very real pact. And so it is that He shows
him His secrets as to a true friend who serves Him through
love and not through fear, as a slave might. Thus He Himself
says to His apostles: *Jam vos dixi amicos, quia quaecumque
audivi a Patre meo, nota feci vobis* (John xv. 15). Now I say that
you are My friends, for I make known to you all things that I
have heard from My Father. To a pure soul, whose palate is
cleansed from the defilement of sensual love, Holy Scripture
is a life-giving and refreshing food whose flavour is very

² The accepted fourfold interpretation of the schoolmen was summed
up in the doggerel verses

> *Littera gesta docet, quid credas allegoria,*
> *moralis quid agas, quo tendas anagogia.*

There are really two senses, the literal and the spiritual, or figurative,
the latter being divided into three according to the nature of the interpretation. All the senses are not to be found in every passage of the Bible,
hence Hilton's qualification, "If the matter allows of it". Presumably his
mystical is the allegorical and his heavenly the anagogical sense.

agreeable to the mind which ruminates it well, because there is hidden in it the spirit that informs all the powers of the soul, and fills them with heavenly and spiritual delights. He has need of good teeth who will eat this bread, for lovers of the flesh and heretics cannot reach its inner nature. Their teeth are unclean and so they cannot taste it. The teeth signify the interior senses, which in lovers of the world and heretics are unclean. They would like to come to the true knowledge of Scripture by the subtlety of their natural intelligence, but they cannot do so. Their intelligence is corrupted through original sin as well as actual, and it has not been rectified by grace. They can never do more than gnaw on the outer bark, and whatever their claims, they never taste the inner flavour. They are not humble and pure, or friends of God, and therefore He does not reveal His secrets to them.

The secret of Scripture is kept sealed with the signet of God's finger, which is the Holy Ghost, and so without His love and His leave no man may obtain it. He alone possesses the key of knowledge, as the Scripture says (Isa. xxii. 22). And He is Himself the key, and He lets in whom He will through the inspiration of His grace, and does not break the seal. That is what God does to those who love Him. He does not do it to all in the same measure. He does it especially for those who are inspired to seek truth in the Scriptures and who, having applied themselves to serious study, give themselves up to fervent prayer. These may find the truth when God is pleased to reveal it to them.

See, then, how grace opens the eyes of the spirit and enlightens the intelligence beyond the weakness of corrupt nature. Whether the soul reads Scripture, or hears it, or reflects on it, it receives, as I said before, a new ability to understand it and appreciate its truth. And it gets, too, the ability to find a spiritual sense in what is said literally. And that is not surprising, for it is the same spirit, namely the Holy Ghost, who interprets it for the consolation of a pure soul and who originally inspired it. And through this grace the uneducated can, and in fact do, grasp the substance, the real truth and the spiritual flavour of Scripture, as well as the educated. Admittedly they may not understand so many details, but that is not necessary. And when the soul is given this ability and this illumination by grace, it will sometimes wish to be alone, free from the interference of creatures, so as to be able to make free use of the instrument that it has at its disposal, that is its reason, to understand the truth that is in the Holy Scriptures. And then words and interpretations and texts enough will come to mind to give it an ordered and steady occupation.

And only by experience can a soul know what consolation and spiritual joy, what savour and sweetness, these illuminations may bring—interior perceptions, secret knowledge, and sudden touches of the Holy Ghost. And I believe that a man receiving these will not fall into error, if spiritual pride and over-great subtlety of intellect do not cloud his interior senses. David, I think, rejoiced in this sort of experience when he said: *Quam dulcia faucibus meis eloquia tua, super mel ori meo!* (Ps. cxviii. 103). How sweet are Thy words, O Lord, to my palate, more than honey to my mouth. That is, O God, Thy words in Holy Scripture, when grace brings them to mind, are sweeter to my palate, that is to the affections of my soul, than honey to my mouth. It is indeed good to see God thus without any laborious study.

This manner of seeing Him, as I said before, does not reveal Him as He is, but clothed in the images of works and words, *per speculum etiam in aenigmate*; through a glass and in an image, as the apostle says (1 Cor. xiii. 12). God is infinite power, wisdom, and goodness, justice, truth, holiness, and mercy, but what He is in Himself none can apprehend. He can only be seen in His works by the light of grace. His power is seen in the creation of all things out of nothing, His wisdom in the order in which He disposes them, His goodness in saving them, His mercy in forgiving sins. His holiness can be recognized in His gifts of grace, His justice in the punishment of sin, His truth in the rewarding of good works. All this appears in Scripture, and the soul sees it together with all His other attributes.[3] And indeed the light that grace throws on Holy Scripture and other inspired books[4] is nothing else than a series of delightful letters[5] which pass between the soul which loves and God who is loved, or, to speak more accurately, between God the true lover and the souls which He loves. He has a great love for all His chosen children who are enclosed in the clay of this mortal life, and therefore, though He dwells high above them in the midst of the delights of the Godhead, He remembers His people and visits them often with His spiritual presence, and consoles them by His communications in Holy Scripture, driving depression and weariness, doubts

[3] It seems possible to see in this paragraph a reference to the highest of the Gifts of the Holy Ghost, that of Wisdom, which enables us to see all things in their relation to God. The mind viewing created reality refers it back to the Creator. Hilton expresses it the other way round by passing from the consideration of God in His various attributes to the manifestation of them in the world.

[4] *Other inspired books.* "Other writing that is made through grace". The inspiration of the Scriptures is formally attested by the Church, but it may be presumed, I suppose, that the Fathers were often enlightened by the Gift of Understanding and their works in a real sense inspired or "made through grace", though there is no formal attestation of the fact in their case. In the Middle Ages the claim was made unhesitatingly for Origen, St Gregory, and St Bernard. See *The Study of the Bible in the Middle Ages* by Beryl Smalley (Oxford, 1952), p. 12, for references.

[5] St Augustine (Enarrat. in Psalm., lxiv, n. 2, P.L., xxxvi, col. 774) describes the Scriptures as letters sent from God to the soul. *Misit inde ad nos epistolas Pater noster, ministravit nobis Scripturas Deus.*

and anxieties, from their hearts, and making them rejoice in Him, truly believing His promises and humbly awaiting the fulfilment of His will.

St Paul said: *Quaecumque scripta sunt, ad nostram doctrinam scripta sunt, ut per consolationem Scripturarum, spem habeamus* (Rom. xv. 4). All that is written for our instruction is written that we may have hope of salvation through the consolation of the Scriptures. And it is one of the effects of contemplation to see God in the Scriptures when the eyes of the spirit have been opened. The clearer the vision in this contemplation, the greater is the love which it inspires. A very slight taste of this knowledge of Scripture will make a soul that enjoys it set little value on all the seven liberal arts or all worldly knowledge. For the end of this knowledge is the salvation of the soul in everlasting life, and the end of the other is only vanity and passing delight—unless grace turns it also to salvation.

THE FORTY-FOURTH CHAPTER

Of the secret voice of God which is heard in the soul, and how it may be recognized. How the illuminations which grace brings to a soul may be called the words of God

THESE new experiences that a pure soul undergoes are indeed good, and if the soul were entirely occupied with them, it might be said truly that it was to some extent reformed in feeling, yet even then not fully. For God will show still more and lead it to an even greater intimacy. He will speak to it with greater familiarity and love, and the soul will hasten to follow the movements of grace. For the prophet says: *Quocumque ibat spiritus, illuc gradiebantur et rotae sequentes eum* (Ezek. i. 20). Wherever the spirit goes, there the wheels go

following it. The wheels signify the true lovers of God.
These are, as it were, round in virtue, without any angle of
malice, and they turn easily inasmuch as their will is docile
to the movements of grace. They follow its inspirations, as
the prophet says. But before they do this they have a sure
test whereby they can recognize the voice of grace in order
that they may not be deceived by any illusion of their own or
of the devil. Our Lord said of those who love him: *Oves
meae vocem meam audiunt, et cognosco eas, et cognoscunt me meae*
(John x. 27, 14). My sheep hear My voice, and I know them
and they know Me. The secret voice of God is true and
makes the soul true. There is no pretence or illusion in it,
no pride or hypocrisy, but gentleness, and humility, peace,
and love, and charity; it is full of life and grace. Sometimes,
when this voice sounds in us, it is of such efficacy, that the
soul leaves whatever it is doing, prayer, speech, reading, or
meditation, and every sort of bodily activity, in order to
listen to it alone. It listens in great peace and with feelings
of love, entirely removed from all remembrance of earthly
things.[1] And in the peace of this experience God reveals

[1] This appears to be a description of rapture or ecstasy in the full sense,
and I take it that it is within this experience that the divine action manifests itself in a variety of ways, which Hilton will describe later. It may be
convenient to summarize them here.

(1) Some sort of revelations of our Lord, in which, he says, Jesus
shows Himself "sometimes as an awe-inspiring ruler, sometimes
as a father to be revered, sometimes as a spouse to be loved".
(chap. 44).

(2) A revelation of the nature of rational souls both elect and reprobate (chap. 45).

(3) A revelation of the nature of angels; first of the damned and after
that of the blessed (chap. 45).

(4) Another revelation of our Lord; first of His humanity and then of
His divinity (chap. 46).

(5) A revelation of the Trinity (chap. 46).

It is not difficult to equate these experiences in general with the visions

Himself sometimes as an awe-inspiring ruler, sometimes as a father to be revered, sometimes as a spouse to be loved.[2] This experience fills the soul with a reverent and loving contemplation which gives it greater joy than it has ever known before. It is conscious of such great security and peace in God, of receiving such favours from His goodness, that it wishes always to be in this state and never to give itself to any other exercise. It seems to touch God, and through the power of that ineffable touch all its ills are cured and it is confirmed in its state, reverently contemplating Him alone, as if nothing existed but God and itself. It is supported by nothing but the favour of His goodness which it knows it has received.

Often this experience is not inspired by any text of Scripture, and the soul formulates few words, though it may make use of words to give expression to the love, or adoration, or other feelings that arise in it. When it is actually enjoying this experience the soul is completely detached from the

---

described by St John of the Cross in the second Book of *The Ascent of Mount Carmel*, and it is tempting to see in the last two (4 and 5) St Teresa's experiences described in the Seventh Mansion of *The Interior Castle* (chap. 2, 1 and 2), where she describes two visions of our Lord (particular visions occurring at a very advanced stage of her mystical experience, it is to be noted), which seem to correspond with those described by Hilton, and referred to under 4 above. However this may be, our Lord under one aspect or another is likely to be the object of visions, and we need not be surprised at this reference of Hilton's or at those given under 1 above. More remarkable perhaps is the similarity between what he has to say about the revelation of the Trinity—and the soul begins to perceive a little of the mysteries of the Blessed Trinity (chap. 46, p. 306)—and St Teresa's description of the same thing (*Interior Castle*, Seventh Mans., chap. 1, 9). The question of the revelation of the nature of angels and of souls (2 and 3) is more difficult and is discussed in the Appendix.

[2] *Exigit ergo Deus timeri ut Dominus, honorari ut pater, et ut sponsus amari.* St Bernard *In Cantico*, Serm. LXXXIII, n. 4, P.L., CLXXXIII, col. 1183.

love of the world, and even at other times it gives little thought to worldly affairs, for it is too much occupied in other ways. And to a soul in this state grace will bring certain illuminations, words of God and sight of spiritual truths. For the purpose of all the divine action in a soul is to unite it to Him in the most perfect love. And because that cannot be brought about suddenly, God, who is Love, and of all lovers the most wise, makes use of various expedients to bring it about. In order to wed the soul truly to Him He uses the language of a lover. He reveals His treasures, He makes great presents, and promises still greater; He caresses the soul, often visiting it with great graces and spiritual consolation. I cannot describe all these favours in detail, and it is not necessary, but nevertheless I will say something as grace inspires me.

First of all, to a pure soul whose eyes have been opened to the perfection of love, spiritual truths are revealed, not that the soul should rest in them, and seek no further, but that through them it should be led to seek and love Him who is above all, paying no attention to anything outside Him.[3] You ask what these spiritual truths are that I speak of so often, and I reply that they are all the truths of Holy Scripture, and a soul that by the light of grace understands Scripture, sees the spiritual truths about which I have been speaking.

[3] This passage is an important commentary on what Hilton has to say about mystical experiences properly so-called, and puts them in their right perspective. They are not ends in themselves, but, as he said above, means used by God to wed the soul to Himself.

THE FORTY-FIFTH CHAPTER

*How grace in opening the spiritual eyes gives the soul wisdom
and makes it capable of seeing in humility and truth the various
degrees in the Church militant, and the nature of angels, and
first of all of the fallen angels*

NEVERTHELESS, there are other spiritual truths which the
light of grace reveals to the soul, and they are these. The
nature of rational souls and God's just dealings with them,[1]
the nature and activity of angels, the blessed and the reprobate; finally the knowledge of the Blessed Trinity in so far
as grace reveals it.

Scripture says of the spouse in *The Canticle of Canticles*:
Surgam, et circuibo civitatem; et quaeram quem diligit anima mea
(Cant. III. 2). I shall arise and go about the city and seek Him
whom my soul loves. That is, I shall raise my thoughts and
go about the city. The city signifies the universality of creatures, material and spiritual, which under God are governed
by the laws of nature, of reason, and of grace. I go about this
city when I consider the nature and causes of material creatures, and the gifts of grace and the joy of spiritual ones. And
in all these things I seek Him whom my soul loves. It is
good to see God in the material world with the inward
eyes, to see His power, His wisdom, and His goodness in
governing it, but it is much better to see Him in spiritual
Beings, and first in rational souls, both the elect and the reprobate.[2] It is good to see how in His mercy He calls the

---

[1] Hilton's word here is *gracious* which might be taken as referring
literally to grace and the phrase might be rendered "the effects of God's
grace in them". In a more general sense applied to the divinity it could
mean compassionate or benignant. In translating it *just* I have rather
stretched the meaning and have really interpreted it in the light of what
he goes on to say in the next paragraph.

[2] Hilton's emphasis on these revelations about the souls of men and

elect; how He draws them back from sin by the light of His grace; how He helps and teaches them, chastises and consoles them; how He justifies, purifies, nourishes them, and makes them glow with love and light by the plenitude of His grace. And He does this not to one soul only, but to all His elect, according to the measure of His grace. With regard to the reprobate, He shows how justly He abandons them and leaves them in their sin without doing them any wrong; how He recompenses them in this world, letting them have their way, and afterwards punishes them for all eternity.

This is to have a vision, though still an imperfect one, of the Church Militant upon earth; to see how black and ugly it looks in the reprobate, how beautiful and how lovely in the elect. And all this spiritual vision is nothing else than the sight of God, not in Himself, but in the secret works of His mercy, and in His severe and just judgements, revealed and renewed each day to rational souls. And beyond this, to see with the eyes of the spirit the pains of the reprobate and the joy and happiness of the elect is very consoling. For a pure soul cannot see truth without great delight and ardent love.

There is revealed, too, the nature of angels; first of the fallen and then of the blessed.[3] It is a great source of satisfaction to the pure soul when grace reveals the devil a helpless captive bound by the power of God so that he can do no harm. The soul sees him, not in corporeal form, but spiritually; it sees his nature and his malice, and as it were pulls him to pieces; scorns and despises him, and sets no store by his malice.[4] Scripture tells us to do this when it says: *Verte*

---

the nature of angels is unusual and presents some difficulty. The whole matter will be found discussed in the Appendix.

[3] See n. 2 above.

[4] Hilton's attitude to the devil is paralleled in St Bernard's Sermon XIII on the psalm *Qui habitat* (P.L., CLXXXIII, col. 238), and in *The Revelations* of Julian of Norwich, chap. 13.

impium, et non erit[5] (Prov. xii. 7). Turn the wicked, that is the devil, upside down and he shall be as nought. The soul is amazed that the devil has such great malice and so little power. No creature is so powerless as he is, and therefore it is great cowardice on the part of men to fear him so much. He can do nothing without God's leave, not so much as enter into a swine, as the gospel says (Matt. viii. 32). Much less, then, may he harm a man. And if God does give him leave to trouble us, it is only in His wisdom and His mercy that He does so, and therefore let us welcome God in Himself and in His messengers. The soul is no more afraid of the blustering of the devil than of the stirring of a mouse. The devil is furious if we dare say no to his suggestions, but his own malice closes his mouth. His hands are bound, as of a thief deserving condemnation and to be hanged in hell, and the soul accuses him and condemns him justly according to his deserts. You need not be surprised at this, for it is what St Paul meant when he said: *Fratres, nescitis quoniam angelos judicabimus?* (1 Cor. vi. 3). Brethren, do you not know that we shall judge angels? that is, those who have become wicked spirits through malice, who were created good in nature. This judgement is already foreshadowed in contemplative souls, for they already share in some degree in all that will afterwards be done in truth by God.

It is a great shame and disgrace to the devil to be treated thus by a pure soul. He would gladly escape and he cannot, because the power of God[6] prevents him, and that is more painful to him than all the fire of hell. The soul turns to

---

[5] The Vulgate text has *Verte impios et non erunt*.

[6] The Underhill text has, "For the might of the eyes holdeth him still," and in a footnote her MS. 9 (Lambeth 472) is quoted as reading, "the holi gooste hooldeth hym stille." The Orchard text has, "for the might of the Highest holdeth him still." I have given what appears evidently to be the sense.

God then with great humility, with heart-felt praise and
thanks for saving it in His great mercy from the malice of so
deadly an enemy.

THE FORTY-SIXTH CHAPTER

*How the soul sees the nature of good angels in the light of the
same grace, and how it knows in the manner that is proper to it
here how Jesus is God and man, exalted above all creatures*

AND after this by the same light the soul may see the beauty
of angels, the excellence of their nature, the immaterial
character of their substance, how they are confirmed in
grace and everlasting happiness; it may see the distinction
of orders and of individuals amongst them, how they live in
the light of truth and are on fire with the love of the Holy
Ghost in proportion to the dignity of their order; how they
see and love and praise God ceaselessly in blessed peace.
There is no corporeal vision, nor yet an imaginative one, in
all this activity, but it is entirely spiritual both in its manner
and in its object.

Then the soul begins to know these blessed spirits intimately. They show great care and solicitude in helping it,
they teach it as masters, and often free it from illusions by
their presence. They graciously illumine the soul and console it with sweet words suddenly heard, and if it falls into
any spiritual sickness, they care for it and minister to all its
wants. St Paul says of them: *Nonne omnes sunt administratorii
spiritus, missi propter eos qui hereditatem capient salutis?* (Heb.
i. 14). Do you not know that all the holy spirits are ministers
sent by God for those who shall receive the heritage of salvation? That is, the elect. As much as to say: you must know
that all these spiritual operations, words and reasons brought

to the mind, and other precious helps, are brought about by the ministry of angels when the light of grace shines abundantly in a pure soul.[1] It surpasses the power of man to relate these experiences in detail, the illuminations, the graces, and the consolations that pure souls receive through the help and the society of blessed angels. The soul takes such pleasure in beholding them that it would like to attend to nothing else. But with their help it sees still more. For the knowledge that a soul receives when it has been purified rises above all this, even to the contemplation of the blessed nature of Jesus. First it sees His glorious humanity and how it is justly exalted above the nature of all the angels; and then it attains to His divinity,[2] for knowledge of creatures leads to knowledge of the creator, and the soul begins to perceive a little of the mysteries of the Blessed Trinity.[3] And this may well be, for the light of grace accompanies it, and as long as it keeps in that light it cannot err. The soul does indeed see, in the manner that is appropriate to it here, the unity of substance and the distinction of Persons in the Blessed Trinity, and many other truths in connection with this mystery which the doctors of the Church expound in their writings. For you must know that in the light of grace a pure soul may see the very same truths concerning the Trinity that are expounded by the holy doctors. But I will not say much about this for there is no need.

The soul feels great love and great joy in the contemplation of this truth, when it attains it through a special grace—

[1] See Appendix.

[2] Visions and revelations of our Lord are, of course, what might be expected, and their is ample confirmation for their occurrence in the writings of other mystics.

[3] This intellectual vision of the Trinity seems to be paralleled in St Teresa's experiences. See *The Interior Castle*, Seventh Mans., chap. 1, *Complete Works* translated and edited by E. Allison Peers (London, 1946), vol. II, p. 331.

for love and light are both found in a pure soul. No love that it gets from contemplation touches God so directly as this love does, for it is the highest knowledge of Jesus, God and man, that grace can give us.[4] And so it enkindles a more ardent love than the knowledge of any other thing, material or spiritual.

These revelations of the whole of creation and of God, the creator and conserver of the universe, which grace brings about in the soul in the way I have described, I call the words and speech of God to His true spouse. He reveals mysteries and gives rich gifts out of His treasury, and decks the soul in them becomingly, so that she need not be ashamed to appear before the face of God her spouse in the company of her fellows. All these loving communications between God and the soul may be called the hidden word, of which Scripture says: *Porro ad me dictum est verbum absconditum, et venas susurri ejus percepit auris mea* (Job iv. 12). This is indeed a hidden word to me and my ear has perceived the veins of its whispering. The inspiration of God is a hidden word, for it is concealed from those who love the world and shown to those who love Him. It is through it that a pure soul easily perceives the softly murmured words in which He specially reveals His truth. For every revelation of truth felt with interior savour and spiritual joy is a secret whispering of God in the ear of a pure soul.

[4] It is difficult to be sure of the meaning of this passage. He would seem still to be talking of the vision of the Trinity—"wonder great love feeleth the soul with heavenly delight in beholding of this soothfastness," he says shortly before—and his remark that the soul comes nearer to God in this experience than in any other is in keeping with this, but he goes on, "for this knowing only is worthiest and highest in itself of Jesu God and man." We have seen that he habitually uses the name Jesus when he is referring to the Father, but it is curious that he should introduce "Jesu God and man" here, as presumably the vision of the Trinity is of a higher kind than any which includes the humanity of Christ.

He who would perceive these soft whisperings of the spirit must have great purity of soul, humility, and all the other virtues, and be half deaf to the noise of the world. This is the voice of God of which David said : *Vox Domini praeparantis cervos, et revelabit condensa* (Ps. xxviii. 9). The voice of God makes ready the harts, and He will reveal the thickets. That is : The inspiration of God makes souls as light as harts that spring from the earth over the bushes and briars of worldly vanity. And He reveals the thickets, that is, He shows them His secrets which can only be seen by sharp eyes. This contemplation firmly grounded in grace and humility makes a soul wise and burning with desire for the face of God. These are the spiritual truths that I spoke of before, and they may be called a new experience of grace. I only touch on them here a little for the guidance of your soul. A soul that is pure and is brought by grace to this sort of activity may see more in an hour than could be written in a large book.

APPENDIX

REVELATIONS OF SOULS AND ANGELS

(See Bk. II, chap. 44, n. 1, nos. 2 and 3)

AT the beginning of chap. 45 (Bk. II) Hilton says, "Never-theless, there are other spiritual truths which the light of grace reveals to the soul, and they are these. The nature of rational souls and God's just dealings with them, the nature and activity of angels, the blessed and the reprobate." In fact, when he goes on to describe these experiences it appears that these revelations are not of the nature of souls but only of God's dealings with them, that is of justification and re-probation (pp. 302-3). This does not seem generally to form part of the experience of the mystics though in the *Spiritual Canticle* St John of the Cross does speak of the soul being initiated into the deep mysteries of God and man.

> "And then we shall go forth to the lofty caverns of the rock . . ." The rock of which she here speaks, according to S. Paul, is Christ. The lofty caverns of the rock are the lofty and high and deep mysteries of the wisdom of God which are in Christ, concerning the hypostatical union of human nature with the Divine Word, and the corre-spondence to this which is the union of men in God, and in the agreement which there is between the justice and mercy of God as to the salvation of the human race in the manifestation of his judgements. (St John of the Cross, *Spiritual Canticle*, stanza xxxvii. *Complete Works*, trans-lated and edited by E. Allison Peers (London, 1934), vol. II, p. 385.)

This knowledge only comes at the summit of mystical ex-perience, in the so-called spiritual marriage, and from the way St John speaks of it, it would seem that the soul, though not yet enjoying the beatific vision, does yet see these things *in Verbo*. It may be that this is what Hilton means. The preceeding passage in chapter 45 (p. 302) perhaps suggests it:

> Scripture says of the spouse in *The Canticle of Canticles: Surgam et circuibo civitatem; et quaeram quem diligit anima mea* (Cant. III, 2). I shall arise and go about the city and seek Him whom my soul loves. That is, I shall raise my thoughts and go about the city. The city signifies the universality of creatures, material and spiritual, which under God are governed by the laws of nature, of reason, and of grace. I go about this city when I consider the nature and causes of material creatures, and the gifts of grace and the joy of spiritual ones. And in all these things I seek Him whom my soul loves. It is good to see God in the material world with the inward eyes, to see His power, His wisdom, and His goodness in governing it, but it is much better to see Him in spiritual Beings.

However this may be, St Bernard seems to teach the possibility of another kind of experience on a much lower level. He perhaps comes nearest to Hilton's teaching when he distinguishes between the contemplation of God and the contemplation of the blessed in heaven, both angels and saints. In Sermon LXII *in Cantica* he says that it is *in foraminibus petrae* that the soul contemplates God himself, but *in cavernis maceriae* the creatures of God, souls and angels. "In the hollow places of the wall", he says, the soul may "now revisit the patriarchs, now greet the prophets, now join itself to the august assembly of the apostles, now mingle in the choirs of the martyrs; and beyond this it may with the speed of thought survey the condition and the abodes of the blessed powers from the least angel to the cherubim and seraphim, as far as each one's devotion leads it". (*Nunc quidem patri-archas revisere, nunc vero salutare prophetas, nunc senatui immis-ceri apostolorum, nunc martyrum inseri choris; sed et beatorum virtutum status et mansiones a minimo angelo usque ad cherubin et seraphin, tota mentis alacritate percurrendo lustrare, prout quem-que sua devotio feret.* P.L., CLXXXIII, col. 1076.) Then, after describing the further experience which is directly of the Godhead itself, he says: "Thus it is clear that there are two sorts of contemplation; one is of the condition and felicity and glory of the heavenly city, where that great multitude of celestial citizens is engaged either in activity or leisure; the other is of the majesty, eternity, and divinity of the king himself. The former is in the wall, the latter in the rock" (*quae cum ita sint, duo liquet contemplationis genera esse; unum de statu et felicitate et gloria civitatis supernae, quo vel actu, vel otio ingens illa caelestium civium occupata sit multitudo; alterum de regis ipsius majestate, aeternitate, divinitate. Illa in maceria, ista in petra.* P.L., CLXXXIII, col. 1077).

This passage has certain similarities to the one from Hilton quoted above and one is tempted to think that Hilton must have been familiar with it, but the differences are per-haps more marked. St Bernard confines the object of this sort of contemplation to the occupants of the heavenly city; Hilton apparently thinks of it as of the souls of the just and of sinners on earth, and he extends it to the devil. "It is a great source of satisfaction to the pure soul when grace reveals the devil a helpless captive bound by the power of God so that he can do no harm" (chap. 45, p. 303). He expatiates upon the contempt the soul will feel for the devil, and his attitude is paralleled in St Bernard's Sermon XIII on the psalm *Qui habitat* (P.L., CLXXXIII, col. 238), though the latter does not suppose any vision or revelation.

The fact is that these passages in both authors present some difficulty. Revelations about the fate of individual souls are not uncommon in the lives of the saints, and there is ample Scriptural warrant, to go no further, for the appearance of angels upon particular occasions, but contemplation as such is always regarded as being of the Godhead, and this kind of subsidiary contemplation, envisaged apparently as forming a not inconsiderable part of the soul's experiences, is difficult to account for, but St Bernard makes the distinction and Hilton may well have had it in mind. It is interesting, incidentally, to note that this vision of the state of angels and of souls is referred to in three of the minor works attributed to Hilton, thus reinforcing the probability of the attribution. (See *Minor Works of Walter Hilton* (Burns Oates and Washbourne, London, 1929), pp. 97, 142, 184.)

But however this may be, there is one point which deserves further mention and that is the part which Hilton gives to the ministry of angels in these experiences. In chap. 46 he says:

> Then the soul begins to know these blessed spirits intimately. They show great care and solicitude in helping it, they teach it as masters (p. 305).

And again in the same chapter:

> You must know that all these spiritual operations, words, and reasons brought to the mind, and other precious helps, are brought about by the ministry of angels (pp. 305–6, cf. Bk. II, chap. 43, p. 293, and Bk. I, chap. 11, p. 17).

And he even seems to say that the visions of Christ and the Trinity are achieved with the help of angels (chap. 46, p. 306).

This idea of the illumination and assistance of men by angels has its roots very far back in theology and crystallized into the doctrine of angel guardians (see *Dictionnaire de*

Théologie Catholique, tome I, col. 1216 ff). It does not, however, seem to have been taken up by mystical writers with the exception of St Bernard, and it is likely that Hilton derived his ideas from him, for I am not aware of any mystical writer between them who makes use of it. (The debateable subject of Rolle's "angels' song" falls into another category. Ruysbroeck in *The Adornement of the Spiritual Marriage*, Bk. II, chap. 24, seems to grant the possibility at least in the case of imaginative visions, but he lays much less emphasis on it.) In Sermon XXXI on *The Canticle* St Bernard is explaining how the angels are solicitous for the spiritual welfare of men, and he describes the angel as follows:

> A faithful servant, who knowing the love that he and man both bear to God is not jealous, but seeks the Lord's rather than his own gratification. He is the intermediary between the two objects of his love, offering up service, bringing back rewards. He encourages the one love, satisfies the other. And at intervals, though rarely, he brings the two objects of his love together, whether by carrying up the one or leading down the other. For indeed he is an inmate and well known in the palace, standing in no fear of being denied access, and he daily sees the face of the father. (*Fidelis paranymphus, qui mutui amoris conscius, sed non invidus, non suam quaerit, sed Domini gratiam: discurrit medius inter dilectum et dilectam, vota offerens, referens dona. Excitat istam, placat illum. Interdum quoque, licet raro, repraesentat eos pariter sibi, sive hanc rapiens, sive illum adducens: siquidem domesticus est et notus in palatio, nec veretur repulsam, et quotidie videt faciem patris.* P.L., CLXIII, col. 943.)

This passage would seem in a general way to attribute mystical phenomena to the ministry of angels as Hilton does, and similar ideas are to be found in St Bonaventure *Solilo-*

quium, cap. 1, n. 7), but In Sermon XLI on *The Canticle* St Bernard refers again to this ministry of angels in a passage of great interest. He describes how the soul even in this life can have some sort of knowledge of the divinity:

> While yet the state of faith endures and the substance of the clear Light is not yet made manifest, the contemplation of pure truth can yet anticipate its action in us, at least in part. . . For when something from God (divinitus) has momentarily and, as it were, with the swiftness of a flash of light, shed its ray upon the mind in ecstasy of spirit, whether for the tempering of this too great radiance, or for the sake of imparting it to others, forthwith there present themselves, whence I know not, certain imaginary likenesses of lower things, suited to the meanings which have been infused from above, by means of which that most pure and brilliant ray of truth is in a manner shaded, and becomes both more bearable to the soul itself, and more capable of being communicated to whomsoever the latter wishes. I think that these images are formed in us by the suggestions of the holy angels, as, on the contrary, evil ones without any doubt are "innoculations" (*immissiones*) by bad angels. And very likely in this way is fabricated, as by the hands of Angels, that mirror and enigma through which the Apostle saw, out of such pure and beauteous imaginations; in such wise that we feel both the Being of God, which is conceived as pure and without any phantasy of corporeal images; and we attribute to angelic ministration whatever kind of elegant similitude wherewith It appeared worthily clothed withal (*Serm. in Cant.*, XLI, 3 and 4).

This passage is commented upon by Abbot Cuthbert Butler in *Western Mysticism* (London, 1922), pp. 153–4, and I have made use of his translation. It would seem to offer a solution of the perennial problem of the mystics, the translation of the perception of spiritual reality, "the most pure and brilliant ray of truth", into "intelligible species"—to use the scholastic terminology—"more bearable to the soul itself", and capable of being expressed in a language intelligible to others. The idea that the species under which it is apprehended are supplied by the angels is said by Butler to be "a piece of purely personal speculation, which did not find a place in the tradition of mystical teaching". This remains true on the whole, but it would seem that this particular theory of the ministry of angels in mystical experience advanced by St Bernard was taken up by Hilton, and it is of particular interest to find a passage in one of the minor works attributed to him which appears to provide exactly the same solution as St Bernard provides to the problem of reducing an ineffable experience to intelligible terms. In the little treatise *Qui habitat* we find it said of angels:

They may not make the light of grace in thy soul, for that falleth to God only himself; for he, through his unseeable presence maketh might, light, and love, and giveth to thy soul. But angels by their presence ghostly shall help thee and comfort thy soul much when thou art in this grace. For they stop out this press of unclean spirits. They cleanse the soul from fantasies and vain imaginations, and *they form fair likenesses in words and in reasons and temper the light of grace sufferably* in feeding of thy soul. They stir thine heart to the love of all goodness, and, if thou offend by frailty, readily they blame thee: thou shalt bear it no further, for they will suffer no sin to rest in thee. They comfort thee in bodily disease and tell thee of the joys of heaven wondrous privily, that thou shouldst not think too heavy the prison of this life (*Minor Works of Walter Hilton*, London, 1929, pp. 151–2).

The thought of this passage corresponds closely to that of St Bernard in the passage quoted above and the general similarity between the whole treatise and portions of *The Scale* leaves little doubt that Hilton was its author (cf. also for a more general exposition of the ministry of angels, St Bernard's sermons XI–XIII on the psalm *Qui habitat*, P.L., CLXXXIII, col. 225–38).

It is perhaps worth noting that Hilton says, "There is no corporeal vision, not yet an imaginative one, in all this activity, but it is entirely spiritual both in its manner and in its object" (chap. 46, p. 305). In other words, in the later terminology, they are intellectual visions which, as St John of the Cross says, "do not (as do those that are corporeal and imaginary) communicate themselves to the understanding by way of the corporeal senses; but, without the intervention of any inward or outward corporeal sense, they present themselves to the understanding, clearly and distinctly, by supernatural means, passively—that is to say without the commission of any act or operation on the part of the soul itself" (*The Ascent*, Bk. II, chap. 23, *Complete Works*, translated and edited by E. Allison Peers, vol. 1 (London, 1934), p. 185).

Finally, we may note that the doctrine about the ministry of angels is quite explicit in the treatise *Of Angels' Song* (Horstman, *Richard Rolle of Hampole and his followers* (London, 1895), vol. 1, p. 178), which is generally attributed to Hilton, and the matter is further complicated there by the introduction of the phenomenon, whatever it may be, which has given its name to the treatise. It is naturally of interest in view of the emphasis that Rolle laid upon it, but as it is not mentioned in *The Scale* it must be considered to lie outside the scope of the present work.